Academic Writing in a Global Context

'This book takes the exploration of academic writing and publishing in new directions, not least in the array of methodological and theoretical constructs developed. Through their research Lillis and Curry have provided rich perspectives into the ways texts are shaped, who is involved in this process and where this happens.'

Suresh Canagarajah, *Pennsylvania State University, US*

'*Academic Writing in a Global Context* will transform understandings about English as an international language for academic knowledge production. It challenges established views of the relations between scholarship, language and location, revealing the political issues which pervade the field. The research with scholars in four countries is rigorous and relevant, grounded and ground-breaking.'

Roz Ivanič, *Emeritus Professor of Linguistics in Education, Lancaster University, UK*

Academic Writing in a Global Context examines the impact of the growing dominance of English on academic writing for publication. The authors explore the ways in which the global status of English is affecting the lives and practices of multilingual scholars working in contexts where English is not the official language of communication, throwing into relief the politics surrounding academic publishing.

Drawing on an eight year 'text-oriented ethnography' of the experiences of fifty scholars working in Southern and Central Europe, this book explores how the dominance of English as the medium of academic publishing is influencing practices of knowledge production and evaluation. Analysis and discussion focus on the trajectories of texts towards publication, the involvement of 'literacy brokers', scholars' participation in local and transnational networks and institutional systems of evaluation and rewards.

This book will be of interest to postgraduates and professionals in the fields of academic literacies, applied linguistics, world Englishes, language and globalization, and English language teaching.

Theresa Lillis is a senior lecturer in language and communication at the Centre for Language and Communication, The Open University, UK. She is author of *Student Writing: Access, regulation, and desire* (Routledge, 2001), and co-author and editor of several books including *Redesigning English* (Routledge, 2007).

Mary Jane Curry is associate professor of language education in the Margaret Warner Graduate School of Education and Human Development at the University of Rochester, US. She co-wrote *Teaching Academic Writing: A Toolkit for Higher Education* (Routledge, 2002).

Academic Writing in a Global Context

The politics and practices of publishing in English

Theresa Lillis and Mary Jane Curry

Routledge
Taylor & Francis Group

LONDON AND NEW YORK

First edition published 2010
by Routledge
2 Park Square, Milton Park, Abingdon, Oxon OX14 4RN

Simultaneously published in the USA and Canada
by Routledge
711 Third Avenue, New York, NY 10017

Routledge is an imprint of the Taylor & Francis Group, an informa business

© 2010 Theresa Lillis and Mary Jane Curry

Typeset in Baskerville and Gill Sans by
Book Now Ltd, London
Printed and bound in Great Britain by
CPI Antony Rowe, Chippenham, Wiltshire

British Library Cataloguing in Publication Data
A catalogue record for this book is available from the British Library

Library of Congress Cataloging in Publication Data
Lillis, Theresa M., 1956–
Academic writing in global context / Theresa Lillis and Mary Jane Curry.
    p. cm.
1. Education—Research. 2. Academic writing—Study and teaching.
3. English language—Globalization. I. Curry, Mary Jane. II. Title.
LB1028.L44 2010
370.72—dc22
2009043903

ISBN10: 0–415–46881–7 (hbk)
ISBN10: 0–415–46883–3 (pbk)
ISBN10: 0–203–85258–3 (ebk)

ISBN13: 978–0–415–46881–7 (hbk)
ISBN13: 978–0–415–46883–1 (pbk)
ISBN13: 978–0–203–85258–3 (ebk)

Dedicated to Pam Burns *who saw us embark on this journey and with whom we wish we could have shared this moment. With love.*

Contents

Illustrations

Tables

Figures

Maps

Acknowledgements

First and foremost, we wish to thank all the scholars who have given so generously of their time, texts, thoughts, and interest over the more than eight years that we have worked on this study. This book represents just a snippet of all that we have learned personally and academically from you. Thank you.

In sustaining this research over a lengthy period we are indebted to many people. We offer our warm appreciation to Wendy Stainton-Rogers who inspired us to begin this research project and has provided considerable practical and moral support. Thanks to our colleagues in the Centre for Language and Communication (at the Open University) and at the Warner School (at the University of Rochester), university staff, librarians, and research assistants funded by our universities, the ESRC (RES-000-22-0098 and RES-063-27-0263) and the British Academy. We wish to thank administrative assistant Janet Moore; translators Milan Graf, Carmen García-Lillis, Rogerio Puga and Balázs Szabolics; scholars who have acted as research assistants and transcribers over this stretch of time, Heather Carroll, Jing Che, Liam García-Lillis, Shirley Graham, Gab'sile Lukhele, Anna Magyar, Lisa Lim, Sarah North, Matilda Tang, and Nan Zhang. We have also been helped by librarian Kathy McGowan and designer Christopher Penders at the University of Rochester and Roger Pitfield at the Open University. Our thanks to colleagues from other institutions, Roz Ivanič, Martin Hewings, Mary Scott, Joan Turner and Brian Street, who have offered us critical commentary and different types of support in many ways over the past eight years.

Our particular gratitude goes to Carol Johns-MacKenzie and Rita Chidley who have done much to sustain the project over a long period of time, not only through their meticulous administrative/secretarial work (in the case of Carol) and careful transcription (in the case of Rita) but with their cheerful enthusiasm and encouragement throughout.

We gratefully acknowledge permission to reprint/reuse sections of earlier publications: To *TESOL Quarterly* for: Curry, M.J. & Lillis, T.M. (2004). Multilingual scholars and the imperative to publish in English: Negotiating interests, demands, and rewards. *TESOL Quarterly, 38*(4), 663–688, parts of which have been adapted in Chapter 2 and other sections of the book. To *Revista Canaria de Estudios Ingleses* for: Lillis, T.M. & Curry, M.J. (2006). Reframing notions of competence in scholarly writing: From individual to networked activity. *Revista Canaria de Estudios*

Ingleses, *53*, 63–78, which has been adapted and expanded in Chapter 3. To *Written Communication* for: Lillis, T.M. & Curry, M.J. (2006). Professional academic writing by multilingual scholars: Interactions with literacy brokers in the production of English-medium texts. *Written Communication*, *23*(1), 3–35, which has been adapted primarily for Chapter 4 and for Lillis, T. (2008) Ethnography as method, methodology, and 'deep theorising': closing the gap between text and context in academic writing research. *Written Communication*, 25(3), 353–388, extracts from which have been adapted in Chapter 6.

And of course our love and thanks to our families who have cheerfully (mostly!) accepted our many trips away from home and looked forward to our stories on return; to Guille, Carmen, Liam and Moritz.

1 English and the politics of academic knowledge production

Why academic writing 'in a global context'?

Academic writing for publication takes place all around the world, involving an estimated 5.5 million scholars, 2,000 publishers and 17,500 research/higher education institutions.[1] While research and writing are always locally situated practices, no academic text or publishing activity can be considered in isolation from the many complex global(izing) practices and systems which influence academic text production in powerful ways, not least the ways in which texts are evaluated and disseminated. English plays a central role in such globalizing systems and practices, being considered by prestigious institutions to be the global 'language of Science'[2] and by many participants in text production – including scholars, reviewers, translators, editors – as the default language of Science and academic research and dissemination. This global status of English alongside the documented growth in English-medium publications means that scholars from around the world are under considerable pressure to publish in English. While such pressure is keenly experienced by scholars writing out of non-Anglophone contexts who have to make difficult decisions about which writing to do in which languages, Anglophone scholars often seem unaware of the privileged position they (we) hold, or the invisible benefits that such a position ensures. Wherever academic writing for publication takes place and whoever it is aimed at, such writing is global to the extent that it occurs within a global market (Gibbs 1995a), where texts are quite literally accorded different value, and within a global 'economy of signs' (Blommaert 2005) where English holds pride of place. In this book we explore the impact of the growing dominance of English as the global medium of academic publications – and of evaluation systems governing the academic marketplace – on the lives and practices of multilingual scholars working and living in contexts where English is not the official or dominant means of communication. At the same time, through our emphasis on understanding scholars' experiences and practices in specific contexts, our aim is to contribute to debates and understandings about academic production, and thus knowledge-making practices, in a globalized world.

Key questions the book seeks to explore are:

- In what ways is the global status of English influencing academic text production and exchange in the twenty-first century?
- To what extent can English be viewed as the global 'academic lingua franca'?
- How is the status of English in academic knowledge production maintained and sustained through key national, transnational and supranational institutions?
- How are individual scholars in non-Anglophone contexts responding to pressures to publish in English?
- Which kinds of knowledge are 'staying local' and which are 'going global'?
- What kinds of texts and knowledge 'travel' across national and transnational boundaries?

This book has at its centre a study based on the experiences and practices of 50 scholars from four non-Anglophone 'centre' contexts – Hungary, Slovakia, Spain and Portugal – in two disciplinary fields, education and psychology. The study, *Professional Academic Writing in a Global Context* (PAW) is unique in its methodology, scope and coverage in that it has involved using a text-oriented ethnographic approach in order to track scholars' text production, practices and experiences, in four national contexts and 12 institutions over a period of

Table 1.1 An overview of the PAW research study on which this book is based

Empirical research questions	**Overarching questions** • How is the dominance of English affecting scholars who use languages other than English and live/work in non-English dominant contexts? • In what ways is the position of English as an 'academic lingua franca' influencing academic knowledge production and exchange in the twenty-first century? • Which texts are successful or unsuccessful in being accepted for publication, and why? **About scholars' experiences and practices** • What are scholars' experiences in writing and publishing their research in English? • What meanings does publishing in English have for scholars? • What pressures do scholars face in this enterprise? • What barriers to publishing in English do scholars encounter? • What does and doesn't get published, and why?
Methodology	Text-oriented ethnography. The collection and analysis of a range of ethnographic and text data to explore the production of texts in their contexts. (See *Methodological Tools* across the book.)

Table 1.1 (Continued)

Number of key participants	50 scholars
Number of key institutions	12 (where scholars are primarily based)
Data sources	<ul><li>Texts written by participants (approximately 1,192)</li><li>Cyclical face-to-face talk around text (208 recorded sessions)</li><li>Language and literacy history interviews (50 recorded sessions)</li><li>Ongoing email discussions between participants and researchers (approximately 2,000)</li><li>Copies of correspondence between participants and others about texts (colleagues, reviewers, editors – approximately 500)</li><li>Observational field notes/Research diaries (total visits 60)</li><li>Telephone discussions (approximately 15)</li><li>Network diagrams drawn by participants</li><li>Documentary data from four national sites (departmental, institutional and national policy documents)</li></ul>
Key unit of analysis	Text Histories (See *Methodological Tool 1: Text Histories*)
National context	Slovakia, Hungary, Spain, Portugal
Disciplinary focus	Psychology, Education
Length of research study	Eight years and ongoing

eight years. An overview of key aspects of the study is summarized in Table 1.1. Given that researching, writing and securing publication often take a considerable amount of time, the longitudinal approach adopted for the study was essential to capture traces of the histories of text production. A key aim of the study was to document specific 'Text Histories', that is, to explore what happens as texts move from one context to another: this includes both trajectories within local national contexts and trajectories across national boundaries, often – given the high status attributed to Anglophone-centre publications – to Anglophone-centre contexts. Details of the kind of data involved in Text Histories are provided in the box over page, which is the first of six *Methodological Tools* outlined across the book. A core premise in writing the book is that paying attention to specific Text Histories and individual scholars' accounts of their experiences of academic text production helps throw into relief key debates about the broader practices and politics surrounding academic text production in a global context.

Methodological Tool 1: Text Histories

Text History (TH) is a key unit of data collection and analysis that we developed for exploring the trajectories of texts towards publication. The goal is to collect as much information as possible about the history of a text, including the drafts produced, the different people involved – including authors, reviewers, translators, editors and academic colleagues – the chronology of involvement and the nature of their impact on the text and its trajectory.

Each TH involves these key data elements:

- face-to-face interviews with the main author or authors, including discussions of the history of a particular text, such as who was involved, target publication, specific issues/concerns;
- the collection of as many drafts as available;
- the collection of correspondence between authors and brokers, including post-submission broker comments, such as reviews and email correspondence;
- email correspondence and informal discussions with authors.

Examples of two simple text trajectories and the writers and literacy brokers involved (see Chapter 4 for literacy brokers):

Example Text History 1

People involved: A = authors; B = brokers; D = draft

	A1 A2 A3	A1 A2 A3	A1 A2 A3	B1 B2 B3	A1 A2 A3 B4	
Written texts collected discussed and analysed	D1 →	D2 →	D3 →	Submitted →	D4 →	published

Example Text History 2

People involved: A = authors; B = brokers; D = draft

	A1 A2 A3	A1 A2 A3	A1 A2 A3	B1 B2 B3
Written texts collected, discussed and analysed	D1 →	D2 →	D3 →	submitted (revisions requested) ↓
				not resubmitted

Collecting text histories is time consuming – the trajectories of some texts towards submission and publication may involve years – and can only ever be partial. The amount and range of data available for each Text History in the PAW study varies because: 1) the texts are at different stages of trajectories toward publication and are therefore incomplete; 2) scholars vary enormously in their practices of keeping drafts and correspondence about specific texts; 3) scholars vary in the extent to which they report the involvement of others in their text production, for a number of reasons, ranging from the relatively straightforward issue of simply not remembering, to more complex issues of confidentiality, status and anonymity. Given the nature of writing activity, we recognize that no Text History is ever complete, most obviously because drafts are discarded and written exchanges destroyed. However, we think the collection and analysis of the kind of data outlined here is an important way of glimpsing important moments within texts' trajectories toward publication.

The politics of location in academic text production

At the heart of this book is the argument that geopolitical location – of scholars, texts, language – is central to the politics of academic text production, a position which has been gaining in prominence (see Belcher 2007; Flowerdew 1999a, 1999b; Salager-Meyer 1997; Swales 1990, 2004; and set out particularly clearly by Canagarajah 2002a). The specific geopolitical sites of the research study on which this book draws can be variously described as *Europe(an)*, *Southern Europe*, *Central* and *Eastern Europe* as well as through reference to specific nation states – Slovakia, Hungary, Spain and Portugal. In terms of their relationship with the use of English, the four national sites can be described as forming part of what Kachru has referred to as the 'Expanding Circle' of English language users (Kachru 2001), in which English is used as a foreign language and increasingly as an instrumental language in education, commerce and other areas. The 'Expanding Circle' contrasts with the 'Inner Circle', which includes nations such as the United Kingdom, the United States and Australia, as well as the 'Outer Circle', which represents former colonial sites such as India, Singapore and Nigeria, where English is a second or official language (Kachru 1992, 2001). In terms of their economic positioning, the four sites can be described as part of the 'centre', in contrast to the 'periphery' – after World Systems theory (Wallerstein 1991) – where 'centre'/'periphery' are used to indicate the differing material conditions and dependency relations between regions of the world, framed in terms of First and Third Worlds or West-as-centre in contrast to postcolonial periphery.

However, while these linguistic (Kahru's three circles) and economic (centre/ periphery) categories are highly relevant to the study of academic publishing for their descriptive and explanatory power – not least in terms of the privileged position held by the Anglophone centre – they can mask variation within and across regions of the world. Thus the four national sites are examples of 'centre' contexts which are also 'peripheral' in a number of ways (Sousa Santos (1994) uses the term '*semi-periférico*'). Most obviously they are non-Anglophone-centre contexts. They are also contexts where, at the state level, English has historically been granted a relatively low profile with limited opportunities for learning English.[3] They thus stand in contrast to many parts of Northern Europe, such as Germany, the Netherlands, Belgium and Scandinavian countries, where English is often the language of instruction in universities and increasingly the language of PhD dissertations (Ammon 2001; Brock-Utne 2001; Phillipson 2003; Truchot 1994).[4] The economic conditions in some of the sites are less favourable than other centre contexts, for example, in Central-Eastern Europe scholars not only earn lower salaries (as we discuss in Chapter 2) but they often have less funding and time for research and travel, less access to well-equipped libraries and laboratories, and less research assistance and other support, including for writing.[5]

In exploring the politics of location in academic text production, therefore, there are three key dimensions signalled in the above discussion which need to be taken into account: the *geographical* (at the levels of immediate local context such as department, institution, as well as the higher scales of state, region); the *geolinguistic* (the languages used or not used in writing for academic publication and their differential status); and the *geopolitical* (notably the policies influencing research and evaluation systems at local, national and supranational levels). All three are important for understanding what's involved and at stake in academic text production in the specific sites on which this book is based; but they are also important in enabling us to explore the nature of academic text production in a global context in three principal ways. First, the book highlights the differential values attributed to what is viewed as *locally* and *globally* relevant knowledge. Thus, for example, analysis of how articles reporting on Hungarian-based research are evaluated in Anglophone publishing contexts raises issues of relevance not only to Hungarian contexts of research and writing, but to all contexts which are marked in some way as being 'non-Anglophone'. Second, by exploring trajectories of academic text production, the book raises fundamental questions about the values and practices emerging from and being controlled by – predominantly – the Anglophone centre. For example, 'anonymized' peer review still remains a largely 'occluded genre' (Swales 1996), where both the texts and the practices remain hidden from public scrutiny – with written texts often viewed as private documents – while playing a powerful role in text and thus knowledge production and circulation. Third, the book calls attention to the range of geopolitical frameworks and descriptors often used uncritically in discussions about academic text production and which mask understandings, values and practices carried out in their name. A key example is 'international', which is in widespread currency in everyday usage, public discourse and research literature yet, as we discuss in the book, is a particularly powerful 'sliding signifier', coming to index far more than 'concerning two or more nations' (the *Concise Oxford English Dictionary Online* defines 'international' as: 'adjective 1 existing or occurring between nations. 2 agreed on or used by all or many nations'[6]). 'International' in the context of academic publishing is, rather, often used as a proxy for 'English medium', and together 'English' and 'international' constitute an important indexical cluster used to signal 'high quality'. Throughout the book we aim to make clear how we are using terms and from whose perspective: in the case of 'international' we avoid using it where other terms are less ideologically ambivalent – and use terms such as *transnational* and *supranational* – and when we do use it, we do so with 'scare quotes' to signal its contested status.

The politics of location in our research: brief reflections

In the spirit of ethnography as a reflexive science (Burawoy 2003) and in an attempt to situate this particular work on literacy (see Menezes de Souza 2008), we offer some notes on the politics of location with regard to us as researchers and our research writings. To write about this in detail would be another book; what follows are some points which stand out to us.

How did this research come about?

We met through being based in the same centre for three years at a UK university. We had each worked before on issues of access, identity and participation relating to student academic writing – Theresa in the United Kingdom and Mary Jane in the United States. What we shared therefore was an interest in the politics of academic writing, practices of inclusion, exclusion, and a familiarity with key positions and literature (notably New Literacy Studies, the work of Pierre Bourdieu and critical reproduction theorists such as Michael Apple) as refracted through our very different geographical, disciplinary and institutional bases. A senior colleague from psychology in our university became aware of our interests and shared her perspective on the specific issues Central European scholars faced in securing English-medium publications. It is fundamentally due to her interest in our work with academic literacies and the initial contacts we made with some Central European scholars, through her, that we began to imagine what kind of a research project this could be. We then called upon our own contacts in Southern Europe to establish Spain and Portugal as research sites.[7]

How do the politics of location affect our research?

Most obviously, we are working from the Anglophone centre – at the beginning in one UK institution and later in a UK and a US institution. This means that (although we, like many centre scholars, complain about too much work, not enough time etc.) we have decent salaries, good resources and opportunities for seeking grant funding. This economic security of salary and resource base has gone a long way towards making this research possible. We are also both 'native' speakers of English – although of different varieties and from different social backgrounds – and thus recognize the benefit we gain from this privilege at this moment in history.

Funding and the politics of English

In seeking funding from research bodies, we think we have been the beneficiaries to some extent of people's 'misrecognition' of the problem we are exploring. Thus while we have received some very insightful reviewer comments on applications which have helped to steer our thinking, we have also been aware of underlying

ideological positions which have benefited us while being at odds with our own positions. Two obvious positions go something like this: 1) 'English is the lingua franca of
science – therefore everyone should be writing in English and maybe such research
can find out ways to make this happen'; 2) 'If people have problems with getting work
published, it's a problem with language or writing so let's find out what the linguistic problems are and resolve these.' But it's also the case that the taken-for-granted
position of English as the global language of Science can work against our (or others') attempts to secure funding for research in this area; focusing on English as the
medium of publication can be seen as not interesting (or worth funding) precisely
because it's taken as a given that people should be publishing in English. If there is a
problem, then it can be resolved by people working to improve their English. (There
is no need for research.)

During the course of the research we have applied for some 13 grants from
eight funding bodies and have been successful in six of these. In seeking funds, we
have noted a difference between US and UK funding agencies – perhaps not surprisingly, Europe is not on the United States' agenda and it has proved harder (actually, impossible) to secure grants from US funding bodies. However, we have been
lucky in that both of our own institutions have actively supported the research –
by enabling us to apply for and secure small amounts of funding for travel, graduate research assistants and transcription – an absolute necessity in any attempt to
do longitudinal qualitative research.

Publishing on publishing in English

Our location in two of the dominant Anglophone academic centres has not
exempted us from the need to be cognizant of the types of target journal to which
we should submit papers from this project. Because of the need to continue to seek
funding to keep the research going for as long as possible (because of its longitudinal
nature) and to meet institutional requirements, in Mary Jane's case, to earn tenure at
her US university, we have had to consider the ranking/status of our target journals
even as we have deepened our awareness of the geopolitics of academic publishing.
In this respect it is salutary to note that a paper we are particularly happy with (Lillis
and Curry 2006b), which is published in an English-medium Spanish journal – in
contrast to our Anglophone-centre publications – has rarely been cited.

We have a more fundamental concern, however, which relates to the value
attributed by Anglophone-centre publishers to the topic we have been researching:
is it valued for the reasons of access and equity that spurred us to pursue the
research, or to some/a large extent because of a process of exotic 'othering'? We
think that both dimensions have been in play at different moments in our work
history and reflect some of the tensions we discuss with regard to scholars' publications in Chapter 6.

The global position of English in journal publications

While a wide range of academic texts are produced for publication, a key focus
in this book is the production of academic journal articles. The reason for focusing so centrally on journal articles is the high status they are attributed in local,

national and transnational evaluation systems. Quantifying the exact number of journals and articles being produced globally is far from straightforward, as the categories used for such quantification vary across systems of counting. The most comprehensive listing of journals, Ulrich's Periodicals Directory, gives the current annual total of 'academic journals' as 66,166 (Ulrich's 2009a).[8] Mabe calculates that 'for most of the last three centuries the growth rate of active peer reviewed scholarly and scientific journals has been almost constant at 3.46% per annum. This means that the number of active journals has been doubling every 20 years' (Mabe 2003: 193).[9]

The status of the journal article as an indicator of scholarly performance is growing, despite the disciplinary variation that exists in the publication types preferred by scholars – that is, natural scientists publish more of their work in journals than do social scientists, who also write books, book chapters, reports and other genres (Hicks 2004). While the elevated status of the journal article (compared with other text types) may be contested by some scholars (often depending on discipline), this status looks likely to grow given the move towards the use of bibliometric systems for the evaluation of academic performance across disciplines in many contexts of higher education, in particular through the use of the 'impact factor', an issue we discuss in detail below.

The ever-growing status of the journal and journal articles is paralleled by the ever-growing use of English as the medium of such articles. As with the annual statistics on journal publication, establishing a precise figure for the linguistic medium of journals published is not straightforward. However, some indication of the linguistic medium – and the dominance of English – can be gleaned by considering a number of key sources. Ulrich's Periodicals Directory indicates that 67% of the 66,166 academic periodicals included are published using some or all English (Ulrich's 2009a). Table 1.2 summarizes key figures on academic journals and their linguistic medium. The predominance of English-medium journals in some sources of bibliometric statistics signals the near-complete integration of English into particular types of journals, especially in certain disciplines. For instance, according to the Institute for Scientific Information (ISI), more than 95% of indexed natural science journals and 90% of social science journals use all or some English (Thomson Reuters 2008a). Similarly, English is the language of more than half of the 4,654 social science journals comprising UNESCO's DARE database of social science periodicals (UNESCO DARE 2009). The differences in numbers between these sources can to a large extent be accounted for by the different criteria used for inclusion, brief notes on which are included in Table 1.2.

Resource input and academic output

The history of the rise of English as a dominant global language of publication has much in common with the rise of English more widely, notably its link in the last century with the economic power of the United States (for discussions, see Graddol 1997, 2006, 2007; Pennycook 1998, 2007). With regard to academic writing and publishing, two specific aspects are important to consider which are

Table 1.2 Summaries of global journal publication statistics from Ulrich's Periodicals Directory (2009b)

Category	Number	Notes on categories
Total periodicals published globally with 'active' status	223,527	Ulrich's periodical categories are 'active', 'ceased' or 'forthcoming'. Here Ulrich's total count has recently had a considerable and intentional jump: 'In addition to the tens of thousands of regular updates that are applied throughout the year to Ulrich's records, more than 14,700 individual serial titles were added to the Ulrich's knowledgebase in 2006. Among these are thousands of European, Asian, and non-English publications in a variety of formats – from newspapers and magazines to Open Access journals and other e-serials'.
		http://www.ulrichsweb.com/ulrichsweb/news.asp, accessed January 2010
Academic/scholarly journals in all languages	66,166	Ulrich's categories are 'Academic/scholarly', 'Newspaper', 'Newsletter/bulletin', 'Consumer' and 'Trade/Business-to-business'. All languages can be included by leaving blank the search criterion 'Language'.
Academic/scholarly journals with some English	44,343	'Some English' is the only category available for searching how many journals are in the medium of English. 'Some English' can include anything from the abstracts/keywords to the entire journal.
Refereed academic/ scholarly in all languages	25,864	'Refereed' is a category that exists within the system and can be used as a search term.
Refereed academic/ scholarly journals with some English	22,910	See above
Refereed academic/ scholarly in Mandarin Chinese, Hindi/Urdu, Spanish, Arabic, Russian, Portuguese, Bengali, French, Japanese, German (often with some English as well)	7,110	We compiled this figure by searching Ulrich's for journals published in the 10 most commonly used languages in the world in addition to English.
Refereed academic/ scholarly in Spanish, French, German, Portuguese, Chinese – and no English	2,383	These journals are identified by excluding English from search criteria.

Note: We have included notes on the categories to give an indication of how definitions and selection criteria can influence the figures produced.

perhaps the most obvious ways in which the politics of location are linked to research and academic text production: first, the link between financial input and academic output, both of which were led by the United States until recently; second, the increasing influence globally of the US-based ISI (now part of Thomson Reuters) and the development of the 'impact factor' for evaluating academic output. We devote considerable attention to the latter in the section below because, as we discuss in this book, it is influencing text production practices in highly significant ways which often remain largely invisible (particularly at the current moment, we believe, to those working in the social sciences and humanities).

Since World War II, the United States has been the leader in overall research investment (from both government and private sources) in terms of total expenditures as well as percentage of its Gross Domestic Product (National Science Foundation 2007a). In 2005 the US share of global research expenditures was approximately 35%, while the European Union had the second largest share at 24%, followed by Japan at 14% and China at 8% (OECD 2008: 1). However, research investment by other regions is growing, particularly China, which has increased research spending by more than 50% since 1995 (EurActiv.com 2006; Zhou and Leydesdorff 2006: 100; see also Shelton and Holdridge 2004).

Research publications remain highly concentrated in a few countries, with more than 80% of world scientific articles coming from the OECD area, nearly two-thirds of them G8 countries.[10] In parallel to its research investment (Gross Expenditures on Research and Development, or GERD), the United States traditionally produced the largest share of science and technology publications until the mid-1990s, when it fell below that of the European Union even as the EU's share of global publications also decreased. The US share of total world scientific article output fell between 1995 and 2005, from 34% to 30%, as did the European Union share, which declined from 33% to 31%, whereas the Asia-10 share increased from 13% to 20% (National Science Foundation 2007a).[11] This 'triad' of the United States, European Union and Asia still dominates scientific journal production, totalling 81% of world share in 2000, up from 72% in 1981. However, other global regions are increasing their share of output:

> While scientific publications are concentrated in a few countries – over 80% of the articles in science and engineering published worldwide are from the OECD area – growth has recently been faster in emerging economies. Scientific articles from Latin America have more than tripled since 1993 and those from south-east Asian economies (Indonesia, Malaysia, the Philippines, Thailand and Vietnam) expanded almost three times over the period.
>
> (OECD 2009b)

But whilst the United States has lost its front-runner position, few individual countries besides China are gaining much in terms of world share of research output (UNESCO Institute 2005; see also OECD 2008). Of course, figures are constructed around states and economic regions of the world as defined by the

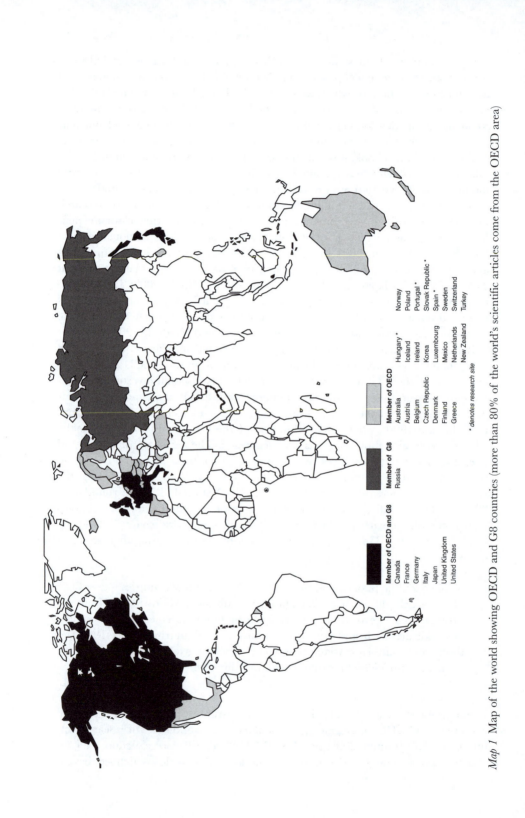

Map 1 Map of the world showing OECD and G8 countries (more than 80% of the world's scientific articles come from the OECD area)

Member of OECD and G8
Canada
France
Germany
Italy
Japan
United Kingdom
United States

Member of G8
Russia

Member of OECD
Australia
Austria
Belgium
Czech Republic
Denmark
Finland
Greece

Hungary *
Iceland
Ireland
Korea
Luxembourg
Mexico
New Zealand

Norway
Poland
Portugal *
Slovak Republic *
Spain *
Sweden
Switzerland
Turkey

* denotes research site

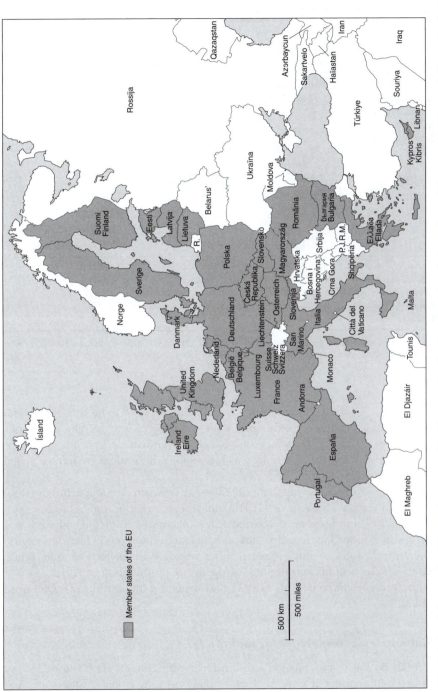

Map 2 Map of Europe showing member states of the European Union. The four sites of the study are Magyarország (Hungary), Slovensko (Slovakia), España (Spain) and Portugal.

Member states of the EU

500 km

500 miles

Table 1.3 Comparison of Research and Development (R&D) spending in relation to academic publishing output in selected regions of the world

Location	R&D as percentage of GDP	Share of world article output (natural, social and behavioral sciences)	Number of ISI indexed journals (SCI and SSCI)
United States	2.68% (2007)	30.2%	3,504
Asia (Japan, China, Singapore, S. Korea, Taiwan)	2.61% (2007)	16.5%	378
European Union	1.78% (2006)	31.5%	3,826
Africa	0.14%, except for Morocco, S. Africa, Tunisia, Uganda, which have between 0.75–1.25% (2008)	0.9% including S. Africa (see below); 0.6% excluding S. Africa	34 (Egypt, Ethiopia, Kenya, Nigeria, S. Africa)
Japan	3.39% (2006)	8.6%	181
United Kingdom	1.78% (2007)	6.9%	1,930
China	1.49% (2007)	4.2%	89
South Africa	0.95% (2006)	0.3%	28
India	0.71% (2004)	1.7%	49

Sources: National Science Foundation (2007b); OECD (2007; 2008; 2009a); Thomson Reuters (2008); UNESCO (2005); World Bank (2008).

compilers (e.g. OECD and UNESCO) and therefore need to be considered with caution and seen alongside other information. A point of obvious relevance to our focus here is that figures which emphasize the growth and output at a pan-regional level mask the differences within regions: indications of intra-regional variation are illustrated in Tables 1.3 and 1.4.

These brief overviews highlight the disparity between developed and developing global regions in terms of GERD and research output, most starkly, representation in ISI indexes. As noted above, few locations outside the United States, European Union, Japan and China are robustly represented. The figures also give an indication of intra-regional differences. Consider, for example, South Africa which accounts for one-third of the article output of all of Africa, as well as the notable differences in GERD and article output within the European Union.[12]

Bibliometrics, impact factor and the ISI

Journals do not simply provide a forum for the dissemination of knowledge but are a key component of systems of evaluation operating globally. This system has

Table 1.4 Research and development spending in relation to academic output in the four
study sites

Location	R&D as percentage of GDP	Share of world article output (natural, social and behavioural sciences)	Number of ISI indexed journals (SCI and SSCI)
Spain	1.20% (2006)	2.4%	53
Portugal	1.18% (2007)	0.4%	1
Hungary	0.97% (2007)	0.4%	15
Slovak Republic	0.47% (2007)	0.1%	14

Sources: National Science Foundation (2007b); OECD (2007; 2008; 2009a); Thomson Reuters
(2008b); UNESCO Institute; World Bank (2008).

been most powerfully shaped and defined by the work of Eugene Garfield,
founder of the Institute for Scientific Information (ISI), who in the 1960s set out
to create a systematic way of determining which journals were most important in
the natural sciences (and later the social sciences and the arts and humanities) and
to construct a 'map of the journal network as a whole' (Garfield 1972: 471). To
do so, Garfield devised the impact factor (IF) to help him select journals for the
indexes he created, the Science Citation Index (SCI, created in 1964) and later
the Social Sciences Citation Index (SSCI) and Arts and Humanities Citation
Index (AHCI). ISI indexes now form part of the Web of Knowledge (www.thom-
sonreuters.com), which includes other indexes (e.g. Current Contents, Medline)
and creates products such as Journal Citation Reports, which calculate impact
factors for journals included in the SCI and SSCI (e.g. those publishing three
years or more).

As created by Garfield, the IF was originally defined as the ratio of the number
of citations to 'source items' (e.g. articles or other types of text) in a particular
journal in one year to the number of articles published by that journal in the pre-
ceding two years. Thus:

citations to X journal in year Y (e.g. 2010)

articles/reviews published in X journal in years Y−1 (2009) and Y−2 (2008)

The resulting ratio, or impact factor, is recalculated annually by ISI for its reports
(Rousseau 2002). Important to note therefore is that the IF both determines the
inclusion of particular journals in indexes, and in a cyclical manner, helps contribute to the higher status of a journal.

While the IF is seen as the dominant bibliometric for journal quality and
enjoys widespread use around the world, there is growing recognition of its
limitations. A fundamental critique of the model overall is that citations are a
shallow measure of research quality or impact. Specific criticisms have also

been made of the operationalization of the model. The IF's two-year window of calculation was determined after Garfield analysed how long citations were made to articles only in the fields of biochemistry and biology; therefore disciplines with longer lag time to publication or slower dissemination of knowledge are disadvantaged (Cameron 2005; Monastersky 2005). In response to this latter criticism, the ISI now additionally calculates five-year impact factors to provide a more accurate indicator of the impact of a journal over time. Other criticisms of IF include, as follows: the IF rises with the number of journals published in a discipline and the number of articles published in a particular journal (Cameron 2005), thus advantaging larger size; higher IF journals tend to receive more submissions than other journals; highly cited articles can raise the IF of a journal in a particular year (Monastersky 2005), skewing the averages; authors can engage in excessive self-citation and deliberate citation of other authors publishing in the same journal; mistakes in reference lists indicate that they are not reliable indicators of sources (Cameron 2005); journals can pressure authors to cite other papers from the same journal and limit authors' citations to competing journals; publication of review articles, editorials and other genres that include many citations, particularly self-citations, can also increase a journal's IF (Begley 2006); journals with 'well-funded public relations offices' can distribute to the media research findings published in their journal, thus increasing their visibility and citations (Monastersky 2005).

Further biases that may result from the IF include: narrowly specialized journals as against multidisciplinary journals (Rousseau 2002); and certain types of article such as methodology as opposed to empirical or theoretical articles (Peritz 1983). The IF may result in bias against applied research that might not be discussed in high-IF journals which privilege basic research (Begley 2006). IF may reinforce 'science nationalism', in which authors cite journals from their own contexts (Ajayi 2004: see Chapter 6). Larger negative effects of the IF include influencing the types of research that are funded, if editors of high IF journals publish articles on certain topics to garner more citations (Monasterksy 2005), and influencing library subscriptions in favour of higher IF journals. The use of IF to evaluate the publications of individual scholars, mentioned above, has also been seen as biased against women, who are cited less frequently than men in some fields (Cameron 2005).

Perhaps the most worrying development in the history of the use of IF is that it has taken on a life of its own, and is increasingly being used for a range of immediately consequential purposes, such as judgements about hiring, tenure and receiving grants, 'despite the fact that such usage can be misleading and prejudicial' (Cameron 2005: 105; see Seglen 1997 for use in Italy, the Nordic countries, Canada and Hungary). In some of these uses, the IF is not based on one journal but is used to create ratings or IFs for individual scholars, by calculating an average of the IF of the journals in which they have published over a given period. IF is also used to evaluate academic departments and to assess the visibility of particular institutions (Rousseau 2002).

Table 1.5 ISI index journal counts as percentage of Ulrich's coverage

Journal counts in ISI indexes		Journal counts in Ulrich's		% of journals in ISI as compared with Ulrich's
Total ISI journals 2009	*16,183*	Ulrich's 'Academic/ scholarly' journals in all languages	*66,166*	24%
Science Citation Index (expanded version)	*6,650*	Ulrich's 'Scientific and Technical' journals	*43,905 active/ forthcoming*	15%
Social Sciences Citation Index	*1,950*	Ulrich's 'Social Science' journals[1]	*9,388 (2009)*	20%

Source: Thomson Reuters (2009); Ulrich's Periodicals Directory (2009a); UNESCO DARE

Note:
As aggregate numbers for social science periodicals are not available from Ulrich's (personal communication), here we have combined search results for these social science fields: archaeology, anthropology, communications, education, economics, geography, history, linguistics, political science, psychology, social sciences and sociology, recognizing that some of these fields may be categorized as belonging to other areas. For more on the challenges of calculating journals totals and coverage, see Nederhof and van Wijk 1997.

ISI, journal selection process and English

Selection is central to ISI indexes and ISI staff review approximately 2,000 new journals annually, selecting only about 12% of submissions and monitoring included journals (Testa 2003). By comparing the number of journals listed in Ulrich's Periodicals Directory with those in ISI indexes, it is possible to estimate the percentage of existing journals that are selected for inclusion in ISI indexes (see Table 1.5). Garfield defends the selective nature of these indexes by positing the 'concentration effect' (1997: 639), which he claims allows ISI to cover the top publications despite limiting the number of journals included. According to Garfield, despite the ongoing growth of specialized journals, 'only a small fraction account for most of the articles that are published and cited in a given year' (1997: 186). Journal selection for ISI indexes is purported to be an open process in which anyone can propose journals to be included. Selection criteria include existing 'citation data, journal standards, and expert judgment' of ISI staff (Garfield 1997: 185). Journal standards include: meeting the established schedule and frequency of publication (timeliness is the most important standard); meeting 'editorial requirements for abstracts, titles, and references set by professional associations of publishers and editors' (Garfield 1997: 185), including English-language abstracts (Testa 2003); and other aspects such as: 'peer review of submissions, editorial board membership, and the reputation of the publisher or sponsoring society' (Garfield 1997: 185). Geographic diversity is another consideration: 'To meet the needs of its international subscriber base, Thomson ISI seeks to cover journals with international diversity among authors of both source articles and cited articles' (Testa 2003: 211). In evaluating new journals, ISI editors 'examine the publishing record of the journal's authors and editorial board members, noting where their articles have been published and if their work has been cited' (Testa 2003: 212).

Despite these seemingly open criteria for all journals, there is strong criticism that ISI indexes are heavily biased toward English-medium journals published in Anglophone contexts (Crespi and Geuna 2008; Van Leeuwen *et al.* 2001). As Katz (1999: 2) identifies, ISI databases provide:

> international coverage, [but] they have a certain amount of bias. They contain more minor US journals than minor European journals, and non-English language journals are not as comprehensively indexed. From a non-English speaking world perspective bibliometric indicators represent only international level, predominantly English language, higher impact, peer-reviewed, publicly available research output.

Most journals that do not publish in English are excluded, thus English-language journals tend to enjoy higher IFs, which in turn contribute to the ongoing privileging of English. This dominance of English as the global language of science in ISI databases is viewed unproblematically by ISI, as its website states:

> English is the universal language of science at this time in history. It is for this reason that Thomson Scientific focuses on journals that publish full text in English or at very least, their bibliographic information in English. There are many journals covered in Web of Science that publish only their bibliographic information in English with full text in another language. However, going forward, it is clear that the journals most important to the international research community will publish full text in English. This is especially true in the natural sciences. In addition, all journals must have cited references in the Roman alphabet.
>
> (Thomson Reuters 2008a)

And Garfield (1997: 641) explicitly offers a view on the location of academic text production in relation to 'vernacular' languages, by describing the state of publishing in the global south:

> Many Third World countries suffer by publishing dozens of marginal journals whose reason for being is questionable. I have urged them to combine the best material into larger regional journals to achieve a critical mass. In addition, their local funding sources need to adopt stringent criteria for publication including international peer review. … Nevertheless, many local journals published in vernacular languages serve a useful purpose for reviewing the clinical and applied literature to the benefit of local physicians and industry.

A number of points are striking about the comments here: the presumed status of English as the medium of academic/scientific communication; the criticism levelled at journals described as 'marginal' which do not fit into the kind of network knowledge system valued by ISI; the carving up of which kinds of knowledge might be best disseminated in 'vernacular' languages. While we are not suggesting a simple cause and effect relationship between the position of one, admittedly powerful, institution such as the ISI, and what is happening in academic text production globally, it is striking that some of the distinctions made by Garfield and ISI about which kinds of knowledge should be circulated where – and in which medium – do indeed seem to be playing out, as we discuss in particular in Chapters 5 and 6.

A social practice approach to academic text production in a global context

Our overarching theoretical position in this book is that academic writing, including the focus of this book – academic writing for publication – is a social practice. A social practice approach to literacy conceptualizes reading and writing as fundamentally social activities; *practice* can be thought of as a 'bridge' notion, linking specific instances of written language use by the individual, as a socially situated actor, with both the 'context of situation' and the 'context of culture' (Malinowski 1923) in three central ways. First, practice signals that specific instances of language use – spoken and written *texts* – do not exist in isolation but are bound up with what people do – *practices* – in the material, social world. Second, ways of doing things with texts, practices, become part of everyday, implicit life routines both of the individual, *habitus* in Bourdieu's (1991) terms, and of social institutions. Third, and at a more abstract level, the notion of practice offers a way of linking everyday and routinized activities of reading and writing with 'the social structures in which they are embedded and which they help to shape' (Barton and Hamilton 1998: 6; see also discussion in Lillis and Scott 2007). Literacy as social practice stands in contrast to an autonomous notion of literacy whereby literacy is viewed as a single and universal phenomenon with assumed cognitive as well as economic benefits (for the distinction between autonomous and ideological notions of literacy see Street 1984, 2004, 2005) and where analytically the focus tends to be solely or primarily on the text (see Horner 1999). This focus on literacy as a *practice* rather than a *textual* phenomenon is a key epistemological and methodological move in work widely referred to as 'New Literacy Studies' (NLS), which explores the wide spectrum of literacy practices of human endeavour, from literacy practices at home and in formal schooling, to practices associated with specific locations such as prisons and workplaces (for overview, see Heath and Street 2008; see also Barton *et al.* 2000).[13]

Scholar Profile 1: Géza, Psychology, Central Europe

Géza is an associate professor working in a medium-sized department. He is 53 years old and has been working as an academic for 28 years. Apart from a brief period in counselling, he has always been involved in academic work. In recent years his research has drawn predominantly on social psychological paradigms.

Like most academics in post-communist countries, where the salary is *insufficient for appropriate living*, Géza has additional jobs. Beyond his one full-time academic post, he works regularly for nongovernmental and governmental organizations (training and service in the areas of communication, decision-making processes, organizational and project development), teaches in another institution (partly for free) and is a commentator on national radio. He loves all his work but wishes there was less or that he had more time to do it all, *it's so exciting and so exhausting at the same time.*

Géza describes himself as *a cosmopolitan person*. His family background includes strong links with Hungary, Germany and Slovakia and he was brought up speaking Czech, German and Slovak. He also speaks Russian and a little French. Over the past 15 years, Géza has increasingly been using English in his academic work, particularly for publishing. He is happy with his level of English. While he is confident that he can produce the kind of writing he wants and he no longer aspires to be a *perfect English scientific writer*, he is aware of significant limitations for his academic writing – mainly for publishing in 'international' journals.

Géza's academic/research work is forged out of a close-knit local team who collaborate on institutionally and nationally funded projects, as well as some 'internationally' funded projects and cooperation with transnational organizations. He has established strong ties with some UK scholars in his field, some enduring for over 10 years. He also has considerable transnational links with both individual scholars and institutions.

Géza has a considerable number of publications in one of his home languages as well as a growing number in English. His publications reflect his theoretical and applied interests: in addition to academic and professional publications he has written textbooks for practitioners. At one level this means that he is committed to sharing his understandings generated from his research with both academics and practitioners, most notably, within health and education. However, at a more fundamental level Géza makes no such distinction in his work, his overall interest being to make a useful contribution to *changing the world*. Thus, for example, he views the research methodology he and his colleagues have developed not only as a means of data collection but as a tool to be shared with practitioners who can effect change in their specific contexts.

While traditions and nomenclature vary, the phrase 'academic literacy/ies'[14] is increasingly used to refer to a social practice approach to the study of the range of academic literacy practices associated with academic study and scholarship, with the writing of students at university level attracting the largest part of research inquiry to date (for recent overviews see Lillis and Scott 2007; Russell *et al.* 2009).[15] Academic literacy/ies research explicitly draws on New Literacy Studies and construes academic writing as being rooted in specific cultural traditions and ways of constructing knowledge (Bazerman 1988; Lea and Street 1998; Prior 1998); as embedded in power relations (Canagarajah 2001; Jones *et al.* 1999); as involving issues of differential access to material or 'non-discursive' resources (Canagarajah 1996; Curry 2001; Curry and Lillis 2004); as well as questions of linguistic and ethnic identity (Bizzell 1992; Curry 2002; Gee 2001; Ivanič 1998; Lillis 2001). Following NLS, an academic literacies approach therefore challenges any simple distinctions between academic texts and the contexts in which they are rooted and points to the need to look in detail at how texts are generated, by whom and with what consequences. In so doing, and of direct relevance to the focus of this book, it stands in contrast to the strongly textualist tradition towards the academic writing of users of English as an additional language, reflected most strongly in the transnational enterprise and pedagogy of English for Academic Purposes (for recent useful overview of EAP approaches see Hyland 2006; for critiques of a predominant focus on text see Benesch 2001; Canagarajah 2002b; Lillis and Scott 2007). However, in resisting a textualist stance, it is important to note that we are of course concerned with the detail of texts – most specifically, to explore how specific textual features are foregrounded and evaluated in trajectories of production and publication. In this respect, we recognize that there is much work to be to done in order to develop contextually grounded text analytic tools. For while a social practice perspective usefully takes the analytic focus outwards, as it were, from text to context, there is no parallel move circulating back from context to text, which can potentially leave the text–context divide intact, and keep text analysis within the realm of traditions of textualist-formalist approaches. In this book we argue for the need to develop context-sensitive meditational (in addition to referential) categories which can help us move beyond this dislocation between contextual understandings and formalist categories (see Chapter 6).[16]

In adopting a social practice approach to professional academic writing – both in carrying out research and in writing this book – we draw on the central positions and notions in NLS outlined above. However, we also emphasize and modify some key notions which have emerged as particularly significant in seeking to understand what's involved in academic writing for publication; some of these are familiar dimensions in NLS, such as literacy *mediation*, which we take up in the context of academic writing for publication as 'literacy brokering' (Lillis and Curry 2006a) and network brokering (see Chapter 3); other dimensions have been less widely discussed in NLS, such as the privileged position of English globally and the impact of this privileged position on knowledge making. Here we provide an overview of those dimensions to a social practice approach which we see as central to discussions in this book.

The mediation of literacy

Academic writing is rarely an individual process or product but is mediated in a number of ways at both immediate and more distant levels. This is a point long since recognized about literacy practices more generally, where the phenomenon of people being involved in text production, reception and negotiation is captured in the notion of *mediation*. Most mediation is conceptualized at the level of inter-action between individuals – for example a child acting as a 'family interpreter' (Faulstich Orellana *et al.* 2002: 4), a father writing down the address of a television contest for his son (Baynham and Maybin 1996), public 'scribes' who fill out official forms or write letters for others (Kalman 1999). But there has also been some emphasis on the institutional and political nature of mediation. Brandt (2001), for example, examines how institutions such as churches, prisons and schools interact with economic and social changes to 'sponsor', that is, foster or constrain the learning and uses of literacy in the United States across the twentieth century. In tracking the impact of individuals other than authors on academic text production, we focus on individual activity but acknowledge that such activity is always refracted through political and institutional conditions governing academic text production in a global context (see Canagarajah 1996, 2002a), which in many ways are played out at the level of textual interventions and which we capture in the term 'literacy brokering'. What is done and by whom to academic texts has significant consequences: consequences for 'success' in the sense of securing publication, but also consequences for knowledge production and dissemination globally – what gets published, by whom, where and why.

Academic writing and the global status of English

While diversity has been at the centre of academic literacies research with regard to student writing – most evidently through discussion around voice and identity (for examples, see Halasek 1999; Ivanič 1998; Lillis 1997, 2001, 2003; Lu 1987, 1994; Spack 1988/1998; Thesen and Van Pletzen 2006) – the status of English in academic communication has received comparatively little attention, leading to what might be referred to as an (invisible) *English* bias in academic literacies research. At the same time, in related applied linguistic fields, there is considerable debate about the nature and status of English as a lingua franca (ELF) (e.g. Jenkins 2007; Seidlhofer 2001) and specifically as an 'academic lingua franca' (EALF) at the beginning of the twenty-first century (for examples see Crystal 2003; Graddol 2006; Huttner 2008; Hyland 2006). The ELF/EALF position, as does work in World Englishes (see e.g. Berns 2005; Rajagopalan 2009; Sano 2002), usefully emphasizes the fact that there are far more users of English as second, third and fourth language as compared with those as a first language (about three to one) and questions the privileged status of the English spoken/used by 'native speakers' above the varieties of many other users of English around the world. However, the over-emphasis on celebrating English as a lingua franca or academic lingua franca, with any implied neutral or positive perspective on its potential to provide opportunities for sharing communication across national borders, can mask a number of important critical dimensions, some of which we have discussed in this chapter: 1) the different conditions under which English-medium aca-demic texts are written, circulated and evaluated (see Swales 1997; Tardy 2004); 2) the evaluation systems in play which ensure that different contexts of English-medium text production are differentially evaluated, most notably English-medium national as compared with English-medium 'international' publications (an issue we discuss in Chapters 2 and 6); and 3) what we refer to as *textual ideologies* – clusters of views held about the nature of language, the writer, his/her location, the status s/he is granted as a user of English (native, non-native, L1, L2 speaker etc.), particularly as enacted by gatekeepers such as reviewers and editors who play a significant part in trajectories towards publication (see Chapter 6).

What's in a name? The politics of labelling

In using labels to describe scholars and their practices in discussions in this book we are aware of considerable limitations but we have attempted to take into account ethical, theoretical and representational dimensions. With regard to the ethical, we have consulted scholars about which geolinguistic labels they prefer (e.g. Hungarian, Central European); with regard to the theoretical, we have sought to use terms which reflect our principal concerns with the politics of location in academic text production, such as multilingual, Anglophone/non-Anglophone-centre, local national languages, rather than available frameworks for positioning scholars primarily in terms of any presumed status in terms of English usage – L1, EAL and so on (although we recognize that 'non-Anglophone' immediately may sug-gest negative positioning); with regard to representational, we have aimed to rep-resent scholars as individuals with specific histories, while also construing them as sharing specific constraints and challenges within the current context of the global status of English for academic publishing (for recent discussion around the labelling of 'EAL' writers, see Flowerdew 2008 and response by Casanave 2008).

Enunciative modalities, English and knowledge making

The politics of knowledge making have for some time been made visible through studies of the sociology of science (e.g. Latour and Woolgar 1986; Knorr-Cetina 1981) and foregrounded in some work on academic text production (see Bazerman 1988; Myers 1990). But while clear links have been established between rhetorical practices in the construction of knowledge and in particular disciplinary knowl-edge making (Bazerman 1988; Halliday and Martin 1993; Hyland 1999, 2000; Prior, 1998), less attention has been given – as in academic literacies research more generally – to the impact of the dominance of English on the rhetoric of knowl-edge making in a global context. A notable exception is the work of Canagarajah (2002c), who offers an auto-ethnographic account of his own production experi-ences as a Sri Lankan scholar, along with critical accounts of other scholarly endeavours, situating and theorizing these in terms of centre/periphery relations.

It is important to bring the politics of English to the centre of debates around knowledge construction and to explore how 'conversations of the discipline'

(Bazerman 1988) are refracted through the politics of language and location. Our aim in this book is to explore this refraction, drawing on two disciplinary fields: psychology and education. These are important fields for exploring the politics of location for a number of reasons. Epistemologically, in many ways, both disciplinary fields reflect the complex and contested nature of academic knowledge building in the twenty-first century, facing towards natural sciences, social sciences and the humanities (see discussions for example in Nisbet 2005; Stainton-Rogers 2004), including the rhetorical practices associated with a range of intellectual traditions. In addition, both psychology and education have an applied dimension which firmly situates research within local contexts while at the same time (often) drawing on theoretical discourses that aspire to universality. A focus on these disciplinary areas therefore foregrounds complex questions about which kinds of knowledge can be most usefully circulated where, and how locality connects with knowledge evaluation systems operating globally.

In their trajectories towards publication, not only do texts move translocally – shifting from one location to another – the evaluation systems within which they travel also shift. Exactly how texts are evaluated as they travel is crucial in the high stakes game of academic writing for publication, in particular article publication. Here authoring or 'voice' (after Blommaert 2005: 69) is particularly important:

> Voice in the era of globalisation becomes a matter of the capacity to accomplish functions of linguistic resources translocally, across different physical and social spaces. Voice, in other words, is the capacity for semiotic mobility – a capacity very often associated with the most prestigious linguistic resources ('world languages' such as English, literacy and more recently multimodal internet communication) and very often denied to resources ranking lower on the scales of value that characterise orders of indexicality (minority languages, 'unwritten' languages, dialects and so forth).

Voice then is not simply a matter of production but of 'uptake' (Blommaert 2005): a text's status, meaning and value are dependent on how it is read, by whom and where, and through which textual ideologies (for further discussion see Chapter 6). How, and whether, voice is granted is influenced by the more powerful enunciative modalities at play in any particular discursive site: enunciative modalities are not just (different) ways of speaking and listening (writing and reading) but they signal who has the right to occupy particular kinds of speaking positions within a specific discursive regime (see discussions in Fairclough 1992, after Foucault 1972). In Chapters 5 and 6 in particular we explore the question of speaking rights in relation to knowledge claims.

Social and cultural capital in academic text production

The notion that the language and literacy practices privileged by academia constitute and lead to further cultural capital is a point that permeates much work on students' academic literacy practices in higher education (see e.g. Brammer 2002; Curry 2003, 2007; Nomdo 2006; Rose 1989). Similarly, the professional academic text production and evaluation practices that we discuss across the book can be usefully illuminated by drawing on Bourdieu's (1985, 1990, 1998) theory of different forms of capital (i.e. economic, cultural, social, symbolic). While cultural capital refers to the symbolic goods transferred and created within the family, the notion of social capital offers an understanding of how access to resources beyond the family is negotiated and sustained:

> social capital is the aggregate of the *actual or potential resources which are linked to possession of a durable network of more or less institutionalized relationships of mutual acquaintance and recognition* – or in other words, to membership in a group. … These relationships may exist only in the practical state, in material and/or symbolic exchanges which help to maintain them.
>
> (Bourdieu 1985: 248–249, our emphasis)

As we discuss particularly in Chapter 3, networks across local and transnational contexts play an important part in sustaining scholars' text production activity. Networks both constitute a form of social capital and provide a chief means of access to capital, allocating or facilitating access to tangible and intangible resources (Lin 2001; Portes 2000). Of particular importance are the 'durable' networks that Bourdieu describes, which are often critical for supporting multilingual scholars in gaining access to resources and connections for high status publishing.

Globalization 'from below'

As already stated, academic writing for publication cannot fail to be located and positioned globally within a global knowledge economy and a *global economy of signs* (Blommaert 2005). The approach in this book, in line with NLS and academic literacy/ies research more generally, is to adopt an ethnographic approach, focusing on scholars' practices and experiences by drawing on a range of data sources collected and examined over an extended period of time. A range of data from the PAW study is used across the chapters in this book to illustrate what's involved in the politics and practices of academic text production; it includes extracts from discussions with scholars, extracts from texts they have written, detailed accounts of the trajectories of their texts towards publication (including stories of rejection and acceptance), correspondence between authors, reviewers and editors, and official departmental and national documentation.

In adopting this text-oriented ethnographic approach (see also Table 1.1), the aim is to explore globalization 'from below' (Falk 1999), and to be wary of grand claims made about globalization, such as an emphasis on the transformative potential of 'communication highways', or postmodernist discourses which emphasize diversifying/hybrid practices, claims often resulting from globalization viewed through the First World (see discussions in Bahri 1997; Baumann 1998; Burawoy 2000; Canagarajah 2005; Falk 1999).[17] In part, the approach adopted therefore connects with Robertson's (1995) emphasis on processes of 'glocalization' or Appadurai's (1996) notion of 'vernacular globalization' to indicate how the local is always influenced by processes occurring at a macro level and vice versa as a way of challenging totalizing accounts of globalization.

A notion that has been unexplored in academic literacy/ies research and is particularly helpful in exploring translocal text production and evaluation is the metaphor of 'scales' – mentioned in the quotation by Blommaert above – used by critical geographers and taken up by anthropologists and sociolinguists exploring global(izing) processes (see Blommaert, Collins and Slembrouck 2005). The metaphor of scales offers a way of understanding how local practices are keyed into global processes in a relationship of hierarchy. Blommaert (2005) argues that sociolinguistics has traditionally focused on horizontal metaphors (such as *distribution, spread, community, networks*) to explore difference and diversity across time and space and that what is additionally required is a metaphor which can take account of the vertical dimension.

> Scales offer us a vertical image of spaces, of space as stratified (and therefore power invested); but they also suggest deep connections between spatial and temporal features. In that sense, scale may be a concept that allows us to see sociolinguistic phenomena as non unified in relation to a stratified, non-unified image of social structure.
>
> (Blommaert 2006: 4)

Across the book we include both horizontal and vertical dimensions in exploring academic text production because: 1) they are evident in scholars' accounts and practices; 2) analytically, these dimensions are necessary to understand academic text production. While both dimensions are threaded across the book, the discussions in Chapters 2 to 4 adopt a predominantly horizontal framing, drawing on notions of *community, diversity* and *networks*, whereas Chapters 5 to 7 foreground a predominantly vertical framing, focusing on ideologies of Science and knowledge and power. The most obvious scales in play in academic text production are those making a shift from national to 'international' – which while problematic as descriptors, clearly signal a hierarchical relationship in terms of value within systems of production and evaluation. Where the existence of such scales becomes particularly visible is when attempts are made to 'jump scales' (after Uitermark 2002: 750, discussed in Blommaert 2005). The most obvious example of scale jumping is when scholars aim to move from one socially defined academic publication space (national) to another ('international' Anglophone centre). We consider some of the tensions around scale jumping in academic text production in Chapter 6.

A final key point we would add is the value of ethnography not only for exploring 'from below' what is currently happening, but also for imagining future possibilities. Sustained engagement with scholars and institutions over an extended period of time enables both 'thick description' (Geertz 1973) – that is, to observe and collect everything that may prove (potentially) to be significant, building up a detailed picture of places, people and resources – and 'thick participation' (Sarangi 2006, 2007) – which involves 'a form of socialisation in order to achieve a threshold for interpretive understanding' (Sarangi 2006: 73). Thick description and participation enable the researcher to explore what's significant and at stake for writers at specific sociohistorical moments and at the same time enables us to get glimpses of what Burawoy (2000: 32) calls globalization as imagination (as one of the three dimensions of global ethnography): 'Global imaginations reconfigure what is possible, turning globalization from an inexorable force into a resource that opens up new vistas.' What people do and aspire to do, how they imagine both the local and the global, can offer some ways of imagining future possibilities for academic writing production, dissemination and evaluation. This is the focus of the concluding chapter in the book.

How this book is organized

The book has four main themes which cut across all chapters: the global status of English; the geopolitics of academic text production; the relationship between local and global knowledge production; and the politics of participation in academic knowledge production, including issues of access to, and use of, a range of resources (human, linguistic, material).

Chapters 2 to 4 examine key aspects of academic text production in a global context by focusing in detail on scholars' interests, practices and experiences of engaging in academic text production for publication. Chapter 2 provides an overview of the publishing activity of the 50 scholars who are at the centre of this book, documenting the different communities they are writing to and for, and exploring how the status accorded to English is sustained through institutional and national systems of evaluation and rewards and is impacting on the publishing decisions scholars make. While Chapter 2 focuses on academic text production primarily through the lens of the individual scholar, Chapters 3 and 4 shift the emphasis towards text production as a networked activity. The focus in these chapters is on the ways in which scholars are managing and negotiating the complex and time-consuming tasks of sustaining publication activity in English, alongside writing in a number of languages and for a range of communities, by working within and across networks and by involving a range of 'literacy brokers' directly in text production. Chapter 3 focuses on text production as a *networked* activity, foregrounding the importance of participating in networks at local and transnational levels for securing the resources necessary for publication, particularly in Anglophone-centre journals. In Chapter 4 we direct our attention to the role played by specific participants in this networked activity, that of *literacy brokers* – friends, academic colleagues, editors, translators, proofreaders – and look in some detail at the impact these make on texts and their trajectories towards publication in significant ways. Specific Text Histories are tracked from initial drafts in local contexts through to submission, publication or rejection in Anglophone-centre contexts.

Chapters 5 and 6 pick up on some of the themes raised in earlier chapters to focus on academic texts as knowledge making, exploring in particular the question of what gets valued, where and by whom, in trajectories towards publication. These chapters mark a shift away from the predominantly horizontal analytic lens evident in Chapters 2 to 4 to consider the vertical axis, with an emphasis on the boundaries and stratification at work between Anglophone-centre and non-Anglophone-centre scholars, including a discussion of how these boundaries key into traditions of Enlightenment Science. Chapter 7 concludes the book by exploring some of the challenges in developing a more equitable model of academic text production and evaluation, illustrating some of the ways in which both centre and periphery scholars are currently seeking to open up multidirectional knowledge exchange. These include drives to invent/sustain local knowledges through local national/transnational journals, innovative practices in Anglophone-centre journals seeking to actively include non-Anglophone and/or peripheral scholars, and publishing practices which seek to transform knowledge exchange, such as open access journals.

Throughout the book, we label the data extracts included in terms of mode and/or medium in order to provide basic information to the reader about the data source; thus Discussion is used to indicate spoken interaction between researchers and scholars. Other labels include Email, Draft, Written Reviews, Field Notes and so on. Where we focus on particular Text Histories involving a range of data, we have labelled these TH1, TH2 and so on in the chapters in which they appear, using a gloss for each TH to indicate our principal emphasis in each case.

There are two additional features in each chapter: *Methodological Tools* and *Scholar Profiles*. In each chapter we include an outline of a specific *Methodological Tool* we have used in the research project on which the book is based and which is illustrated in the chapter in which it occurs. The reason for including these *Methodological Tools* in the book is that a key concern in our research has been to develop methodologies for researching academic writing for publication. The six tools we have included, which relate to aspects of both data collection and analysis, reflect some of our attempts and we hope will contribute to discussions about how to develop research methodologies in this area (see Figure 1.1 for a list of the tools included in the book). In addition, 14 *Scholar Profiles* are included across the book to give a (brief) sense of some of the scholars who took part in our study and their priorities, interests and experiences in writing for academic publication. We present these as stories in their own right but it is important to note that their stories and our understanding of them are crucial to the arguments and explorations in this book as a whole.

Ethics and anonymity

Ensuring anonymity has been a central concern of our involvement with scholar-participants over the past eight years. This is not as straightforward as might at first be assumed, because although we can provide pseudonyms for scholars, the extracts we include of their published texts and descriptions of their research might make them identifiable. This is particularly the case if a scholar is working within a

Chapter 1	**Methodological Tool 1:** Text Histories
Chapter 2	**Methodological Tool 2:** Talk around texts
Chapter 3	**Methodological Tool 3:** Analysing academic research networks
Chapter 4	**Methodological Tool 4:** Text-oriented heuristic for tracking changes made across drafts
Chapter 5	**Methodological Tool 5:** Ways of viewing talk/communication around academic texts
Chapter 6	**Methodological Tool 6:** Drawing on the concepts of indexicality, orientation and scales

Figure 1.1 List of Methodological Tools.

relatively small academic subfield specialism. In order to preserve anonymity, in consultation with scholars, we have therefore adopted a range of approaches to naming scholars and texts: in overview lists of scholars, we use numbers; in discussing Text Histories relating to a scholar sometimes we use a pseudonym and sometimes a brief gloss (e.g. a psychology scholar from Portugal); in referring to geopolitical region, we sometimes use the national descriptor such as Spain or Portugal and sometimes a larger regional descriptor, such as Southern Europe; in extracts of texts we have sought to remove lexical items that might easily identify the scholar involved. In making these decisions our aim has been both to secure anonymity and at the same time to provide a rich picture of scholars' activities, perspectives and practices. We have not included discussions of THs which scholars felt might jeopardize relations or opportunities for future publication.

Note to the reader

In crafting this book we have constructed a narrative that aims to move from the predominantly descriptive – with Chapters 2 to 4 seeking to represent how individual scholars are getting on with the 'business as usual' of text production – to the more discursive and polemical – Chapters 5, 6 and 7 – exploring issues surrounding current academic text production in terms of knowledge production and scientific traditions. We have also included a number of discrete data extracts and additional related information marked off from the main body of the text, including extracts from data sources, *Methodological Tools* and *Scholar Profiles* as well as chunks of information that we consider useful to the overall discussions and analysis (for example, on evaluation criteria, numbers of journals, national research investment figures, details on open access journals). These are inserted in the chapters according to where they seem most relevant. The book is therefore constructed to a large extent with a linear text model in mind. However, if you are someone who prefers to start with debate and the larger picture, rather than description and detail, you may want to begin reading at Chapters 5 to 7, and return later to read from Chapter 2. We know that readers do not tend to read academic books from page one through to the end so we have tried to make each chapter and each discrete chunk of additional information meaningful in their own terms. We hope you will choose a way through the text that most suits you.

Suggestions for further reading

For recent overviews on academic literacy/ies as a research frame, see the paper by Theresa Lillis and Mary Scott (2007). For work in applied linguistics whose focus on the research article in particular sowed the seeds of future areas for exploration, see John Swales (e.g. 1985, 1988, 1990). The work of two writers on the politics of English in scholarly publishing have been – and continue to be – powerful: the work of Françoise Salager-Meyer (see e.g. 1997, 2008) whose work particularly on medical publishing has been in the vanguard in foregrounding the consequences of unequal access to English-medium publishing by multilingual medical researchers; and Suresh Canagarajah (see e.g. 2002a, 2002b) who has brought together debates around the politics of academic writing and global flows of knowledge to the centre of US disciplinary writing frames – notably, composition and TESOL – as well as transnationally. In developing our core methodological tool of *Text Histories* we were influenced by the paper by John Flowerdew (2000) in which he tracks the publishing experiences of a Hong Kong scholar. Later we came across the work of Jan Blommaert (2006) on transnational text trajectories, which (drawing on Michael Silverstein and Greg Urban's *Natural Histories of Discourse*, 1996) opened up ways of theorizing academic text (and knowledge) trajectories.

2 Writing for publication in a globalized world

Interests, regulations and rewards

Introduction

This chapter focuses on some of the everyday decisions that multilingual scholars working outside Anglophone-centre contexts face in writing for publication, a theme echoed across this book. We explore scholars' choices and commitments in writing for academic publication in relation to linguistic medium and geo-academic communities, in the context of the growing dominance of English as the medium of global scholarly exchange. A key focus is on the ways in which scholars' choices and decisions are refracted through formal and informal systems of rewards and regulations operating at a number of institutional levels – departmental, national, transnational – and in which the privileged status of English is increasingly being codified. We illustrate how scholars respond to these pressures in multiple and complex ways, with variations across individuals, geographical locations and academic disciplines, as well as scholars' variable access to the resources needed to support academic publishing.

This chapter:

- Explores the interests of scholars working outside Anglophone-centre contexts in publishing their research in English and in other languages;
- Documents the pressures that multilingual scholars experience as refracted through local national and institutional structures and how scholars negotiate reward systems;
- Foregrounds the implicit and explicit codification of the status of English and other languages in institutional practices;
- Explores what is at stake for scholars as they make decisions about producing academic texts in English and/or other languages.

Scholar Profile 2: Sonja, Education, Slovakia

Sonja is a 47-year-old associate professor in education, specifically in the area of language learning and teacher training. She is employed on a full-time basis in one university in Slovakia. This is now her sole occupation: in the past, because of the relatively low salaries in Slovakia, she also worked part time at another university and at a private school.

Sonja uses Slovak as the medium of everyday communication but also uses English daily in her teaching, as well as for reading, writing and email communication. She knows both German and Russian well, although currently uses both little, and also some Hungarian. She studied English at school and at university but had little opportunity to use English before 1989:

> During socialism, you know, there were not enough opportunities to use English. At the beginning I tried to do translation work, something like that, but there weren't many jobs, not many opportunities and therefore, for, I don't know, 13 to 15 years, I didn't use English almost at all. Only after the revolution, after '89, I had a teaching job and I then had to begin to study English again.
>
> (Discussion)[1]

Sonja has published some papers and proceedings mainly in Slovak as she is predominantly interested in communicating research to Slovak professionals – teachers of foreign languages as well as those educating teachers on the teaching and learning of foreign languages. Her main publishing outlet is a Czech journal which publishes Slovak- and Czech-medium papers. While publishing mainly in the medium of Slovak, she also publishes in English, albeit to a lesser extent. She recognizes that publishing in English is considered higher status, however the main driving force behind her writing and publishing in English is the opportunity it offers to share her ideas more widely, beyond the national context. She always asks a 'native' speaker (from a university background) to proofread her English-medium texts and thinks that the biggest challenge she faces is to get the paper to 'sound' English. Proofreaders tend to tell her *it's OK but it doesn't sound English; grammatically it's OK but a native speaker would never write it like this.*

Sonja is keen to write in Slovak and English about her research on the teaching of foreign languages and in particular how models of second and foreign language learning need to take account of different national contexts and practices. But Sonja finds it difficult to get the time to do research or write. Although about 40% of her full-time post is meant to be allocated for such activities, the reality of her heavy administrative load means that there is very little time to do research and to write for publication.

Writing for different communities

Scholars' publication practices

The pressure to publish is central to scholarly life in the twenty-first century across all disciplines and national contexts, captured in the widely used phrase 'publish or perish'.[2] As discussed in Chapter 1, the number of scientific/scholarly publications, particularly journals, steadily increases each year, with English now dominating as the medium of publication in many fields. In addition, in evaluating scholars' work, many institutions are increasingly using formalized systems for measuring academic productivity such as the inclusion of journals in Anglophone-centre indexes. In this highly competitive global academic marketplace, all scholars face difficult decisions about where and how to direct their energies towards research and writing activities. However, as this chapter illustrates, one decision that most scholars in Anglophone-centre contexts take for granted – that English will be the linguistic medium of their publications – is far more complex when faced by the many multilingual scholars around the globe.

The multilingual scholars whose experiences form the basis of this book represent a breadth of experience as academics, but all work at university level and are conducting research and writing for publication in one of two disciplinary fields, psychology or education. Tables 2.1 to 2.4 provide an overview of the scholars from each geographical location, their academic field, academic position and years working in the academy.[3]

All of the scholars (except for the 3 graduate students) hold PhDs (and in some cases additional academic titles/degrees such as *agregação* in Portugal or *habilitáció* in Central Europe)[4]. Many have studied English formally and use it to greater or lesser extents. Only a few (eight of the 50 scholars) have had extended stays in Anglophone-centre contexts, but some have visited the United Kingdom or the United States for short periods. The majority of scholars therefore have developed their knowledge of English in their local contexts, often through their own – rather than institutionally supported – efforts (see *Scholar Profiles* in this chapter

Table 2.1 Overview of Slovak scholars

Scholar	Position – academic	Years in academy	Academic field
SK1	Assistant professor	2	Psychology
SK2	Assistant professor	5	Psychology
SK3	Assistant professor	5	Psychology
SK4	Assistant professor	27	Education
SK5	Associate professor	15	Education
SK6	Associate professor	24	Psychology
SK7	Associate professor	27	Psychology
SK8	Associate professor	28	Psychology
SK9	Associate professor	28	Psychology
SK10	Associate professor	30	Psychology
SK11	Professor	30	Psychology
SK12	Professor	30	Education

Table 2.2 Overview of Hungarian scholars

Scholar	Position	Years in academy	Academic field
HU1	Graduate student	2	Psychology
HU2	Graduate student	5	Psychology
HU3	Assistant professor	2	Psychology
HU4	Assistant professor	4	Psychology
HU5	Assistant professor	5	Psychology
HU6	Assistant professor	7	Psychology
HU7	Assistant professor	8	Psychology
HU8	Assistant professor	17	Education
HU9	Associate professor	15	Education
HU10	Associate professor	19	Psychology
HU11	Associate professor	20	Psychology
HU12	Professor	25	Psychology
HU13	Professor	45	Psychology
HU14	Professor	25	Psychology
HU15	Professor	35	Psychology

Table 2.3 Overview of Spanish scholars

Scholar	Position	Years in academy	Academic field
SP1	Graduate student	3	Psychology
SP2	Assistant professor	2	Education
SP3	Assistant professor	3	Psychology
SP4	Assistant professor	8	Psychology
SP5	Assistant professor	8	Psychology/Education*
SP6	Assistant professor	11	Psychology
SP7	Associate professor	10	Psychology/Education*
SP8	Associate professor	14	Psychology
SP9	Associate professor	19	Education
SP10	Associate professor	18	Psychology
SP11	Professor	23	Psychology

Note: *Institutional location includes both psychology and education.

Table 2.4 Overview of Portuguese scholars

Scholar	Position	Years in academy	Academic field
PT1	Assistant professor	9	Education
PT2	Assistant professor	10	Psychology
PT3	Assistant professor	17	Education
PT4	Assistant professor	17	Psychology
PT5	Associate professor	10	Psychology
PT6	Associate professor	14	Education
PT7	Associate professor	15	Psychology
PT8	Associate professor	15	Psychology
PT9	Associate professor	23	Education
PT10	Associate professor	25	Psychology
PT11	Associate professor	28	Psychology
PT12	Professor	30	Education

and across the book). A number of younger scholars have participated in European Union exchange initiatives, such as the ERASMUS Programme, to study for a few months in other European countries, with English typically the medium of academic commuication.[5] As Tables 2.5 to 2.8 summarize, the majority of scholars are actively publishing their work in the three most prestigious categories of publication – books (85), book chapters (469) and journal articles (1,008) – and in a number of linguistic media.

Table 2.5 Publishing record of Slovak scholars

Scholar	Publication category	Local national language	English	Other languages
SK1	Books	2		
	Book chapters	3	2	
	Articles	5	1	1 French
SK2	Books	0	0	
	Book chapters	4	0	
	Articles	1	4	
SK3	Books	0	0	
	Book chapters	2	1	
	Articles	0	5	
SK4	Books	0	1	
	Book chapters	6	0	
	Articles	4	0	
SK5	Books	0	0	
	Book chapters	1	0	
	Articles	3	1	
SK6	Books	3	0	
	Book chapters	4	0	
	Articles	19	5	
SK7	Books	0	0	
	Book chapters	0	0	
	Articles	1	7	
SK8	Books	7	0	
	Book chapters	9	0	1 Russian
	Articles	14	9	2 French
SK9	Books	2	0	
	Book chapters	9	3	1 German
	Articles	19	7	2 French
SK10	Books	1	1	
	Book chapters	6	1	
	Articles	12	10	
SK11	Books	2	0	
	Book chapters	5	9	3 French
	Articles	25	19	3 French
SK12	Books	1	0	
	Book chapters	2	0	
	Articles	10	0	

Table 2.6 Publishing record of Hungarian scholars

Scholar	Publication category	Local national language	English	Other languages
HU1	Books	0	0	
	Book chapters	15	0	
	Articles	10	5	
HU2	Books	0	0	
	Book chapters	1	0	
	Articles	2	10	
HU3	Books	0	0	
	Book chapters	2	0	
	Articles	0	2	
HU4	Books	0	0	
	Book chapters	1	0	
	Articles	1	13	
HU5	Books	0	0	
	Book chapters	4	0	
	Articles	0	6	
HU6	Books	0	0	
	Book chapters	5	3	
	Articles	4	1	
HU7	Books	0	0	
	Book chapters	8	3	
	Articles	4	1	
HU8	Books	0	0	
	Book chapters	0	1	
	Articles	0	2	
HU9	Books	6	0	
	Book chapters	14	1	
	Articles	36	11	
HU10	Books	4	0	
	Book chapters	13	5	
	Articles	16	11	
HU11	Books	3	0	
	Book chapters	1	1	
	Articles	4	3	1 French
HU12	Books	3	0	
	Book chapters	13	1	
	Articles	39	40	
HU13	Books	0	0	
	Book chapters	5	19	
	Articles	9	9	1 Italian
HU14	Books	0	1	
	Book chapters	1	5	
	Articles	9	25	
HU15	Books	9	4	1 Italian
	Book chapters	37	16	2 French
	Articles	54	32	1 French
				1 German

Table 2.7 Publishing record of Spanish scholars

Scholar	Publication category	Local national language	English	Other languages
SP1	Books	0	0	
	Book chapters	0	1	
	Articles	1	3	
SP2	Books	2	0	
	Book chapters	5	0	
	Articles	1	2	
SP3	Books	0	0	
	Book chapters	0	1	
	Articles	2	3	
SP4	Books	1	0	
	Book chapters	16	0	
	Articles	5	0	
SP5	Books	0	0	
	Book chapters	6	0	
	Articles	5	3	
SP6	Books	3	0	
	Book chapters	8	0	
	Articles	4	1	
SP7	Books	0	0	
	Book chapters	4	1	
	Articles	15	16	
SP8	Books	1	0	
	Book chapters	18	0	
	Articles	13	0	
SP9	Books	9	0	
	Book chapters	21	7	
	Articles	1	7	2 Catalan
SP10	Books	0	0	
	Book chapters	1	0	
	Articles	9	8	
SP11	Books	3	0	
	Book chapters	5	3	
	Articles	17	12	1 Catalan

The overview of publications in Tables 2.5 to 2.8 shows that, even given the individual differences in publications records, most scholars are publishing in more than one language, including, most obviously, scholars' local national or community languages. All but one of the 50 scholars have published in the local national language and 40 are publishing more in local national languages than in English or other languages. In addition to publishing in the local national language, 45 have published in English; and 14 have published in other languages. For scholars in Slovakia, Hungary and Portugal, after English, the most common

Table 2.8 Publishing record of Portuguese scholars

Scholar	Publication category	Local national language	English	Other languages
PT1	Books	2	0	
	Book chapters	1	2	
	Articles	30	4	2 Chinese
PT2	Books	0	0	
	Book chapters	0	0	
	Articles	4	1	2 Spanish
PT3	Books	1	0	
	Book chapters	3	1	
	Articles	9	0	
PT4	Books	0	0	
	Book chapters	0	0	
	Articles	2	0	
PT5	Books	0	0	
	Book chapters	10	6	
	Articles	1	4	
PT6	Books	0	0	
	Book chapters	8	1	
	Articles	6	1	
PT7	Books	3	0	
	Book chapters	6	4	
	Articles	22	8	
PT8	Books	0	0	
	Book chapters	0	0	
	Articles	8	15	
PT9	Books	2	0	
	Book chapters	2	6	
	Articles	23	8	1 French
PT10	Books	0	0	
	Book chapters	14	0	
	Articles	24	0	
PT11	Books	4	0	6 French
	Book chapters	31	6	3 Spanish
	Articles	48	24	1 Italian
				5 French
PT12	Books	5	0	
	Book chapters	2	9	
	Articles	57	15	1 French

language of publication is French; for scholars in Spain the additional language mentioned is Catalan.[6] Of the total, to date 39 scholars have published more, or equally, in articles than in books or book chapters; 11 have published more book chapters than articles or books.

The tables present a useful snapshot of scholars' publishing activity, indicating that in addition to publishing in local national languages, English is clearly significant as a medium of academic publishing. However, the tables do not adequately represent the complex range of audiences – or communities – for whom many multilingual scholars are writing, or the nature and significance of English-medium publications in their academic lives. For instance, the column labelled 'Published in English' obscures the different contexts in which such writing takes place, the purposes and audiences of such writing, and the different status that different types of English-medium publications hold. In order to explore some aspects of this complexity, we draw on the notion of 'community', which has been widely invoked in studies of academic writing, and proves useful in beginning to characterize the kind of publishing activity – and therefore knowledge production – in which multilingual scholars engage. We turn briefly to consider three specific dimensions of 'community' – *discourse, practice* and *speech* – all three of which have fed into our characterizations of the communities that scholars are writing for and which we summarize in the next section.

Discourse, practice and speech community/ies

The term 'community', placed alongside the prominent qualifiers of 'discourse', 'practice' and 'speech' is obviously problematic, not least because of the homogeneity and idealization that these phrases imply, including the downplaying of asymmetrical relationships (see Barton and Tusting 2005; Ivanič 1998; Prior 1998, 2003). 'Community' is an example of what Blommaert (2006) refers to as a *horizontal metaphor* or lens which dominates the sociolinguistic study of language. There is clearly a need to include a vertical dimension to the notion of community, an issue we return to in Chapters 5 and 6. However, we consider this predominantly horizontal framing of 'community' – taking account of the three dimensions of discourse, practice and speech – to be a useful heuristic, close to scholars' own accounts, for beginning to characterize the different kinds of writing for publication that scholars are involved in, and the audiences that these are directed towards.

Discourse community proves particularly useful for emphasizing the discourses associated with a specific disciplinary group or community, notably the specific texts and genres (e.g. Johns 1997; Swales 1990, 2004), whereas *community of practice* emphasizes the activities or practices associated with particular groups and the ways in which individuals engage in them (Belcher 1994; Wenger 1998). Research in academic literacy studies draws on both notions to explore the relationship between texts and practices, that is, the ways in which people learn the rules governing both texts and practices and thus participate in their maintenance and development (Candlin and Hyland 1999; Flowerdew 2000; Myers 1990; Prior 1998). In aiming to characterize who scholars are writing for, notions of discourse community and community of practice are clearly important, but it is also important not to lose sight of a third

notion of community, that of *speech community* (Hymes 1974), which helps to foreground, in particular, the significance of linguistic medium in academic text production. Although the notion of speech community has limitations – particularly that it
implies a focus only on the spoken word – it is important for the very reason for which
it has often been dismissed in academic literacy research: it foregrounds the importance of the relationship between the individual and his or her local sociolinguistic
context. The local sociolinguistic context is often minimized in discussions of discourse communities, where 'discourse' is used to emphasize written texts. Swales, for
example, in his influential discussion of the distinction between speech and discourse
community, makes two key claims. The first is that, in contrast to speech, 'literacy takes
away locality and parochiality' (Swales 1990: 24). The second is that the functions of
speech as compared with (written) discourse are fundamentally different:

> In a sociolinguistic speech community, the communicative needs of the
> group, such as socialization or group solidarity, tend to predominate in the
> development and maintenance of its discoursal characteristics. The pri-
> mary determinants of linguistic behaviour are social. However in a
> sociorhetorical discourse community, the primary determinants of linguis-
> tic behavior are functional, since a discourse community consists of a group
> of people who link up in order to pursue objectives that are prior to those
> of socialization and solidarity.
>
> (1990: 24)[7]

The claim that literacy removes locality and parochiality and the sharp distinction made between 'communicative' or 'social' and 'functional' needs has been
strongly challenged in New Literacy Studies (see Gee 1992; Street 2003) and there
are specific points which are important to bear in mind with regard to our focus on
academic text production. First, and perhaps most obviously, it is the fact of belonging to a particular speech community yet having to engage with a number of different speech communities that adds to the sheer number of communities that
multilingual scholars are writing for. Second, the complexity of the writing tasks in
which scholars are engaged can only be recognized if these tasks are understood in
terms of working within linguistic, academic and epistemological traditions related
to the local – departmental, national, regional – as well as to transnational and
'international' communities. Third, the question of 'participation', a key descriptive
and metaphorical trope in writings on discourse communities and communities of
practice, is clearly bound up with scholars' everyday patterns of communicative
activity, in particular speech communities in which research and writing activity
takes place. The relationship between individual scholars, their commitment to their
local as well as to 'international' research communities is an important strand in
understanding what's involved and at stake in publishing in a global context and is
discussed in Chapters 5, 6 and 7. Here, we simply wish to stress that ignoring
the notion of speech communities in explorations of academic literacy practices
masks a significant aspect of the interests driving the research and writing activity
of scholars who are working in languages in addition to English.

Scholar Profile 3: Kriszta, Psychology, Hungary

Kriszta is a 42-year-old associate professor, head of her department. She has been working as an academic for some 20 years in a predominantly experimental paradigm. She is passionate about her academic work and devotes considerable energies to developing both 'basic' research and its applications to hospital settings.

Her research and writing involve working closely with two academics in the same field in her department – one of whom in particular is a highly respected scholar in the field in many parts of the world – as well as with postgraduate research students and, in applied research, hospital doctors. Kriszta acknowledges the considerable mentoring the senior scholar has provided throughout her academic career – from her position as undergraduate and postgraduate student, through to her current position as head of department. The renowned status of the senior scholar has also led to some invitations to write for some English-medium journals. As her career has progressed, Kriszta has been increasing her submissions to high status English-medium journals.

Kriszta enjoys language learning both formally and informally – she studied Russian and Italian at school – and is an enthusiastic user of English. In addition to Hungarian and English, she uses Spanish for ongoing academic research with scholars from several Spanish-speaking countries, Mexico and Spain. While critical of her English language competence, she is relatively comfortable with using English for teaching – she teaches several programmes in the medium of English at her university, involving students from a number of non-Anglophone sites, such as Norway, Greece, Sweden and Israel – and research writings.

> I think that my English is enough. Not very good, excellent, but it's enough. I mean, earlier ... it was a suffering for me that I couldn't express myself as I wanted but nowadays as I prepare for the classes and make some English notes etc. I can much more easily express myself.
>
> (Discussion)

Her growing sense of confidence with English doesn't mean that she produces her English-medium academic texts alone. She often involves others – mostly a colleague within the group who has spent considerable time in the United States and who checks carefully through drafts, making revisions to both form and content. Kriszta has a considerable number of publications in Hungarian and a growing number in English. She sees English-medium publishing as central to the systems structuring academic work:

> If you apply for a grant or if you summarize your scientific record in your CV you simply put that 'I am the first author of this number of articles in English and second author in that number etc. etc.' So this is the measure of the quality in a sense.
>
> (Discussion)

The communities that multilingual scholars are writing for

In characterizing the range of audiences scholars are writing for, below, we therefore work with all three notions – discourse, practice and speech. From scholars' publishing records – including the information in Tables 2.5 to 2.8 – set alongside discussions, texts (see *Methodological Tool 2: Talk around texts*) and documentary data, such as curriculum vitae and departmental reports, we can characterize the communities scholars are writing for along several key dimensions: disciplinary, geolinguistic and applied versus theoretical. While acknowledging that any set of labels will oversimplify the intended audience for specific texts, and that the descriptors used, such as 'local' and 'international' are highly contested, as we discuss throughout this book, we have characterized seven communities for which scholars are writing, aiming to take into account these different dimensions.

National academic community in the local national language

The national academic community is a principal target for many scholars, as Tables 2.5 to 2.8 indicate, and for the most part involves writing in the local national/state language: Slovak, Hungarian, Spanish or Portuguese. Some scholars in Spain also write in one of the additional four official languages. Most scholars in the study are keen to contribute to local research 'conversations' (Bazerman 1988) by writing for the national academic community. National publishing outlets such as academic journals are often broad in scope, publishing a range of research articles on different topics and using very different paradigms. For example, Margarida, a Portuguese psychologist, edits a Portuguese-medium journal which is aimed primarily at the national research community and has both a psychological and broader social sciences remit, as indicated in the journal's description: '*A revista* [XX] *publica artigos e notas de investigacão, revisão ou discussão teórica, nos domínios da Psicologia e das outras ciências sociais, humanas e do comportamento*' (The journal [XX] publishes articles and research notes, reviews and theoretical discussions, in the fields of Psychology and other social human and behavioural sciences).

National applied community in the local national language

By 'applied community' we mean writing aimed at practitioners such as teachers, clinical psychologists, health professionals – that is, audiences who many scholars see as potentially direct users of their work. Although not indicated in our tables, many scholars have published applied texts, which are generally written in the local national language. What is important to note is that some scholars distinguish between the readers of their applied and their more theoretical writings, along local-national and 'international' lines. Through their applied publications in local national languages, many scholars hope to improve the quality of psychological and educational practice in their local contexts. In fact, some scholars who have attained high levels of success publishing in research journals have come to

Methodological Tool 2: Talk around texts

To explore scholars' perspectives on writing for publication, there is a need for a methodology which provides a lens not only on writers' perspectives on texts at one moment in time, but also on the various moments along their trajectories toward publication. Our approach therefore is to use *talk around texts* methodologies aimed explicitly at developing 'long conversations' (Maybin 1994) between writer and researcher.

Talk around text involves cyclical dialogue between the researcher and the scholar over a period of time, involving face-to-face discussion as well as ongoing communication via email (and less commonly in our research, via telephone). Beginning with a literacy history interview (as in Barton and Hamilton 1998), autobiographical accounts of a scholar's language and academic literacy learning are explored, so that current practices and perspectives can be understood

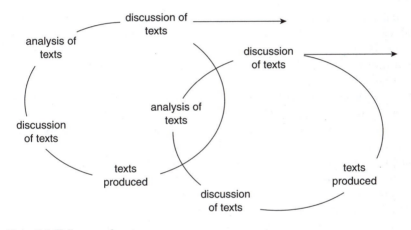

Figure 2.1 Talk around texts.

within the broader sociohistorical context of an individual's life (and academic writing) trajectory. Subsequent discussions focus more centrally on specific texts that a scholar is writing or has written and the issues surrounding the production of such texts, including details of the involvement of others. The cyclical nature of such dialogue around texts also enables the researcher to bring her analysis of texts and the events surrounding their production back to the writer for discussion and the chance for the scholar to offer his or her perspectives on the analysis.

'*Talk around texts*' = focus on text as object (content, form), as process (who was involved when, where, why) and as capital (what it is worth in the academic economy).

reconsider the focus of their professional energies and have intentionally shifted to aim their publications at local applied audiences. For example, Kriszta, a Hungarian psychologist, reports:

> Over the years I am more and more for the practical field. Or if it is research, I think it should have some consequences or some parts of applicable techniques or whatever. Otherwise, why do the research? Because the research part [of my work] is so isolated and apart from the very very few persons in the high research level, no one understands even the questions or those paradigms or designs or whatever. And it's a, you know, a club for some people who can discuss the things. But what for?
>
> (Discussion)

National academic community in English medium

Journal publishing in English in national contexts is a common practice in the natural sciences (Gibbs 1995b; Swales 1990). That this phenomenon is also increasing in the social sciences and humanities is partly borne out in our study; English-medium national journals appear to be increasing in the field of psychology, but to a lesser extent in education. The principal reason given by scholars for publishing in English-medium national journals rather than (or in addition to) national journals in the medium of local national languages is to communicate research to a wider audience, which is particularly important for scholars whose first language is not widely used outside the local context, such as Slovakia and Hungary. For instance, Rita, a psychology scholar, writes for the main Slovak English-medium psychology journal, because *this is useful for us because foreigners can't understand Slovak* (Discussion). In some national contexts, such journals also have another important function, that is, as 'exchange capital' for externally published journals, which universities in poorer countries often cannot afford to buy (see Box *The Library Exchange System: An Example from Slovakia*). Within psychology, publishing in English-medium national journals is a variable phenomenon across the four different contexts studied, being greatest in Slovakia, and decreasing as we move from Hungary to Portugal to Spain. The differences can in part be explained by the 'small' versus 'big' status of languages: the number of speakers of Slovak are approximately five million worldwide whereas Spanish speakers are estimated at 330 million. Thus the lower proportion of the Spanish psychology scholars contributing to national English-medium journals may at least in part be because of the greater number of Spanish speakers worldwide and the wider availability of Spanish-medium journals in Spain and Latin America.

'International' academic community in the local national language

Writing in a local national language for publications that are produced and/or distributed across national boundaries is a phenomenon directly relevant to scholars from Slovakia, Portugal and Spain. For Slovak scholars, the Czech Republic, with which it constituted one political entity until 1993, offers an audience twice the size of the Slovak audience. Given the close similarities between Slovak and Czech language varieties, Slovak scholars can write in Slovak for some journals published in the Czech Republic. Likewise Portuguese scholars look to Brazilian journals as potential outlets. For Spaniards, scholarly journals published in Latin America constitute a transnational community based on a common language. However, some scholars express concern about the geopolitical power relations between these Southern European countries and former colonies, and the dangers in European scholars publishing in such outlets. Education scholar Fidel states:

> We shouldn't export our reforms, our experiments. We could export them to South America but I would feel ashamed of selling a Spanish product in South America. I would understand that as a new way of colonization. I mean, I think they have very good academics there who can do good work.
>
> (Discussion)

Intranational academic community in English medium

Kachru uses the term 'intranational' to indicate the use of English as a 'link language' (2001: 520), that is, as a language used for communication within a state or national boundary where several other languages are spoken. We are using it here to indicate the growing use of English as the medium of communication within formally demarcated political/geographical boundaries, notably, the European Union, but also informal (although with historical antecedents) boundaries, such as Central Europe. While in principle any of the European Union official national languages (currently 23) can be used in reports on research projects, in practice the most commonly used medium is English (Labrie and Quell 1997; Phillipson 2003). Other instances of the use of English as an intranational language are English-medium psychology publications in Central Europe such as the *Journal of Psychology*, published in Croatia, and the English-medium journal, *The New Educational Review*, which began publication in Slovakia, Hungary and Poland in 2000. For Slovak psychology scholar Olivia, such a journal is an ideal target for disseminating research related to the region: *we are working more and publishing more in the Slovak context, and working also at this regional level* (Discussion).

Other national academic community in national languages

As indicated in Tables 2.5 to 2.8, some multilingual scholars also publish in second or third languages in other national contexts: German, Italian, French, Russian, Hungarian, Czech and Catalan. The reasons given for publishing in other national contexts are: 1) to contribute to the networks that scholars participate in within their 'specialist subfields' (Becher 1994: 151); 2) historical relations between different nation-states, which are often reflected in differences along generational lines – for example, older scholars in Hungary and Slovakia are often familiar with Russian and German languages and intellectual traditions; and 3) invitations from journals in other contexts to make contributions or to publish translated versions of previous publications. Denisa, for example, who is from a Czech-speaking family background, grew up also speaking Slovak and studying Russian and French, and later English at school. While Russian scholarship continues to be important to her, particularly for reading, French is currently more central to her interests, given the close ties she has established with a group of French-speaking scholars working in her specialist area. This collaboration has led to several co-authored publications in French.

'International' academic community in English

This category comprises a range of publications produced in English and primarily in Anglophone-centre countries, predominantly the United Kingdom and the United States, and distributed worldwide, including high status publications listed in indices such as the SCI and SSCI. Many scholars are aiming to publish in these journals for a number of reasons. Some see specialized Anglo-American journals as better outlets for their research, because, as Istvan notes, they are *able to give a full forum where I can find the people who are interested in my topic* (Discussion). Some consider publication in Anglophone-centre contexts a significant goal. Diana, a Portuguese education researcher, states:

> I would like very much to publish in these 'international' journals, of course, for professional material reasons, but also because I feel that I can publish in those journals, you see? I have material to do, good work. It's not just to publish though. Besides that, I like the challenges, I like to feel the challenge of doing something that is difficult.
>
> (Discussion)

In general, scholars hope to reach a wider audience than is locally available and to participate in transnational academic conversations. A further major imperative driving scholars' interest in publishing in high status 'international' journals is how these journals are codified in rewards systems operating at departmental, national and transnational levels.

We return to focus on the communities outlined above (particularly the first, third and last) in relation to knowledge making in Chapters 5 and 6. As illustrated in this section (and in the *Scholar Profiles*), multilingual scholars are motivated by a range of personal and scholarly reasons for aiming to publish in English. However, their decisions and choices are also influenced by external pressures, notably the rewards systems under which scholars live and in which the status of English-medium publications plays an increasingly significant role. In the following section we consider some aspects of these systems and tensions surrounding scholars' interests in publishing for different communities and in different languages.

The library exchange system: an example from Slovakia

Journals are expensive products. Subscription costs for individual journals range from between 300 and 1,000 Euros and have been rising rapidly in recent years.* Exchange systems, whereby libraries exchange journals published in their national contexts for journals from others, are particularly important where Gross Domestic Product (GDP) is small and where the national currency has low value on international markets. In Slovakia there are three psychology/social sciences journals published in English or which have regular English-medium issues and are used as exchange for academic materials from other libraries. Libraries involved in these exchanges are referred to as 'exchange partners'. The following details list the number and geographical location of the exchange partners for three Slovak journals.

1 *Studia Psicologia*: Eight partners: Russia (2), US (2), United Kingdom (1), Czech Republic (1), Poland (1), France (1)
2 *Sociologia*: Fourteen partners: Russia (5), Finland (2), Hungary (1), United Kingdom (1), Ukraine (1), Czech Republic (2), Poland (2)
3 *Human Affairs*: Two partners: United Kingdom (1), US (1)

The system relies on considerable interpersonal negotiation, back and forth over what constitutes a reasonable exchange package, as librarians seek to establish 'partners' – institutions which will agree to make exchanges. *It's a big responsibility as you just have to do it alone. It's a lot of work* (Interview with librarian responsible for managing exchange packages). And problems do occur between 'partners', as the librarian illustrates.

> We had a longstanding agreement with the Czech National Academy [of Sciences] that our packages would be on equal terms – for example a package of 20 Slovak journals would be exchanged for a package of 20 Czech journals. Our latest package was 55 for 55. They are our biggest exchange partner. But, last year, suddenly after more than 50 years, we received an email saying that they were changing our exchange agreement: 'We can send you just 20 for your 55.' We were very shocked.
>
> (Interview)

This 50% cut in the value of Slovak items was strongly resisted and involved protracted negotiations between librarians, including senior administrators on both sides. The outcome this time was an agreement to maintain equal packages. No reason was given for the Czech attempt to change the system except the general lack of finance – 'We don't have any money'. Although no money changes hands – that is the point of the exchange system – it seems that the Czech administrators were trying to reduce their exchange capital outlay for Slovakia, perhaps with a view to increasing it elsewhere. As increased demands are faced in one part of the market, these get pushed elsewhere, often onto less powerful partners.

Typically 10 Slovak items are exchanged for two US items. But even this is hard to sustain:

Continued

Last year I had to negotiate with two American libraries and we lost. For some time we have been exchanging packages but they have now said they do not want to exchange on any terms.

(Interview)

The growing shift away from small publishing houses for the production of local journals towards large multinational companies presents problems for library exchange systems in fundamental ways. Currently the exchange system works with hard copy, and although the production of hard copy alongside e-copy is possible, multinational publishers are pushing hard for e-copy only. Such companies determine whether even a small number of hard copies can be produced and regulate the costs of both e- and hard copy.

*These figures are calculated from Springer (www.springer.com/librarians/price+lists? SGWID=0-40585-0-0-0, accessed 5 October 2010) but are comparable with other publishers whose prices range between $200 and $1,600 for journals without expensive graphics.

Situated systems of regulations and rewards

While scholars are clearly continuing to publish in local national and other languages, it is the English-medium publications that are increasingly functioning as a key criterion for evaluation of scholarly activity. Indeed, English-medium publishing features in the full spectrum of key moments in an academic career: from being hired; to obtaining a permanent post, raises and bonuses, and promotions; to assuming responsibilities such as supervising graduate students; and to being awarded grants. Whether the criteria are formal, codified and publicized, or informal, uncodified 'common knowledge', the reward systems within which scholars work increasingly, directly or indirectly, foreground English-medium publications.

The criteria used to evaluate individual, departmental and institutional research activity often include a number of measurable (although far from unproblematic) aspects of scholarly publishing such as: whether a work is peer reviewed; the inclusion and ranking of journals in indices; the impact factor of journals; and raw numbers of citations of scholars' work. Many institutions place an explicit premium on 'international' or 'foreign language' publications, as compared with publications designated as 'national or 'domestic'. Thus texts published in other national languages, such as French-medium books and articles published by a Slovak scholar, can carry higher status than national publications in the medium of local national languages. However, the meaning of 'foreign' or 'international' varies across contexts, and scholars' accounts strongly signal the ways in which 'international' functions as a sliding signifier: English-medium publications tend to be valued the most, even if this is not explicitly stated in official documents. As Aurelia, a Portuguese education scholar, summarizes: *If it's Spanish, then you see, well, it is not international, it is Spanish. Or if*

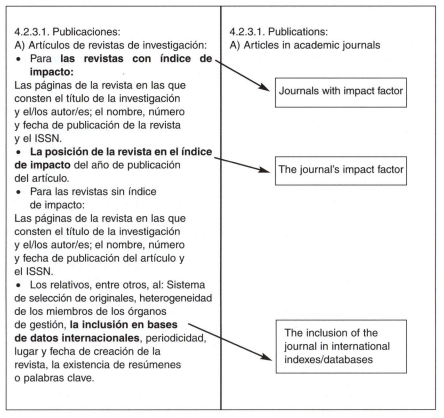

4.2.3.1. Publicaciones:
A) Artículos de revistas de investigación:
- Para **las revistas con índice de impacto:**
Las páginas de la revista en las que consten el título de la investigación y el/los autor/es; el nombre, número y fecha de publicación de la revista y el ISSN.
- **La posición de la revista en el índice de impacto** del año de publicación del artículo.
- Para las revistas sin índice de impacto:
Las páginas de la revista en las que consten el título de la investigación y el/los autor/es; el nombre, número y fecha de publicación del artículo y el ISSN.
- Los relativos, entre otros, al: Sistema de selección de originales, heterogeneidad de los miembros de los órganos de gestión, **la inclusión en bases de datos internacionales**, periodicidad, lugar y fecha de creación de la revista, la existencia de resúmenes o palabras clave.

4.2.3.1. Publications:
A) Articles in academic journals

Journals with impact factor

The journal's impact factor

The inclusion of the journal in international indexes/databases

Figure 2.2 Extract from Spanish evaluation document.

it is Brazilian it is not international! But if it is English, then it is international (Discussion). The meanings carried by 'international' are multiple, sometimes denoting any publication outside the national context, but more often indicating an English-medium publication outside the immediate local context. In some cases 'international' is reserved for referring specifically to journals included in Anglophone-centre indices such as the SCI and the SSCI. From the perspective of Ernesto, a Spanish psychologist, not just the inclusion but the ranking of journals in specific periodical indices carries significant weight in his institution:

> The institutional reward does not depend on the language, but on the ranking of the publication in the Social Sciences Citation Index at least in psychology. Given that the highest publications in this ranking are in English, this is why they are rewarded.
>
> (Email)

Ernesto's comment signals how the – common – institutional conflation of language of publication with the status and perceived quality of a journal publication might come about. Since the majority of publications indexed in the SCI are published in English, criteria that award more points for SCI-indexed journal publications implicitly value English over other publications in other languages. Likewise, 'English' – regardless of whether or not included in the SCI/SSCI – in practice often comes to index 'high quality'.

The value attached to English for employment and promotion

While the denotational meaning of 'international' varies – both within and across sites and moments of practice – the symbolic and cultural capital attached to what gets labelled as 'international' pervades academic reward systems. This is illustrated in Figure 2.2, an extract from an official Spanish evaluation document on academic employment and promotion where 'internacional' and 'indices de impacto' are foregrounded. Although 'English' is not explicitly identified – as is the case in most official documentation – the fundamental criterion to publish in indexed journals point to the inherent privileging of English, because of the bias of these indexes towards English-medium journals (see Chapter 1).

Detail on how differential value of linguistic medium for publications works in practice, in relation to the hiring process, is provided by Spanish education scholar Guillermo:

> For the new [employment] contracts, you need to be accredited, and you are required – you need to have two or three, of what they call 'international' or impact publications – 'internacionales de impacto' – it could be a French publication or it could even be a Spanish publication. Let's put it this way. If it's in English, then it's considered that it has impact, just because it's in English. If it's in French, then they have to look into it, and oh, yeah, this is an international prestigious journal – and in Spanish then you know they're going to look at it with X-Rays to see to make sure it has impact.
>
> (Discussion)

Guillermo's comment signals a continuum of prestige for the languages used in academic publishing. In the Spanish higher education hiring criteria, as in the Portuguese case presented by Aurelia above, there is a near-automatic conflation of 'international' with English, even if an English-medium journal does not have an official impact factor. Along similar lines, Figure 2.3 shows how criteria for promotion to the 'academic doctorate' issued by the Hungarian Academy of Sciences privileges 'foreign' publications, with the number of points awarded to different types of publication increased by two if these are 'foreign language publications'.

Similar criteria including the 'foreign'/national distinction, are illustrated in Figure 2.4, which shows a document used in a Slovak institution to quantify a

Researcher note: The academic doctorate is a degree beyond the PhD awarded to senior scholars who have published and been cited extensively, particularly in Anglophone-centre indexes. There are two paths toward this degree, either to have published eight articles included in the indexes PsycINFO or SCI, each of which needs to have garnered eight citations, or to amass a total of 120 points, as indicated here:

Monographs	10 points*
Edited research volumes	6 points*
Book chapters	4 points*
Refereed academic journals	4 points*
International conference proceedings	2 points*

* Two extra points for foreign language publication

Figure 2.3 Extract from document providing criteria from the Hungarian Academy of Sciences for the academic doctorate [Hungarian original].

psychology scholar's productivity during the previous five years for purposes of promotion. For this review, this psychology scholar was required to include publications in the previous five years, with an interim stage, 'since the last reclassification.' This document accompanied his curriculum vitae, on which he had indicated, for each co-authored publication, the percentage of the work for which he was responsible.

Figure 2.4 shows how publications in journals included in foreign indexes (SCI and Current Contents) top the hierarchy, followed by publications in indexed Slovak journals, then by publications in non-indexed foreign journals and conference proceedings, and finally by Slovak non-indexed journals and proceedings. A premium is clearly placed on publishing articles in indexed journals, preferably 'foreign' publications, which again in practice often amounts to English-medium publications.

A clear distinction in institutional systems of evaluation, therefore, is made in terms of the cultural capital of each different type of publication, which in some contexts impacts directly on reward systems. Thus, in one Slovak institution, scholars' publications are awarded a specific number of points – 'hard points' – for academic publications: within these, more points are awarded for papers in English-medium international journals listed in citation indices than for Slovak-medium journals even in the same indices. These points, as well as 'soft points' awarded for other publications and activities are *essential for sustaining the status of the department,* considers the head of department. He sees them as functioning as an important motivational tool for scholarly production, but he also recognizes the anxiety they provoke during scholars' annual review: *Every December, it's a very bad time for everyone because they have to come, and say what they have published, and they are nervous* (Discussion). Scholars' anxiety is not surprising because their already small salary may be significantly reduced if their publications profile is weak. Academic

An overview of selected quantitative data about the applicant, serving for his/her reclassification into the qualification grade IIa (Title of document)			
	Total	Since the last reclassification	In the last 5 years
Number of own scientific works published in foreign CC [Current Contents*] journals	3	2	2
Number of own scientific works published in Slovak CC journals	3	3	2
Number of own scientific works published in foreign journals other than CC and in proceedings	4	4	3
Number of own scientific works published in Slovak journals other than CC and in proceedings	30	30	12
Number of book monographs	2	2	2
Number of chapters in books	3	3	2
Number of abstracts from international conferences and similar	11	11	6
Number of SCI citations	2	2	2
Number of citations other than SCI	6	6	4
Number of citations in diploma, candidate and doctoral works	14	14	14
Requested lectures abroad (number)	5	5	5
Participation in foreign scientific projects (number of times)	3	3	3
Leader of a scientific project (number of times)	2	2	2
Participation in scientific projects (number of times)	3	3	2
Teaching (number of hours per year)			approx. 15/year

Figure 2.4 Slovak promotion document completed by a psychology scholar seeking promotion to associate professor [Slovak original].

Note:

*Slovak scholars mention Current Contents as the preferred index for their publications; in fact, some use an adjective, 'currented', in discussions of what value a particular journal will have in their reward systems. According to its publisher, 'Current Contents® is a current awareness database that provides easy access to complete tables of contents, bibliographic information, and abstracts from the most recently published issues of leading scholarly journals' (Thomson Reuters 2009).

salaries in Slovakia generally consist of a base and a bonus – with the bonus being anything from 30 to 100% of the base – and the bonus is calculated on an evaluation of scholars' activity, including publications.

Thus where a scholar's publications are considered too few or too low status, salary can be decreased immediately by up to 30%. (See Table 2.9 for salary figures across the four research sites.)

Figure 2.5 shows an extract from an evaluation document from another Slovak institution, which categorizes publications on the basis of 'territoriality', or place of origin, and 'qualification of the document', meaning how the publication is ranked. Two additional evaluation criteria, peer review and inclusion in indexes, are also embedded in this document. In this instance, the criteria relate to scholars in the field of education, where, in contrast with psychology, using such criteria constitutes a much more recent, but growing, practice.

While a codified system for evaluating academic output in the field of education in this national context – as in other fields – has been in existence for some time, in

Table 2.9 Annual academic salaries in four sites, equivalent to euros, adjusted for local cost of living

	Slovakia	Hungary	Spain	Portugal
Faculty salary, annual basis	9,178 euros	15,812 euros	34,908 euros	29,001 euros

Source: European University Institute 2009.

Directive No. 13/2005-R

Article 4

Criteria for the Categorization of Published Documents

(1) The categories of published documents are represented by three-letter codes. The documents are categorized by:
   (a) their originality and their type and function;
   (b) their bibliographical standard and character;
   (c) their territoriality and qualification ...

(4) The third letter signifies the territoriality and qualification of the document.
   (a) A – documents published by foreign publishers (publishers on the territory of the Czech Republic have been considered foreign since 1 January 1993).
   (b) B – documents published by domestic publishers (publishers on the territory of the Czech Republic were considered domestic until 31 December 1992).
   (c) C – foreign current journals and reviewed edited collections/proceedings.
   (d) D – domestic current journals and reviewed edited collections/proceedings.
   (e) E – foreign non-current journals and non-reviewed edited collections/proceedings.
   (f) F – domestic non-current journals and non-reviewed edited collections/proceedings.

Figure 2.5 Extract from Slovak evaluation document [Slovak original].

Resources needed	Specific issues
Time	Time needed for maintaining and developing English, requesting publications directly from authors, additional time spent on writing in English, writing for publication in several languages.
	Time limited particularly when scholars have more than one job.
Brokering	Costs for translation and/or time spent on editing, proofing at every stage of process.
Library/Anglophone centre publications	Limited resources overall including access to centre journals, books and databases, payment for interlibrary loans.
Travel, conferences for networking	Limited institutional or personal funds available in some contexts.

Figure 2.6 Key resource issues for English-medium text production.

2008 the system was revised and given a new institutional impetus and direction. The core premise that there should be an evaluation system has remained the same since the socialist era. What have changed are the formal features of the coding system, with the current emphasis on the amount and quality of output (research and publications), in contrast to a previous predominant emphasis on years of service.

The updated codified system is incorporated into institutional procedures, where academic publications form part of promotion criteria and annual salary awards. The head of a Slovak education department sees some advantages to having publications included in the reward system: *The new system will help me a bit – to reward people who are trying hard to publish and that's important* (Discussion). At the same time, she is concerned about the effect that this shift in the reward structure will have on the type of publication that scholars invest in producing, particularly given the resources that she and her education colleagues have access to (see Figure 2.6 for additional resource demands faced by scholars):

> Whatever is international is of a much higher value. Absolutely. But doing research in language, linguistics and education, at the international level is very difficult. We don't have the resources or conditions for that. I don't get a sabbatical to work on my research.
>
> (Discussion)

It is important to note that the criterion 'international' here – international was used in the scholar's discussion while 'foreign' is the term used in the Slovak document (Figure 2.5) – is understood by the head of department to mean 'non-domestic', published in other national contexts (that is, not simply English-medium publications). This distinction accounts for the details in the document (in Figure 2.5) about the category of texts published in the Czech Republic which, prior to 1992, were 'national' because Slovakia and the Czech Republic formed one national state territory.

> I like the system [set out in the Directive], I think it's pretty good. But it's a system that is applied in all universities in Slovakia – and the people who created the system are much more influenced by natural sciences and it's different in natural sciences because once, if they find a medicine, or whatever, they can apply it all over the world. But it's totally different [in social sciences and humanities]. In studies in England or America for example they may know about teaching English, but *we can't just use it here*. We have to change, we have to do many different things to apply it here. We *can't* just apply it here, we have to take account of our students, our mentality, our system of thinking and everything, and this is the stuff that some people must do. And this is what *I* must do, what I'm doing.
>
> (Discussion: italics = emphasis by speaker)

As with any institutional initiatives, in national contexts the current enactment of the system of evaluation varies from institution to institution. Thus in some institutions the older system of evaluation continues, based on academic qualifications and years of teaching, whereas in other institutions, an increased emphasis on academic (publishing) output is foregrounded.

This head of department's comments illustrate the far-reaching implications of a shift in evaluation policy in terms of the work that she and her colleagues do, her keen awareness of the limitations of the material resources available to them, and the possible ramifications of these changes on the type of work they might therefore produce. We return to issues around which knowledges can and should be produced and disseminated, and where, in Chapters 5, 6 and 7.

Scholars' concerns about the value accorded to different types of publication in institutional evaluations often stem not only from personal concern about remuneration and recognition, but also from their broader academic interests. Indeed, scholars feel under pressure to publish in English for different reasons and at different moments in their lives. Thus while a senior scholar, Istvan, is not specifically motivated by the goal of increasing his salary – even though he recognizes that *in Hungary a researcher's salary level is low comparatively with the French or Swedish* (Discussion) – he is driven by his interest in sustaining his research programme through securing external funding, for which he needs to publish in high impact factor journals – that is, in English. Similarly, while Mercedes, a Spanish associate professor of psychology who is at an earlier stage in her career, does not feel under direct pressure to publish in English, she is acutely aware of the importance of publishing in English, for the promotion review called a *sexenio*. After *six years of research, you have to select five things, but the unwritten rule is if in those six years, the five things you present, two of them are in*

English-language medium, you get the research promotion (Discussion). Mercedes's interest is motivated:

> not for the money, not so much, though probably a little for the prestige that's attached to it, but basically because it gives you many more possibilities of creating a sort of a research structure. To get the scholarships, to get projects, to get that sort of thing.
>
> (Discussion)

The importance of *sexenios* increased with a 2001 Spanish national law on the administration of universities (*Boletin Oficial de las Cortes Generales*, 2001) whereby passing a *sexenio* became a prerequisite to advising graduate students and assessing PhD dissertations and was reinforced as a factor in securing research grants. Mercedes's commitment to working with graduate students and developing research networks therefore means that securing publications in English-medium international psychology journals takes on more importance.

The value attached to English for research funding

Funded research projects are another domain in which evaluation criteria clearly privilege English-medium publications and the status of English in the academic world. Here again, point systems are in play in governmental and institutional funding policies and criteria. The prestige that English-medium publications confer supports scholars' ability to obtain grants in their local context from academic institutions or government agencies. As Julie, a Hungarian education scholar, reports:

> When I apply for grants for the Hungarian Academy of Sciences – that's where the major grants come from – they are interested in publishing activities, and they reward international publishing more than publishing in Hungarian. And we have very few opportunities to publish in Hungarian, so I tend to publish in English.
>
> (Discussion)

Beyond the individual value of a scholar's English-medium publications for receiving grants, English has also made a foothold in the conduct of the grant and research evaluation system itself. In Portugal, the most recent national research review process, overseen by the government body the Fundação para a Ciência e a Tecnologia (FCT), involved evaluation committees comprising only 'international' scholars – 'international' here meaning scholars from outside Portugal – and there was no expectation that such scholars should or would know the local national language, Portuguese. The 'international' nature of the panel therefore dictated the use of English as the medium of communication so that these 'international' scholar-referees could critically read the materials submitted for the evaluation of the research output and evaluate the quality of research centres (units) which are financed nationally. Reports for this evaluation were also required to be

---

FCT Fundação para a Ciência e a Tecnologia

MINISTÉRIO DA CIÊNCIA TECNOLOGIA E ENSINO SUPERIOR

EVALUATION OF RESEARCH UNITS

GUIDELINES FOR EVALUATORS AND EVALUATION FORMS

The current evaluation by FCT aims to determine the level of performance that the Research Units financed under the pluriannual program (base and programmatic) have achieved over the last 4 years (2003-2006).

Eventually, the FCT would like to ascertain the performance of the Portuguese Research Units during this period when compared with equivalent research Units at the International level. Thus, a clear and accurate evaluation exercise, based upon panels of international experts will be carried out.

Of particular importance for the evaluation panels will be to determine whether the Research Units have reached sufficient critical mass to carry out the proposed research and whether the fusion of previous small Units into lager (*sic*) Units has been guided by a logical and sensible aims that can be justified in view of the objectives of the research.

At the end of the evaluation process, the panel will provide an overall grading for each Unit (excellent, very good, good, fair and poor) reflecting the Unit's performance in the past and the future research proposal. Units which are classified as either Fair or Poor will not receive funding from the FCT.

For the evaluation Units will be asked to submit a report in English concerning the work carried out during the relevant period. They will specifically be required to organize their report into a number of individual Research Groups under the leadership of a Responsible Investigator. The Overall Unit Report should reflect the consensus of the panel, integrating the reports and recommendations on different research groups within the Unit into a single document. Its contents will be communicated to the Research Unit coordinator at the end of the evaluation process and will be made public afterwards.

It is **not expected** that any simple computation be applied to derive the final research unit evaluation from the preliminary evaluation form or the site visit.

It is **expected** that the evaluation panel will explain in some detail in the Final Unit Evaluation Report its overall judgment of the Research Unit at the end of the evaluation process, as well as to give specific comments on the different research groups that make up the Unit including the grades attributed to each individual Research Group.

To indicate the relative importance of different recommendations the following qualitative terms should be used: *recommends, strongly recommends, most strongly recommends.*

Figure 2.7 Extracts from FCT Evaluation Guidelines (original version in English).

submitted in English, as seen in Figure 2.7. Scholars are therefore required to submit their reports in English. The evaluation overall emphasises the rising use of bibliometrics across the disciplines in the evaluation of scholars, their programmes and their departments, by government agencies. The field notes included in Figure 2.8 give some sense of the effect on scholars of this shift to the 'international' English-medium evaluation exercise.

Researcher note: Field notes made during a site visit in 2008 point to the considerable anxiety and disquiet around the national research evaluation process taking place in English medium and with no Portuguese scholars included in the panel.

This whole visit (2008) has been coloured by people's concerns, hopes and anxieties around the national evaluation of research activity, organized and administered by the FCT (Fundacão para a Ciência e a Tecnologia) that had been taking place in the previous six months or so and, like all national assessments of research was likely to be highly consequential for individual scholars, research centres and institutions in terms of funding. Of particular concern this time around was the fact that there were no Portuguese academics on the evaluation panels. The panel of academics evaluating the Portuguese scholars' work has long since been 'international' that is, including academics from several (mainly European) universities in addition to Portuguese scholars. But for the first time, in 2007–8 there were no Portuguese scholars on the panels. This meant that all documentation had to be prepared in English.

FCT Story 1: The editor of an English-medium psychology journal: He had been on an FCT research board but had resigned his position because he disagreed with the 'international' only panel. He felt it was 'crazy' to have an 'international' panel who knew nothing about Portugal or Portuguese-based research. Moreover, Portuguese-medium journals don't seem to count – he felt that there should be space for all kinds of academic writing, in all languages.

FCT Story 2: Two scholars with longstanding research collaboration: They felt that their commitment over the years to publishing their work in English as well as Portuguese as the means of contributing to and being part of the international research community was being vindicated by the international nature of the panel. But they had been concerned about who would be selected as the panel members; there was no guarantee of independent review – and if the international member selected to evaluate their work was critical of their paradigm there would be problems. 'International' doesn't guarantee a fairer evaluation than 'local'.

FCT Story 3: The editor of a bilingual academic journal in education: The pressure to publish in English has increased a lot in the last year or so. 'This is a big dilemma for [scholars] working in education. If you write in English you lose … we Portuguese have a poet that says "my country is my language". It does not make sense to be evaluated only in English and only through English publications.'

Researcher reflection in diary: international, academic, independent, foreign, evaluation, small country. What's missing? Portugal.

Figure 2.8 Field notes relating to FCT.

English-medium publications can also help scholars receive funding from agencies outside the local national context, for example, European Union programmes which enable them to participate in cross-national research projects. In a cyclical way, participating in such projects also supports scholars' ability to develop local research activity, by fostering greater collaboration with local colleagues (within and outside their departments) and allowing scholars to recruit graduate students to work on their projects (see Chapter 3). As a Spanish educationalist explains, being involved in an EU funded research project:

> allows me to be in a project in which, first, I can do work with others on a certain issue; and second because with that I get money and that, particularly with the European projects, allows you to hire people, and because no one else in the department is interested in [my topic], I have a chance to get people who are starting to do their PhD, to work for it.

> (Discussion)

Thus across the board, the increase in scholars' reputation and prestige generated by English-medium academic publishing engenders concrete material benefits for scholars, their graduate students and in some cases their departments and other colleagues. On occasion, individual scholars' interests in English-medium publishing may align with institutional and governmental policies and practices that reward disseminating research in English – as in the case of the education scholar above, who welcomed the opportunity to work transnationally; at other times these are in considerable tension, as reflected in Figure 2.8. The tensions surrounding interests, opportunities and obstacles for publishing in English alongside other languages is a theme we return to in Chapters 5 and 6.

Conclusion

Multilingual scholars are responding to the increasing pressure to publish in the medium of English in different ways. Most are aiming to publish in English-medium 'international' journals while maintaining an active publications agenda for a range of communities, in local national languages as well as, in some instances, in other national languages. While there is evidence that 'international' is being used to refer to non-national contexts of publication, the sliding of the signifier *English* towards *international* and vice versa, which is attributed higher status, can mask the higher value being attributed to 'English' in many institutions. The differential value that English-medium publications accrue according to the communities with which they are associated functions as a distinct form of social capital (Bourdieu 1998). Across national contexts, this value is sustained through both formal and informal systems that reward publishing activity variably for the purposes of annual salary, promotion and attracting research grants. Scholars are enthusiastic about their research and often work at building up local research structures, even in contexts where the financial rewards and material resources are limited. At the same time, they are increasingly engaged in writing in English, particularly for high status Anglo-American journals. They are often exhausted, illustrating the sheer amount of work in which multilingual scholars frequently engage. As Canagarajah (1996, 2002a) and Ammon (2001) have noted, the imperative to publish in English places demands on periphery scholars that many Anglophone-centre scholars may not contend with, including access to material resources, the means to achieve sufficient level of English proficiency, and time and mental

energy for writing in multiple languages. In general, institutional policies and practices clearly place a high premium on English-medium publication. When assigned
specific measurement criteria, such as inclusion in indexes and impact factor,
English-medium publishing can appear as an objective measure of research quality (but see Chapter 1 for critiques). In a broader sense, publishing in English functions as a powerful form of symbolic capital (Bourdieu 1991).

It is clear that all researchers face some degree of internal or external pressure
to publish their (our) work. However, for multilingual scholars working outside
Anglophone contexts, these pressures are considerably greater, as in addition to
publishing in local national languages, governmental and institutional imperatives
urging the use of English may make some publishing activities feel compulsory
and have important consequences for how and where scholars invest their time
and energies.

In this chapter, our focus has been on academic text production largely from
the lens of the individual scholar, and on some of the consequences for individual scholars of decisions they make. Yet considerable academic text production
and decisions around text production – including information and access to relevant outlets for knowledge – involves a range of others. In the following two
chapters we explore how scholars are managing and negotiating the complex and
time-consuming tasks of sustaining publication activity in a number of languages
and for a range of communities, by working within and across networks and by
involving a variety of 'literacy brokers' directly in text production.

Suggestions for further reading

For highlighting the key relationship between the material conditions in which
multilingual scholars outside Anglophone contexts work and their ability to publish their scholarship, Suresh Canagarajah's (1996) article on the material or 'non-
discursive' resources is essential reading. For developing methodologies which
place writers at centre stage, see the work of Roz Ivanič on academic writing
(Ivanič 1998, and discussed in Carter *et al.* 2009) and more generally the work in
New Literacy Studies (e.g. see Barton and Hamilton 1998; Street 2003). To
understand how the discursive resources of English additionally constitute a form
of cultural capital, and considerable symbolic power in the global publishing
marketplace, Pierre Bourdieu's (1991, 1998) theories have been especially useful,
alongside academic literacy research which foregrounds the enactment of cultural
and symbolic capital, such as work edited by Lucia Thesen and Ermien Van
Pletzen (2006) and work by Bruce Horner and Min Zhan Lu (1999).

3 Mobilizing resources for text production

Academic research networks

Introduction

Given the number of communities that scholars are seeking to publish for, alongside the increasing pressure to publish in English, meeting the range of demands represents a considerable challenge and struggle. Participation in academic research networks seems to offer a key way for scholars to manage their writing for publication – particularly for publishing in English – within the resource constraints of their daily research, writing and work activity. Indeed, success in English-medium publishing seems to depend largely on the extent to which scholars can mobilize relevant resources via networked activity. In this chapter we explore the dynamics of scholars' participation in a range of networks from which they mobilize people and material resources to support their text production. Such participation includes, in particular, the co-authoring of texts, collaboration around research and a range of network brokering activity. We identify the ways that networks act as social capital, examining the resources to which networks afford access and we highlight the importance of the critical relationship between local and transnational networks for securing high status English-medium text production and publication. Evidence of the significance of different kinds of network activity – in which scholars engage locally and transnationally – calls into question the predominant focus on individual competence in EAP (English for academic purposes) and academic writing research and pedagogy more widely.

This chapter:

- Problematizes the continued emphasis in studies of academic writing and teaching on individual competence and signals the need to shift towards a focus on academic text production as networked activity;
- Explores the significance of links between local and transnational networks for text production;
- Explores the significance and challenges of establishing and sustaining local and transnational networks of activity for successful English-medium text production;
- Points to the different ways in which scholars in networks adopt different network roles (e.g. carrying out research, translating, revising English-medium texts, drafting abstracts);
- Points to the *pivotal* roles of some scholars in and across networks.

'Competence' as individual expertise or networks of activity?

> It's quite difficult [to publish in English-medium journals], not especially because of language, but because of the special scientific culture. Sometimes several of my colleagues complain that since they can't speak in English or can't write in English very well, they do not submit any paper to a journal. And usually I respond that it is mainly not a matter of language, it's a matter of scientific culture, a scientific community, a scientific network.
>
> Gyula, Central European psychology scholar (Discussion)

In identifying a *scientific culture, a scientific community, a scientific network* as highly salient to English-medium publishing, Gyula's quotation above powerfully points to the need to look beyond the individual as the locus of text production and signals the importance of networks as a key resource for supporting multilingual scholars' academic text production.

The idea of academic text production as a networked activity stands in stark contrast to conventional notions of what writers do – both in the popular imaginary and in the fields of English language teaching and of the teaching of writing more generally. Such notions typically picture the writer as an individual creator, one who must possess the full range of knowledge and abilities required for producing texts. Furthermore, academic writing, especially academic writing for publication, is often situated on the far end of a perceived trajectory of difficulty in terms of language learning and use, the assumption being that a certain degree and type of competence necessarily precede the production of academic texts in English. The notion of *competence* here is widely used to refer to the individual capacity to do something effectively with the English language, including writing academic texts (e.g. Burrough-Boenisch 2003; Canagarajah 2002c; Young 2003). In some instances *competence* is explicitly qualified as *communicative*, signalling an ability to communicate appropriately according to context (e.g. Chimbganda 2000; Olson 2002). Likewise qualifiers such as *interactional* (Jenkins and Parra 2003) and *cross-cultural* and *intercultural communicative* competence (Sehlaoui 2001) also signal the importance of contextual knowledge for successful communication. In contrast, an emphasis on knowledge of language is foregrounded in the qualifier *linguistic* competence (Medgyes and Laszlo 2001; Norton and Starfield 1997). Explicit distinctions are sometimes drawn between linguistic (knowledge of grammatical rules) and communicative (rules of use) competence (Berns 1990; Widdowson 1983).

The continued emphasis on individual competence in the research and teaching of academic writing – albeit with a range of qualifiers – brings into relief two linguistic traditions still exerting a powerful influence on understandings about what's involved in academic writing. The first (chronologically) is the cognitivist-Chomskyan tradition, which emphasizes not only knowledge of the grammatical rules governing a language (Chomsky 1957, 1965), but also the notion of an idealized 'native' speaker. The second is the Hymesian tradition, which stresses the importance of exploring speakers' and listeners' (and writers' and readers') knowledge of contextual rules for use in order to communicate appropriately in different social contexts (Hymes 1968, 1971). While the former cognitive tradition is evident in studies of writing, particularly in second language acquisition research (Ching 2002; Firth and Wagner 2003), the latter communicative emphasis has held considerable sway (e.g. Allison 1996; Hall and Eggington 2000; Paulston 1992; Swales 1990). However, while Hymes's contextualized 'communicative competence' has undoubtedly influenced much ELT work, the cognitivist-Chomskyan tradition has cast a long shadow across approaches purporting to be 'context sensitive'. As powerfully argued by Leung, the socially oriented notion of communicative competence 'has been recontextualised in ELT' as a psychological phenomenon (Leung 2005: 138). There are increasing calls for a return to Hymes's descriptive ethnographic intent (see Rampton 1997). Leung argues for ELT to 'take notice of real-world social, cultural and language developments in contemporary conditions and to re-engage with a set of reformulated ethnographic sensitivities and sensibilities' (2005: 119). While Leung's call for a greater recognition of real-world conditions does not argue for a shift away from the central importance attached to individual competence (e.g. Jacoby and McNamara 1999), his emphasis on 'ethnographic sensitivities' signals a need to reclaim Hymes's emphasis on framing communicative activity in terms of networks, individuals and resources:

> One cannot take linguistic form, a given code, or even speech itself, as a limiting frame of reference. One must take as context a community, or network of persons, investigating its communicative activities as a whole, so that any use of channel and code takes its place as part of the resources upon which the members draw.
>
> (Hymes 1974: 4)

Few studies of academic writing have taken up this network perspective since Hymes's exhortation to broaden the focus of research, testifying to the enduring pull of the individual competence perspective. Notable exceptions include the work of Ferenz (2005), who – while sustaining a predominantly individualized focus in terms of text production – draws on social network analysis to explore the influence of the language used in students' social networks on their choice of language for texts such as master's theses. Casanave documents the importance to novice Japanese scholars of cultivating 'networks of contacts' (1998: 194) for publishing and co-authoring opportunities. These scholars actively work to maintain networks that they have partly established during graduate study in the United States (see also Flowerdew 2000). Belcher uses Swales's (1987: 43) term 'off-network' to refer to scholars isolated from centres of power in 'locations with limited resources and perhaps few colleagues' (Belcher 2007: 2). Belcher notes that the support of local colleagues in responding to reviewers and editors is consequential for writers who persist in revising texts multiple times and ultimately achieve publication. These studies help to foreground the fact that text production often relies on the collaboration of a range of people who may not conventionally be considered as having an 'authoring' role, the importance of which is borne out by the scholars' accounts and experiences, as we now discuss (see also Chapter 4 for discussion of literacy brokers).

Scholar Profile 4: Africa, Education, Spain

Africa is a 28-year-old scholar who recently successfully defended her PhD in the field of education and now works as an assistant professor. Hers is a 'European PhD', funded through the Spanish government, which means among other things that 25% of the thesis had to be written in a language other than the national – including autonomous regional – languages. As part of the European PhD programme she was entitled (and funded) to spend up to three months of each of the doctoral study years in a university in any country as long as the focus would be relevant to her doctoral work, whether empirically or theoretically. During the period of her doctoral study therefore she spent three months in research visits to Portugal and Argentina, at universities selected because of their direct relevance to her interests. Her PhD panel involved examiners from three national contexts: Finland, Germany and Spain.

Africa comes from a bilingual French/Spanish family background and loves using and learning languages. In addition to Spanish and French, she began learning English as a young child and is currently learning German and Catalan. She sees English as crucial for her academic work: for reading in her field and for publication, the latter seen as an essential element for securing a successful career.

> It's [publishing in English] much better than just publishing in Spanish, because what you publish in Spanish is just for people who read Spanish, and it doesn't go abroad. If I want to have a big career - I don't know still if I want to – it's very useful to publish in English.
>
> (Discussion)

She works closely with her former supervisor not just on her PhD-related research and writings but also on a number of projects funded at national and European levels of which he is principal or co-lead investigator. As part of this research group activity while still a PhD candidate, Africa worked alongside more senior scholars from disciplines including education, psychology and sociology. Before defending her thesis and through her participation in such a strong local national research group, she had already co-authored articles, book chapters and books in Spanish as well as an article and European Union research reports in English.

Her former supervisor has acted as a mentor not only in her research but also with regard to English-medium publications. He has supported Africa's writing in a number of ways; translating and working on drafts in Spanish towards English, as well as revising English-medium versions of texts. In turn, she has made a significant contribution both to work within the local research team and their transnational links, contributing to data analysis and writings in Spanish and English.

Multilingual scholars' networks

Describing scholars' networks

In our discussions with multilingual scholars, their experiences of working with others in a range of network relationships that connect both directly and indirectly with academic text production emerged as a significant theme. We therefore asked individual scholars to draw a representation of these relationships in a way that would encapsulate, from their perspective, key people connected to their research and writing activity. As indicated by the six example sketches included in Figure 3.1 below and over page, scholars chose different ways of representing these relationships.

While the representations in these sketches clearly differ, they point in particular to the importance attached to the following:

- Links with other individual scholars (all sketches);
- Links within and across different departments, disciplines, institutions (sketches 1, 3, 4);
- Links between countries/contexts (sketches 1, 5, 6);
- Links at specific moments or over certain periods of time (sketch 3);
- Importance of particular scholars (sketches 1, 2, 3, 6);
- Closeness or distance of others in relation to themselves (sketches 1, 2, 3, 6);
- Emphasis on themselves as members of teams (sketches 1, 2, 3);
- Foregrounding of the topic around which link is built/sustained (sketches 1, 2, 3, 4, 6);
- Links between research and writing activity as compared with teaching (sketch 4);
- Ways in which specific writings are connected with specific individuals and/or groups (sketches 2, 4, 6).

Sketch 1

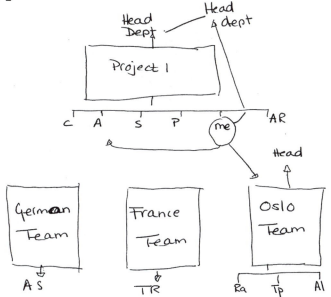

Sketch 2

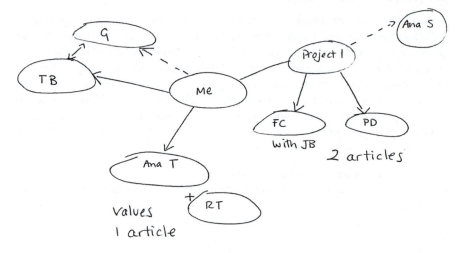

g

TB

Me

Ana T

values
1 article

RT

Project 1

Ana S

FC

with JB

PD

2 articles

Sketch 3

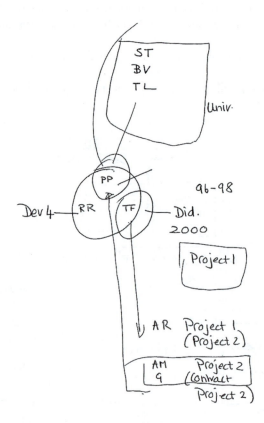

ST
BV
TL

Univ.

PP

96-98

Dev 4 — RR   TF — Did.

2000

Project 1

AR Project 1
    (Project 2)

AM   Project 2
g   (Contract
      Project 2)

Sketch 4

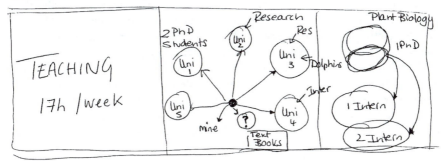

Sketch 5

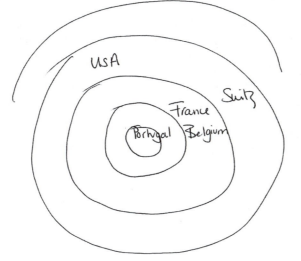

Sketch 6

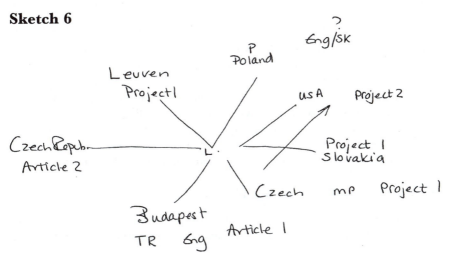

Figure 3.1 Scholars' sketches of their networks.

Scholars' informal diagrams and sketches reflect key features of network activity as discussed by theorists in a number of disciplines, in particular, sociology and sociolinguistics. Features most directly relevant to our discussion are outlined in *Methodological Tool 3*, some of which are evident in scholars' diagrams. Thus, for instance, networks can be described along two domains: structural (features) and interactional (dynamics) (Milroy and Milroy 1992). A key feature of networks is *nodes*, or the members of a network, while the *ties* that connect nodes comprise the interactional domain, or patterns of relationships. Both nodes and ties are evident in scholars' representations. For example, in Sketch 4 the scholar uses lines with arrows to indicate ties emanating from himself to students and colleagues in two departments in his institution, while in Sketch 1 the scholar uses nodes to represent both people and the geographical locations to which she has ties. Networks may include nodes that are connected because of official positions, such as members of an academic department, division, or institution (Sketches 1, 3, 4) but such official entities do not a priori constitute networks. Instead, as the figures indicate, academic research networks can be informal and unofficial, cohering around a particular field, topic or methodology (Sketches 1, 2, 3, 4, 6) or may be more formal and official such as special interest groups of a scholarly disciplinary association, albeit entailing voluntary participation. Sketches 1, 5 and 6 indicate how some multilingual scholars' writing activity is embedded within larger network activity and connections, illustrating how the 'highly clustered' structure of scientific networks often comprises smaller, tightly knit groups that operate within larger networks (Newman 2001: 408).[1]

Scholars' diagrams also illustrate other key network features such as *centrality*, that is, when someone is positioned as central to a network, as in Sketch 1, in which the scholar places the head of her research group in a hierarchical position above all other network members. We prefer the term 'pivotal' to centrality as it more usefully signals the dynamism of relationship between 'central' and other nodes in networks in terms of managing access to resources. Network *clusters* are evident in Sketches 1 and 6, which position both local and transnational research groups as network nodes. The *intensity* of ties is indicated in some sketches by the solid and dotted lines connecting nodes that represent both individual people and a main research group (see Sketch 2).

The scholars' sketches show traces of what Crane (1972) refers to as 'invisible colleges', which link groups of scholars together for the 'exchange of scholarly thought, privilege and much else' (as discussed in Baldauf and Jernudd 1987: 98). The issue of 'privilege' is important here in relation to the function of networks in helping to secure high status English-medium publication, as we discuss in the following sections. Connections between scholars, including the establishment of such 'colleges', have of course been facilitated by the growth of information and communications technologies: email, internet search engines and electronic library databases are used on practically a daily basis by all the scholars.[2]

Resources available through networks

For multilingual scholars seeking to sustain publishing activity across a number of communities, participation in both local and transnational networks seems

Contacts (connections to other scholars, both local and distant)
Information (about local and transnational conferences, grants, publishing opportunities)
Academic materials, such as journal articles etc.
Rhetorical resources (e.g. English-language writing expertise and assistance)
Collaboration on writing (including in English)
Collaboration on research (including the full spectrum of research and writing activities)
Brokering (e.g. connections to publishing opportunities, support with writing and publishing, help in interpreting reviewers' comments, etc.)

Figure 3.2 Resources made available and mobilized via local and transnational academic networks.

to be highly desirable, if not essential. This is particularly important for gaining access to Anglophone-centre-based information and the crucial linguistic and rhetorical resources needed for English-medium high status publishing. As indicated by the scholars, networks thus facilitate access to contacts (including other networks), various types of knowledge and opportunities to use these academic resources. Figure 3.2 lists the main types of resources that scholars mention in relation to publishing activity, which are available and mobilized via networks.

In considering relevant resources, it is important not to underestimate the significance of sharing the most obvious kind of resources – such as research literature – as illustrated in one Central European psychology scholar's account:

> He is a key figure in this field and I met him. I knew his work from the literature and I met him at a conference in München. And I had very short conversation with him in the corridor and he sent me a pile of these articles with some comments. He realises that I am interested in this field and maybe these articles would be helpful and they were absolutely good to have because they were practically an overview of these things. *It is absolutely impossible for me to get access to these materials* and then he sent me the proof copy of his book and things like that. And we had a kind of correspondence as well and it was very remarkable.
>
> (Discussion: *italic* indicates our emphasis)

For scholars working in contexts that offer limited amounts of the material resources many Anglophone-centre scholars take for granted, resources made available via network activities – including the distribution of basic resources such as journal articles in a specialized field – can prove highly consequential.

Methodological Tool 3: Analysing academic research networks

To describe and analyse scholars' academic research networks, the following key notions have proved useful (e.g. Boissevain 1987; Haythornthwaite 1996; Newman 2001).

Structural domain features

Nodes – points or people or actors in a network, comprising individuals or groups of any size

Centrality – the relative position of a node in a network, affecting how much access the node has to resources and power over their flow and other activity*

Clusters – groupings of subsets of nodes within a network, usually representing dense relationships

Range – the number of nodes or clusters in a particular network, and the diversity of these nodes or clusters

Ties – relationships between nodes (flows of information, support, resources, and structural and personal connections), also called edges or lines

Density/sparsity – the extent to which nodes in a network are connected to other nodes

Interactional domain features

A/symmetry – power relations and social status differences between nodes in a network, sometimes related to access to resources

Uni- or *multiplexity* of ties – the various domains in which nodes may be connected, e.g. work, neighbourhood, church, social events, etc.

Intensity – the frequency of contacts between nodes

Durability – the length of contact between nodes in a network, or persistence of ties

Brokering – bridging networks or clusters to facilitate or gate-keep the allocation of resources, including information

---

*While drawing on the notion of centrality, we find the term 'pivot/al' a useful way to indicate the dynamism of the relationships between 'central' nodes in a network and other network members.

Social network analysts have used various graphic representations of these domains and features of networks, finding such graphics valuable for both analytic and presentational reasons (Freeman 2000). An essential choice to make in graphically representing a network is whether to take the 'ego' perspective of one member (Wellman *et al.* 2006) or to present the whole network as determined by an external perspective, such as the researcher's (Mitchell 1986). In the representations of scholars' networks – both their own and those we have designed – an ego perspective is used whereby the network represented is from the perspective of the individual scholar.

How specific network ties may (or may not) provide access to such crucial resources, across local and transnational networks, warrants a deeper focus which we can only briefly touch on here. The network literature frames ties in a strong/weak binary, but emphasizes that having connections to both types of tie are likely to produce the greatest access to resources. Strong ties entail frequent, intense and durable contact, as well as the multiplexity that results when members collaborate in different capacities or contexts or share ties to other networks. However, strong ties, it is argued, can limit a network's range (Portes 1998), thereby restricting access to information and other resources outside the network and acting as 'a conservative force' (Milroy and Milroy 1992: 13). In contrast, weak ties, which are usually more uniplex and heterogeneous, can enable greater flows of resources, particularly types of information or resources relevant in situations such as job hunting. Weak ties represent intermittent or isolated network contacts that may be activated for a specific goal, such as a funded research project that ends within a particular timeframe. The seemingly paradoxical notion of the 'strength of weak ties' (Granovetter 1973, 1983) suggests that people with a broad array of ties to various nodes (e.g. in sparse networks) have greater access to knowledge than do members of dense networks comprising strong ties. In characterizing the types of network activity that seem to support publication in high status English-medium journals, we point to specific instances of strong and weak ties as they occur in networked activity and how these affect text production. Especially important for network members are ties – weak or strong –to nodes who act as brokers – whether in central or marginal positions – and who play a pivotal gate-keeping role as they manage ties and transmit resources within and between networks (see Haythornthwaite 1996; Wellman and Berkowitz 1988).

Characterizing local–transnational network activity in academic text production

In this section we provide four characterizations of the types of network activity in which multilingual scholars engage, signalling in particular the relationship between local and transnational networks and how these relationships affect opportunities for high status English-medium publishing. In these characterizations, we draw on key notions from the network literature discussed above and summarized in *Methdological Tool 3*. We characterize the relationship between local and transnational networks as weak or strong depending on the number of ties, their density, intensity, durability and uni- or multiplexity. That is, we consider how ties between networks are activated, for what kinds of purpose and with what kinds of result. We highlight the pivotal brokering role of some network members, especially between local and transnational networks, and illustrate how local–transnational network activity directly impacts on text production and publication by briefly considering examples of Text Histories.[3]

Scholar Profile 5: Diana, Education, Portugal

Diana, 51, has taught at her university for 14 years. Seven years ago she was promoted to what in the local system is called 'auxiliary' professor, a higher rank than assistant professor. Her multidisciplinary research in education includes multiculturalism, language and anthropological approaches. In her specialist subfield Diana's reputation for cutting-edge work is growing: in 2008 she was invited to give keynote speeches at two 'international' conferences. She has collaborated with local colleagues on teaching-related publications as well as some research publications but she generally publishes single-authored texts which she recognizes is a challenge: *I think I am really making progress but it's difficult because I am alone doing that.*

Portuguese is Diana's daily language of communication; she has also studied French, Italian, Spanish and English. Her English is strong: she earned her master's degree in an Anglophone country and has visited there periodically. However, since returning to Portugal, she finds it difficult to maintain English and does not enjoy the effort. The English classes she tried locally seemed irrelevant as they were aimed at younger students preparing for examinations.

Diana has published a considerable number of articles and book chapters in Portuguese as well as textbooks. She has also published in English in Portuguese national journals. She regularly presents at 'international' conferences; most of these have been turned into proceedings papers rather than journal articles. Publishing in high status English-medium journals appeals to her, but she feels she lacks information about suitable target journals. Although she is acutely sensitive to the imperative of English-medium publications for advancement, her motivation for seeking to publish in English is to reach a broad audience interested in her theoretical ideas. Despite her high level of English, she feels challenged to express *very complex thoughts:*

> I do not have the grammar, you see, to write it in English. For example, suppose I start a sentence 'If something or other' then I don't know what is the correct verb tense. And then I start to change the whole structure of the phrase, and get into my English difficulties. And then I get very mad because it's not the way I write, you see. And I was so upset with that, that I stopped writing.
>
> (Discussion)

Diana has been reflecting on how to achieve her goals of developing three distinct strands of her work into English-medium articles for high status journals. Surmounting the conditions of working without close collaborators, lacking knowledge of target journals, and dissatisfaction about her writing abilities in English pose a clear challenge. Recently, Diana was anticipating a six-month sabbatical, but political and economic events in Portugal called into question whether it would be granted.

Network activity 1: weak local–weak transnational

Characterizing the local network: Joaquim is a Southern European associate professor of psychology whose research area bridges psychology and medicine. While his English is strong, so far he has published exclusively in the local national language. For a number of years he has worked with colleagues and graduate students in his institution on various projects. Joaquim is currently engaged in two main projects funded by modest national government grants. His desire for larger grants contributes to the pressure he feels for English-medium publications, which, given their higher status, help secure funding. Thus Joaquim hopes that expanding his local network will provide opportunities for publications and funding. Currently, in order to pursue one main interest, he has convened a local research group of three colleagues at his institution, four collaborators at the hospital where the research takes place (a doctor, a nurse, a nutritionist and a psychologist) and graduate students. His second project involves four colleagues from his institution, graduate students, 10 hospital colleagues and a Swedish scholar (see Figure 3.3 for a diagram of Joaquim's networks). Managing multidisciplinary networks is not easy, however, as researchers' objectives, such as obtaining external funding, do not always mesh with institutional polices, in this case, hospital policies and aims. In fact, Joaquim relates how a previous cross-institutional network, which was characterized by weak ties, disintegrated:

> It was very hard to work alone. Well, in the beginning there was a team and very good intentions and so on, but this didn't work out as I planned and I had to make several changes in the site, and with collaborators in this research in order to get the participants, and everything changed. First the beginning of the project was postponed about one year because the leadership of the hospital was a little bit changed and we had to ask for another authorization from the new director and it took almost one year to get an answer. And then we started, and I came to realize that things were not working, and that I would have to change people. Nothing worked as I planned.
>
> (Discussion)

Lessons from this earlier project have spurred Joaquim to forge stronger collaborations. For both current projects, however, his networks consist predominantly of local members, few of whom have adequate access to the connections, information or resources for English-medium high status publishing. For example, one of his doctoral students drafted a manuscript in the local national language and then translated it word for word into English, leaving Joaquim with considerable work in preparing it for submission. He highlights the need he feels to get support in these tasks: *It's so difficult to do papers in English if we don't have some colleagues or students that are skillful in writing in English* (Discussion). While his network members contribute resources such as disciplinary and research knowledge, experience obtaining government grants, most lack ties that could facilitate publishing. In addition, his networks are *sparse* (see Figure 3.3) with little overlap between them, so Joaquim cannot share work across the two projects. Despite these constraints, Joaquim is making progress toward his publishing goals: a high-status Anglophone-centre journal asked him to revise and resubmit a manuscript he co-authored with a master's student based on her research as part of one of his projects. This preliminary success comes despite the limited range of Joaquim's local network (i.e. few ties beyond the local partner institutions), with few ties to linguistic/rhetorical knowledge and other resources related to English-medium publishing.

Characterizing the transnational network(s): While earning his PhD, Joaquim forged a weak tie to a US psychologist (see TH 3.1). More recently he has travelled to conferences outside his local national site expressly to expand his network, such as a small UK research seminar which has as one objective to *build a network of people researching on this topic* (Discussion). There Joaquim has also met with a Swedish scholar whom he had earlier invited to consult on one of his research projects. Such conference travel requires financial resources, which are limited in Joaquim's context, thus often restricting access to conferences as a way to build networks.

TH 3.1: Seeking network resources to revise an English-medium article

To collect data for his dissertation, Joaquim contacted a US psychologist by email to ask permission to translate and adapt the psychologist's questionnaire. Later, this psychologist emailed Joaquim supportive feedback on his first English-medium paper, based on his PhD dissertation. Joaquim responded to some of these points before submitting the paper to a US journal with a high impact factor. Nonetheless, the paper was rejected, primarily on the grounds that the sample size was too small and too homogenous. Joaquim invited the same US psychologist to co-author the revised paper, but the colleague was too busy. Had this been a stronger tie, co-authorship might have resulted from such an invitation. Next, Joaquim invited a local colleague to help revise the paper.

> A colleague here who did his PhD in the United States – and he's also from statistics – and I, we are going to transform it, to revise the paper and improve it in English and to send to any kind of journal as long as it is indexed and has an impact factor. Maybe send it to the lowest impact factor, doing the opposite strategy [previous strategy was to target a high impact factor journal]. In the end we sent it. I got the answer but after about a year. Classes had begun and we had no more time to work on it.
>
> (Discussion)

Contemplating how to respond to the journal reviews, Joaquim was aware that his limited material resources (access to a larger sample, as requested by a previous reviewer), lack of familiarity with other suitable target journals and time constraints deterred him from revising the article. Ultimately Joaquim abandoned it to pursue newer projects: *It takes a lot of time and also I depend on the help of others and it's not easy* (Discussion). This TH illustrates how working within both weak local and weak transnational networks limits access to resources that can be mobilized around text production and the difficulties involved in building transnational network ties. It also illustrates the often asymmetrical power relations between peripheral individuals and networks and Anglophone-centre scholars and networks: Joaquim called on the US scholar for support (and not vice versa), and in this case the US scholar was not able to offer it.

Joaquim's network diagram (see Figure 3.3, JS = Joaquim) shows his connections in relation to three projects: on the left is Project 1 including members from his institution and a local hospital; on the right, Project 2 involves different institutional colleagues (except for one, JN, who belongs to both projects) and a Swedish scholar (PN) as the only transnational link. The top network circle relates to the TH 3.1, which involved a weak transnational tie to the US scholar (KM) and one

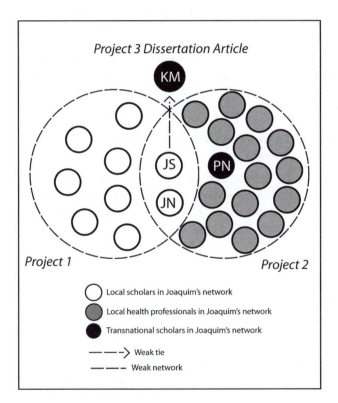

Figure 3.3 Joaquim's networks.

local colleague (JN). A dotted line indicates the weaker status of the top network circle.

Network activity 2: strong local–weak transnational

Characterizing the local network: Fidel is a senior lecturer in education at a Southern European university. He has a high level of expertise in English and has published extensively. Fidel participates in a local network with colleagues and graduate students from multiple departments at his institution in which group members have been researching and publishing together for more than a decade, with Fidel co-authoring at least 14 texts in the medium of the local national language and English. The local network thus comprises intense, durable ties; some nodes share multiplex ties along work and social lines. For several years Fidel and some local network members have been involved in two interconnected funded projects, one national and the other transnational (European Union).

   Characterizing the transnational network(s): Fidel's ties to transnational networks are generally official (that is established through official EU-funded schemes) and generally weak in that they reflect intermittent collaboration projects, such as the current one, which involves scholars from six other national contexts (T1–6 in Figure 3.4). His involvement in the EU project includes brokering the participation of some local network members into the transnational network activity. These ties are activated at different points in the project cycle and for different purposes – for example, to organize conference submissions and to write papers.

TH 3.2: Mobilizing local network resources to submit and publish conference papers

During one of our field visits, Fidel and local colleagues were working feverishly to meet a deadline for the electronic submission of proposals for an international conference. Both national and transnational project teams considered it important to submit proposals, not least as evidence of dissemination of funded research. Field notes document the activity involved in meeting this deadline:

TH 3.2 Example 1

It's early evening, around 6 pm. I'm waiting to interview Fidel [FG in Figure 3.4] about his latest writings. Fidel is busy, walking in and out of his office from his desk to the printer in another office. NO and AC are discussing in Spanish the draft submissions they are preparing for an English-medium European conference. The deadline is imminent and they are all anxious to get these proposals in. Fidel is engaged in several tasks at the same time. He is trying to write a single-authored proposal in English and support NO in producing his single-authored text in English. Fidel sits at his desk. AC comes in and looks at NO's draft and adds comments. I'm there so I offer to look at NO's draft too. The phone rings and Fidel is talking on the phone to MN and they are discussing in Spanish a version of another proposal they are preparing together on behalf of two other colleagues [JK and JL in Figure 3.4], also involved in one of the research projects. Fidel listens and responds in Spanish on the phone as he writes at his computer in English, and MN writes at hers.

(Field notes)

In the event, nine proposals of approximately 1,000 words each were produced to schedule, involving 13 scholars working across two projects: three scholars in the EU project, seven in the national project and three working on both projects. All proposals were accepted and presented. After the conference, six papers were published as proceedings. While the texts produced were drawn from two distinct projects, the extract from field notes above gives an impression of the amount of activity involved and the ways in which members from both projects supported each other's English-medium text production. Fidel draws on the local network as a resource for his own text production: MN, a colleague in the local network, regularly comments on his English-medium texts, including texts for this conference. But Fidel is also an important resource for others within the network. He translates, comments on Spanish drafts in Spanish, comments on English drafts in English and Spanish, and makes revisions to Spanish and English drafts. Example 2 illustrates how Fidel helps move one text from Spanish and English towards submission for the conference.

TH 3.2 Example 2

Draft 1 by junior colleague in Spanish and English	Draft 2 by Fidel in English only
(1) Results of this research **provienen del analisis de un** questionnaire, that it **indaga** about the next points: labour **trayectoria**, initial and continuous formation, **condiciones de trabajo y vision de la profesion**. (2) It will be analyse the relationship **que** existed **entre estos rasgos de los docentes y su concepcion de identidad.**[4]	(1) Our analyses will be based upon the replies of these teachers to a questionnaire which interrogates into the following points: career, initial and continuing training, working conditions, their images of the profession. (2) Teachers' identity will be framed within these features.

The shift involves translation, reformulations at word and phrase levels, and deletions (see Methodological Tool on pages 89–91). Fidel's role in the stages of another text produced for the same conference can be illustrated by considering the text's trajectory (in Example 3), which involved some members of both local and transnational networks.

TH 3.2 Example 3

Three key stages were identified in this TH's trajectory as summarized below:

Stage 1. Research carried out by team and taxonomy generated. Communication is predominantly Spanish medium.

> NO drafts a paper based on developing a new taxonomy in Spanish.
> Taxonomy paper discussed by local team in Spanish.
> Professional translator translates text into English.
> Fidel checks and revises translation.

Stage 2. Written text distributed for discussion among EU colleagues. Communication in English medium.

> OP from Team 1 (T1 in Figure 3.4) comments on taxonomy in English on behalf of the Czech team, which suggested additional type in taxonomy.

Stage 3. Taxonomy revisited; revised English-medium text produced. Communication in both Spanish and English medium.

> Team discuss in Spanish and English.
> NO makes revisions in Spanish in line with OP's suggestions
> Fidel translates new type from Spanish to English for taxonomy.
> NO develops paper further.
> Fidel translates Spanish versions into English.

It is clear that Fidel plays a pivotal brokering role, not only in the research activity taking place in both projects but also in the crafting and drafting of the English-medium academic texts – his own and those co-authored and single-authored by others (as indicated by names on published papers). Fidel links two quite different networks: the strong, intense, durable local network is linked to a weaker, less intense, shorter term transnational network. While the transnational network formed around a specific purpose and did not persist, Fidel's brokering between local and transnational networks enabled members of his local network to gain access to the presenting and publishing opportunities afforded by the transnational network. What is also important to note here is that the transnational ties established through the funded projects seemed to strengthen the local network's internal ties and research and writing in the two local national languages as well as in English.

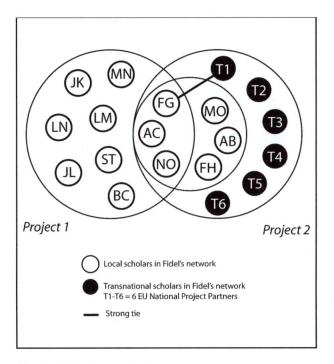

Figure 3.4 Fidel's networks.

Figure 3.4 shows Fidel's overlapping local and transnational networks, with three members involved in both projects. Fidel's network diagram shows participants in the local and transnational projects discussed in the TH. In the left hand circle are members of the local network. Three scholars including Fidel can be considered 'core' to the local network in that they collaborate closely to generate ideas for research activity and publications (see FG, MN and JK in Figure 3.4). Located in the overlap of the circles are colleagues working on both projects.

Network activity 3: weak local–strong transnational

Characterizing the local network: Julie is a Central European associate professor of education with a high level of English proficiency and more than 20 English-medium international publications, compared with a small number of publications in the local national language. She carefully followed advice from her PhD advisor to produce English-medium publications, to: *publish internationally and don't worry about who thinks what about you in* [the local context]. *Make sure you are internationally well known, and things will kind of be arranged for you sooner or later* (Discussion).

More recently Julie became motivated to pursue publishing in the local national language to increase her qualifications for promotion and to obtain her country's highest academic degree (beyond the PhD), the 'academic doctorate':

> Earlier I didn't publish a lot in [national language] but I have to, because our department is very young and we need somebody who could pass this academic doctorate thing, and for that I had to be known locally and then much more known outside. The requirements for university teachers to have this degree is new stuff. You cannot start your department, cannot start an MA programme if you don't have somebody who has this Academy of Sciences doctorate and I'm the person who is closest to this.
>
> (Discussion)

To achieve this new goal Julie needed to build a more robust local reputation, in pursuit of which she developed a local network, not previously a priority. Her new local network comprises graduate students and two colleagues who also have ties to her PhD advisor. Developing the local network was a strategic move in relation to Julie's specific goals. However, rather than being the original engine of Julie's publishing success, her local network is being built on her 'international' (English-medium) publishing experience.

Characterizing the transnational network(s): Julie's PhD supervisor had moved to an Anglophone-centre country, from where he facilitated Julie's publications, first by co-authoring three English-medium articles with her, then by brokering introductions to scholars and editors in Anglophone publishing houses (as indicated in Figure 3.5, Julie's network diagram). Julie directly attributes her success to this relationship:

> I actually learned to publish from him and it was he who pushed me to publish, so without him I wouldn't have because I thought I'm not clever enough for that kind of thing. And then when he left, for a long time he still read some of my papers and we did things together.
>
> (Discussion)

Subsequently, Julie has published prolifically in English, partly as a result of being linked with this broker – her supervisor – who connected her to transnational networks, information and other resources that have supported her success. Julie's network diagram shows both her recently created local network and her extensive transnational network, with Julie at the overlap of local and transnational (see Figure 3.5, JL = Julie). Transnational network members are included in two concentric circles: in the inner circle are members with whom Julie has strong, intense ties, such as her PhD advisor (ZE); in what she calls the 'outer circle' are other contacts from a range of geographic locations (United States, United Kingdom, Japan, Netherlands). Julie's diagram demonstrates a particularly wide-ranging network, based on both durable and intermittent contact with various ties. It is a combination of these strong and weak ties that has facilitated Julie's access to publishing, as TH 3.3 illustrates.

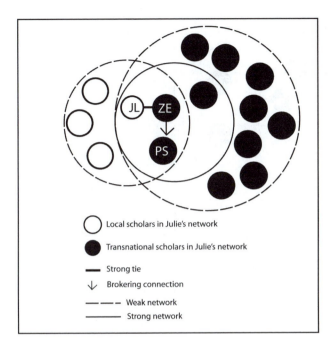

Figure 3.5 Julie's networks.

TH 3.3: Mobilizing transnational network resources for English-medium book publishing

Julie's PhD advisor has acted as a pivotal broker for much of her publishing success. In addition to co-authoring with Julie, he informed her about the opportunity to publish a single-authored English-medium book with an Anglophone-centre company, as she relates:

> When I finished my PhD, my topic was not very well researched because it's very difficult to research, there's a lot of [X] theory behind it that you have to be familiar with. And when my advisor moved to Great Britain he had contact with lots of people and he started publishing books and then he told me he would get me a contract on writing a book on [X] and I wrote a few chapters to see how I can progress. Then when I was writing this book he wrote me an email that an editor is looking for a book in this series and he actually has planned a book – and I contacted him and he said okay, yes, he's interested. And I sent him a proposal, and a sample chapter and that's how it went. I had to restructure some of the things, but that was it.
>
> (Discussion)

Once the proposal was accepted, Julie drew on local but particularly also on transnational network ties to seek feedback on drafts of the manuscript: two local

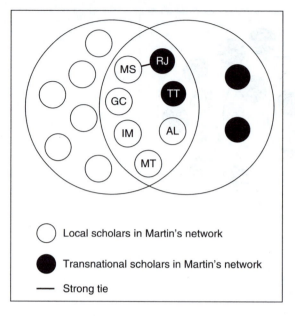

Figure 3.6 Martin's networks.

colleagues, her former PhD advisor, the publishing house editor and an anonymous reviewer. Julie's story highlights how the strong tie to her PhD advisor in her transnational network brokered her links to the weak ties leading to the book publishing opportunity. Despite her initial lack of confidence, Julie's experience with publishing many English-medium texts laid the groundwork for taking on a book project, but the research network created the conditions in which she could gain fairly easy access to the editor. More recently these successes have also helped her develop a stronger local network which has resulted in receiving a large government grant for local national research.

Network activity 4: strong local–strong transnational

Characterizing the local network: Martin and Géza are Central European psychologists who have collaborated for more than 15 years in a strong local network that includes other researchers, graduate students and a departmental translator. They have co-authored, often with additional local network members, some 20 publications in the local national language and in English. As head of the institute where they work, Géza may be characterized as a central node in their network, however, Martin consistently collaborates in research and writing with Géza and takes the lead on his fair share of publications.

Characterizing the transnational network(s): Géza and Martin have a longstanding tie to a British psychologist, Sophie, who with her husband, has been committed to supporting the work of Central European scholars for some time. Sophie has brokered introductions for Martin and Géza to other scholars and has collaborated with them for many years on projects and publications. One of their transnational network ties with a British psychologist, Rudy, was originally forged in the early 1990s by another local network member, Ivan, who initiated this tie by requesting an offprint from Rudy; soon afterwards, Martin, Géza and Ivan met Rudy at a conference. On a subsequent trip to the United Kingdom, Sophie took Martin and Géza to visit Rudy, who invited them to participate in an EU research project involving 10 countries. Although they were not then eligible for EU funding, they secured a small local government grant to participate. Their ties with Sophie and Rudy, as well as others to whom Sophie introduced them, have lasted for more than 15 years, with intermittent contact including visits on both sides, typically funded by the British Academy, and ongoing contact by email. The network activity has resulted in collaborations on a number of projects and publications.

TH 3.4: Mobilizing local and transnational network resources to contribute a chapter to an English-medium book

This book chapter resulted from network participation across local and transnational contexts that provided opportunities to be included in the book and to co-author texts. While the research came out of a 10-country EU collaboration, apart from Rudy, the co-authors came from the local network. The text began as an abstract for a conference that was organized by a Central European university and co-sponsored by institutes in the Netherlands and the United States. The local network's strategy for conference submissions was for all members to submit different single-authored papers. After acceptance, other names were added, both to acknowledge their contributions and to increase their English-medium publications. The local network submitted four papers, two of which were accepted. For the chapter in this TH, Martin was the lead author.

The resulting book was co-edited by the conference organizer – a Central European scholar – and another European scholar at one of the sponsoring institutions, Thomas, whom Martin had previously met at European conferences. The main organizer had ties to two US researchers who connected him to a US publisher, which agreed to publish the book. The call for papers had asked authors to have their work checked by 'a native English speaker'. As a result Martin engaged Rudy early in the writing process, asking him to check his English before the conference (Martin also received input from the local departmental translator). At this point Martin added the names of Rudy and the local network members as co-authors. After the conference, Martin sent the next draft to Thomas, the co-editor. Thomas returned substantial suggestions, with an overall aim of shifting the text from conference paper to book chapter genre, specifically by reducing the number of tables and making the text more of a narrative. Subsequently, Rudy spent two days at the Central European scholars' institute with them working to, as Martin characterized it, *anglicize* the text. Example 1 in TH 3.4 illustrates the kinds of change made to the discussion section during Rudy's visit (for details of categories used to track changes in text trajectories see *Methodological Tool 4: Text-oriented heuristic for tracking changes made across drafts*).

TH 3.4 Example 1: Extracts illustrating revisions to discussion section of chapter

Type of change	Previous text	Changes	Rhetorical/ knowledge significance
Content changes: additions, deletions, replacements of words or sections	p. 16, 'the frequencies were found to'	Additions (in bold): **'for many of the more descriptive indicators** the frequencies **within these samples** were found to *be* **fairly similar to those obtained in larger scale surveys with larger samples'**	Increased specificity serves to mitigate strength of claims.
	p. 17 'the high risk among [X] young people appears to be related to lower levels of thinking about potential threats'	'the **relatively** high risk among [X] young people appears to be related to lower **reported** levels of thinking about potential threats'	Added modifiers mitigate strength of claims.
Argument: claims and arguments made, changes in what is fore grounded/ backgrounded		p. 19 'The most obvious difference between the countries ...'	Addition foregrounds the comparative analysis and sharpens focus on findings of difference.
		p. 19 'Such clear patterns need to be explained'	Establishes rationale for subsequent discussion.
Positioning: explicit reference to position of text in relation to field/ discipline	p. 18 'Being aware of the limitations of qualitative studies using small samples'	'Being **only too** aware . . .'	Emphasizes authors' voices/ awareness of the limitations of their methodology.

Note: We use X and Y in text data to anonymize key lexical items that might identify the scholars.

The revised manuscript was returned to Thomas, who replied with 10 main points to be addressed. At this point Rudy – now back in the United Kingdom – took centre stage in handling revisions, addressing most requests but ignoring a couple of Thomas's points. Martin accepted Rudy's changes, as well as Rudy's decision not to respond to some of Thomas's suggestions. After this draft, only minor changes were made before publication.

This Text History illustrates how their transnational network facilitated Martin's and the local network's access to both the publishing opportunity and to linguistic and rhetorical resources for text production (and earlier, to participating in the multicountry research project). The local network's strength and durability provided a solid foundation for this work to take place. As a broker, Rudy's contributions spanned convening the larger research initiative to becoming heavily involved in English-medium text production, ultimately taking charge of the last stages of revisions. Apart from a four-year wait for the book's publication, Martin expressed satisfaction with the process, including the changes that Rudy and Thomas made to the text and the roles they played in its production.

Conclusion

The idea that text production is a distributed or networked activity is not new (see Bell 2007 for text production in news media), but often goes unrecognized in debates about academic text production. Networks are clearly a significant resource for all academic text production but particularly so for multilingual scholars experiencing significant pressures and constraints in their attempts to publish in a number of languages and for a number of distinct communities. While we have presented here what might be construed as quite static representations of networks, the value of these representations is that they offer traces of scholars' experiences and activity and link these to the production of specific academic texts at specific moments in time.

In contrast to an emphasis on individualized competence, scholars' accounts and practices of text production foreground the importance of networks as the source of considerable material support as well as constituting a form of capital. Strong network activity – whether at local or transnational levels – is often central to research and writing, particularly in enabling the mobilization of a range of resources which are key to securing publication in Anglophone-centre contexts. This point is most clearly evident where networks are weak, as illustrated in the case of Joaquim, whose weak local and transnational networks have not yet provided sufficient support for his efforts to publish in English-medium journals.

Multilingual scholars' participation in a range of different types (in terms of strength and location) of network clearly entails different results in terms of publishing outcomes. Variation exists between scholars and across contexts in entering, participating in, and sustaining networks and the relationship between types of network participation/mobilization and success in Anglophone-centre publishing is complex. An obvious question is: does participation in transnational networks lead to Anglophone-centre publications or vice versa? In some instances such participations seems to occur at the same time and constitute the same phenomenon, as in the case of Julie, whose network broker (PhD advisor) brought her into his transnational networks resulting in immediate opportunities for publication. In other instances, as in the case of Martin and Géza, there is a definite time gap between forging a transnational network and securing Anglophone-centre publication. Furthermore the significance of the local networks cannot be underestimated: local networks can in some instances provide the base not only for strong research activity from which to engage in transnational networks, but also for securing publications nationally and 'internationally'. This was the case with Fidel, whose strong local network ensured that publications were secured in spite of a weak transnational network, which in general offered limited opportunities for publishing for the scholars participating in a specific EU project.

At the same time, it is important to note that scholars who are not publishing in high status English-medium outlets appear to have weaker transnational networks. Variation in the composition and strength of local and transnational networks therefore has important consequences for scholars in terms of accessing resources and in terms of the intensity and durability of the connections and collaborations the network can foster. While local networks provide certain forms of support, they may not facilitate ties to other resources such as information about publishing opportunities, suitable target journals and so on. Transnational networks may be less intense and durable than local networks but – particularly if connected to strong local networks – can provide information, opportunities, and support for English-medium text production, leading to publication.

We return to the question of how scholars might be better supported in their publishing activity in Chapter 7. In the next chapter, we direct our attention more closely to particular types of brokers signalled in this chapter, those who most directly impact on the texts being produced and who we refer to as 'academic literacy brokers'. The focus of the following chapter is to track in some detail the impact of academic literacy brokers on text trajectories toward publication.

Suggestions for further reading

Among social network theorists, Caroline Haythornthwaite (1996) presents a useful introduction to the core concepts of social network analysis and various ways of visually representing networks. Lesley Milroy and James Milroy's (1992) article explicitly bridges approaches from sociolinguistic network mapping and an analysis of power relations in society. Diane Belcher's work (e.g. 2007) on journal practices usefully foregrounds the importance of networking in academic publishing. For the need to reconsider communicative competence in English language teaching – in the light of networked activity – we found Constant Leung's (2005) article to be generative.

4 Texts and literacy brokers

Introduction

As the previous chapter illustrated, published academic texts involve not only those named as 'authors' but also a significant number of others who impact directly, and in a range of ways, on academic texts in their trajectories toward publication. Some of these backgrounded activities and interventions are widely recognized in labels such as 'translating', 'proofreading', 'editing' and 'reviewing' but what goes on under these labels is far more complex than is often assumed or acknowledged. Little systematic or detailed research has been carried out on the nature and impact of these activities in text production whether by scholars who use English as a first or additional language.[1] The aim of this chapter is to make visible the range of interventions and activities impacting directly on text production, which we refer to as 'literacy brokering'. In addition to named authors, a wide range of brokers are involved in English-medium text production, including friends, editors, reviewers, academic peers, and translators. All of these brokers mediate text production in a number of ways, with potentially significant consequences for how texts will be received and evaluated as they travel from one part of the academic globe to another.

This chapter:

- Makes visible the range and extent of brokering activity involved in academic text production;
- Illustrates the challenges and decisions faced by scholars in working with different kinds of brokers;
- Discusses how different kinds of brokers orient to texts and knowledges;
- Illustrates how different brokers impact on specific shifts and changes to texts;
- Discusses how brokering needs to be understood and theorized as a geolinguistic and geopolitical phenomenon which is central to knowledge production and distribution globally.

'Polishing the text': literacy brokering in academic text production

Researcher: Your term polishing, what do you include in 'polishing', or how do you compare it with 'proofreading' or 'editing'?

Géza: They're very different, yes of course. As I mentioned, this friend, he did really, only spelling and grammar corrections, and sometimes a word he would think is not proper. And then there is a polishing that is about, proposing changes, like the proofreader not only checks the language but checks the meanings, and tells you 'It's not clear to me. Is this, wouldn't this sound better if you spoke like blah, blah, blah' and makes another sentence of it. But this is, that's the second step when he changes the structure of sentences, or paragraphs. And the best proofreader is the one who tells you 'Well, I would cut this result and go deeper into the other results because this, this may be interesting for the reader, or give more examples of this, or cut this graph or these pictures.' So this is actually not proofreading.

(Discussion)

What is done and by whom to bits of texts in their trajectories toward submission and eventual (in some cases) publication is far more complex than is usually recognized. As indicated in the scholar's comment above, this complexity is often masked by terms which have widespread currency, such as 'polishing' – a term used widely by scholars in several contexts – or semi-technical terms, such as 'proofreading'. Like many labels used in describing what's involved in academic writing – such as 'revising', 'editing', 'correcting' – such terms are sometimes a useful shorthand for something with which many of us may be familiar at some level (particularly those of us who work in academia and/or publishing). But they can also obscure what is happening and the significance of such interventions in academic text production. An important first step, therefore, is to tease out what is going on in academic text production and publishing by empirically tracking what is being done, rather than starting from (common sense) assumptions about who is involved at different stages and why.

Our starting point is to use 'literacy brokering' as a meta-category to refer to all the different kinds of direct intervention by different people, other than named authors, in the production of texts and to track what is actually involved (see Chapter 3 for 'brokering' relating to network activity for mobilizing resources and people in support of research activity and writing). We use the term literacy *brokering* rather than other less ideologically loaded notions (mediation, sponsoring, shaping)[2] as a way of explicitly acknowledging that intervention in academic texts is not a neutral enterprise, but rather involves participants of unequal status and power. In many instances 'literacy brokers' occupy a powerful position straddling the 'boundaries and peripheries' between communities and groupings (Wenger 1998: 199) and a focus on literacy brokering signals the economic and power dimensions to text interventions and their consequences in the academic marketplace (Bourdieu 1998; Gibbs 1995a; see Chapter 1). In tracking the different kinds of intervention we sought to avoid predetermining the importance of different types of text change but rather aimed to treat texts holistically, characterizing the most salient type of changes. Salience here is a relational notion, related to specific trajectories and publication Text Histories, as is illustrated in the discussion below. A key tool for tracking interventions is summarized in *Methodological Tool 4*.

Methodological Tool 4: Text-oriented heuristic for tracking changes made across drafts

Focus on text data				Focus on interview/email/field note discussions		
Changes made to draft	Draft number and section (e.g., AIMRD C)*	Text reference/ extract	Suggested/ made by? When?	Response by author(s)	Rhetorical/knowledge significance	
					Named author(s) perspective	Researcher comments
1. Additions word/sentence/ section added						
2. Deletions word/ sentence/ section deleted						
3. Reformulation words/phrase/ sentences reworded						
4. Re-shuffling re-organization of sentences/ paragraphs/ sections						
5. Argument claims, evidence, warrants, what is foregrounded, backgrounded						

(Continued)

Focus on text data				Focus on interview/email/field note discussions		
Changes made to draft	Draft number and section	Text reference/ extract	Suggested/ made by? When?	Response by author(s)	Rhetorical/knowledge significance	
	(e.g., AIM-RDC)*					
					Named author(s) perspective	Researcher comments
6. *Positioning* explicit reference to position of paper/ research in relation to field/discipline/ journal (e.g. CARS – Swales 1990)						
7. *Lexical/ Register* levels of formality, discipline, field specific vocabulary						
8. *Sentence-level changes/ corrections* to sentence level syntax, vocabulary, grammar, spelling, punctuation						

Focus on text data				Focus on interview/email/field note discussions	
Changes made to draft	Draft number and section (e.g., AIM-RDC)*	Text reference/ extract	Suggested/ made by? When?	Response by author(s)	Rhetorical/knowledge significance
					Named author(s) perspective / Researcher comments
9. Cohesion markers ways in which sentences / sections linked through for example conjunctions, lexical items					
10. Publishing conventions specific journal or organizational conventions (such as APA American Psychological Association)					
11. Visuals/ Representation of text Formatting, diagrams, bullets					

*A=abstract; I=introduction; M=methods; R=results; D=discussion; C=conclusion

In order to track the impact of brokers on text production, we developed this heuristic for tracking changes made to texts which, while informed by a number of textual and rhetorical frameworks (see e.g. Berkenkotter and Huckin 1995; MacDonald 1994; Swales 1990; Ventola and Mauranen 1991), was directly influenced by the work of Knorr-Cetina (1981) and Gosden (1995).[3]

Scholar Profile 6: Istvan, Psychology, Hungary

Istvan, in his late 50s, is a full professor of psychology as well as the director of an institute at his university's medical school; he carries out multiple lines of experimental research bridging the fields of psychology and medicine. He has been working in academia for more than 25 years; he also has a clinical practice as a psychotherapist and provides graduate-level clinical training. Much of his research involves sustained or short-term collaboration with local colleagues, postdoctoral researchers and about 10 doctoral students in Hungary, and researchers from other European countries, the United States and the United Kingdom.

Although Istvan studied English at university (along with Italian and German), his English proficiency is mixed – a high level for reading academic texts but much lower levels of oral and written production. Given the limited opportunities of Central Europeans of his generation to study abroad, Istvan has not been able to stay in Anglophone countries for more than a few months at a time. Nonetheless, he has published extensively in English resulting to a large extent from his participation in various transnational networks.

Istvan has published considerably in the local national language, but mainly on his practice and clinical work. He values such publishing for building a local reputation which enables him to apply for national grants and serve on national research boards and committees. Furthermore, he is committed to re-establishing what he sees as the high quality of applied work in Hungary, restoring local practice to the level of quality it enjoyed in pre-communist times:

> In the first part of the twentieth century, the quality of Hungarian clinical psychology was recognized in Europe, so psychologists in our country have made a continual effort to enrich this tradition. It provided a stable basis for keeping relative autonomy and democracy in the 'worst of times' and served as a source of change of the social and economic system at the end of the twentieth century.
>
> (Email)

From his experimental research Istvan has published in many English-medium journals with high impact factors, which he sees as *an exciting challenge*. Addressing the international research audience is his priority, given the specialized nature of his research and its relatively small audience in the local national context. Istvan often takes responsibility for drafting English-medium articles reporting on his experimental results; some of his English-speaking students and post-doctoral researchers review his manuscripts before they are sent to his Anglophone colleagues, who sometimes make further revisions to the text. In some cases journal editors have questioned the discrepancy between what they see as a lack of clarity of English expression and the fact that Anglophone colleagues are named co-authors. Istvan's collaboration with these colleagues centres on their shared research interests, rather than on securing help with English.

Types of literacy brokers in academic text production

In the 284 Text Histories we have collected and (re)constructed, a total of 480 academic literacy brokers can be traced to the direct production of texts, that is, they were explicitly identified by scholars as being involved in the production of their texts (see *Methodological Tool 1: Text Histories*). This is a minimum calculation of literacy brokering activity: if we included in these figures references simply made to brokers in a broad, non-specific way, for example, 'this paper was reviewed', 'my friend always checks my drafts', the total number can probably be doubled. Literacy brokering – as an activity outside named authoring – therefore clearly represents a significant dimension to the production of academic texts.

On the basis of the Text Histories analysed we have identified two principal categories of literacy brokers: *language* and *academic* brokers.

Language brokers. These are brokers who are called on primarily because of their knowledge and expertise of the English language. They include professional language brokers – such as translators, proofreaders and English-language specialists, such as teachers of English – as well as informal language brokers. Professional language brokers include people with a range of professional backgrounds, qualifications and expertise, and are paid for the work they do with author(s)' texts. In contrast, the involvement of informal language brokers can be characterized by their personal relationship to the author and include friends, spouses or other family members; they offer unpaid support with the production of texts. Seventeen per cent of all brokers reported were in this category of language brokering.

Academic brokers. These are academics who work in universities or research institutes, often from Anglophone-centre contexts. They can be further subclassified into three main types, depending on how their professional expertise relates to the subfield specialism of a particular text and its authors: a *general academic*, who is not from the same disciplinary area as the author(s); a *disciplinary expert*, who shares the same disciplinary background and interests as the author(s); a *subdisciplinary specialist* (Becher 1994), who is from the same specialist field as the author(s). Some academic professionals can be further categorized according to their specific role or function in relation to the chronological production of a text, for example pre- or post-submission – an academic colleague may offer comments on a journal article before it is submitted to a journal, in contrast to a journal reviewer or editor who would typically be involved post-submission. Eighty-three per cent of all brokers reported fell into this category of academic broker.

The impact of language brokers on texts

The attraction of using professional English language brokers such as translators and English language editing services is obvious; academic writing for publication takes time, academic writing in several languages takes even more time. Shortage of time for research and writing activity is a common complaint by scholars around the world and given, as discussed in Chapter 2, that multilingual scholars are often writing for a range of communities, maintaining and sustaining publication for these constitutes a significant challenge. Being able to call on professional language brokers – such as English language professionals or translators – might seem to offer a practical solution to the problem of regularly transforming research and publications from one language into English-medium texts. However, as the Text Histories below illustrate, language brokering is neither straightforward nor necessarily appropriate for all targets of publication. We use four THs to illustrate some of the difficulties and opportunities surrounding the involvement of language brokers in the production of academic texts.

TH 4.1: A professional translation

This TH centres on a paper originally written in Hungarian. The author had secured permission from the publisher of the original Hungarian version to have it translated (see Chapter 5 for the notion of equivalency in texts). This was the first time – in her 10 years of working on English-medium texts for publication – that she decided to use a translator. Having secured funds for translation, she saw this as an exciting opportunity, both enabling her to continue with other research writing while at the same time making available research in Hungarian to a wider academic readership. However, when the translation was returned, the scholar was extremely concerned about the quality of the translation and contacted us to ask for an opinion on the English version.

TH 4.1 Example 1

> I would like to ask you to have a SHORT glance at this article. My problem is that the text is NOT really English. It is rather a VERBATIM translation of the hung. text, but does not express the meaning of my sentences ... Please give me feedback.
>
> (Email)

The extracts from the 8,070 word paper in Example 2 illustrate that the author's concern is well founded. The English-medium text is hard to understand, resulting from what is clearly a word for word approach to translating the Hungarian-medium text.

TH 4.1 Example 2

Extracts from Hungarian version	English Translations
A szoros értelemben vett gyógyszerkutatások esetében ez az igény érthetö és elfogadható. Azonban így szem elöl tévesztünk egy amúgy, a napi gyakorlatban sokkal inkább hasznosítható lehetöséget.	In the case of the medical research in a narrower sense this requirement is understandable and acceptable. However in this case we lose sight of an opportunity which can otherwise be made much more use of in daily life.
Az imént körülírt szellemben fogant (gyógyszer) kutatások elrendezései tehát igyekeznek elkülöníteni a „valódi' hatást a csak „hit'- vagy „elvárás' mentén kialakuló hatástól.	Therefore the arrangements of the (medical) researches originated in the sense previously described make an effort to separate the 'real' effect from the effect developing only along the 'belief' or the 'requirement'.

| Érdekes megközelítés az ellentétes irányú meghatározás. A hatás kifejlödéséhez szükség van a társas kölcsönhatásra, legalább indirekt formában | The definition from the opposite direction is an interesting approach. Company interaction is necessary for the development of the effect at least in indirect form. |

The author's excitement at having the opportunity to have a text translated – and thus save her time that she could devote to her research and other writings – turned into disappointment and considerable upset, as Example 3 illustrates.

TH 4.1 Example 3

At the moment I HATE the whole project.

First of all I feel sorry for the girl who made the translation.

And: at the beginning it seemed to be an easy/quick project, but it definitely lost its beauty … I need a couple of days to decide what to do.

(Email)

The author had made contact with the translator via a recommendation from a friend. When the author discussed her dissatisfaction with the translation, the translator reacted angrily, not least because she had sent a 'trial' page before doing the full translation. The scholar said in part the situation was her fault because she was *not careful enough, I just had a short look at it, and realized that these are English words, but did not realize that they are not English sentences!* (Discussion). The translator did not recognize the legitimacy of the author's concerns about the text and was unhappy with the author's suggestion to pay half the originally agreed fee. Following this unsuccessful attempt at seeking a translation, the author asked a research assistant to do the translation and to work with an experienced colleague from her academic field, who had lived in the United Kingdom for some 40 years, at crafting the English version. In the end a translation was therefore produced (illustrating the importance of networks for generating resources, as discussed in Chapter 3). However, from the time the original translation was requested and carried out to the time when an acceptable version was produced, three years elapsed. Given the time delay, the author decided against submitting the paper to the English-medium journal she had previously identified, for two main reasons: the content was no longer personally *intellectually interesting* to the author and the paper now appeared *old*, which, given the value attached to 'novelty' in journal publications (see Kaufer and Geisler 1989; see also discussion in Chapters 5 and 6) would mean that considerable work would need to be done in updating the literature, relocating the study and reviewing the argument.

It would be easy to dismiss this specific TH as just one example of poor translation. However, scholars are overwhelmingly dissatisfied and suspicious of using translation; of course cost is one key issue, with many scholars not able to pay the fees that might secure a high quality translation, a point recognized by professional translators. Scholars do not blame translators per se, but rather the fact that it is very difficult to find a translator who is sufficiently familiar with their subfield specialism to produce meaningful texts.[4]

Translation and 'editing' (revisions to English-medium texts) costs vary enormously. For the most part scholars do not use professional translators or 'language editors' because of the costs involved. Some reported using professional translators when they had grant funds.

Some figures mentioned by scholars

50-80 korona per page for language editing (Slovakia)
200 euros for language editing of three versions of a paper (Spain)
700 euros for a 25 page translation (Portugal)

Some figures and comments provided by a professional translators' organization

For translation:

- Rates vary highly by location and by disciplinary field.
- Rates can be higher when a field enjoys high volume in a community (e.g. bio-medical sciences) and there is limited expertise in that field specialism.
- Rates can be as low as 3 cents (euro) per word and as high as 30 per word.

For language editing or 'authors' editors':
Rates vary between 2 cents (euro) a word and 7.5 cents a word.

Figure 4.1 Translating and editing costs.

TH 4.2: An English language professional

In contrast to translators, who tend to be avoided by scholars in our study for both economic and academic reasons, English language professionals are often called upon to work on scholars' texts (in some fields referred to as 'authors' editors', see Burrough-Boenisch 2003; Shashok 1992, 2001, 2008). This TH concerns a short journal article co-authored by three Central European psychology scholars who have been working together for some time on a series of experimental studies focusing on the relationship between language use and brain damaged patients. The paper was written for, and published in an English-medium national journal.

The lead author has used English for her academic writing for some 10 years – before this time her papers had been translated by a professional into English and Russian – and is meticulous in checking sentence level grammar. While relatively confident, like many multilingual scholars she feels that her texts should be checked for grammatical errors by a 'native' speaker of English. A key goal for her is to consider how an 'English reader' engages with the text and to craft the text with this reader in mind. *I think one of my ideas is that I want someone to go through and to tell me how he understands it. What is understandable and what he understands* (Discussion). The broker involved in this text is an Anglophone-centre English language teacher working locally who regularly reads and corrects papers for the lead author, for a small fee and, as in this TH, just before submission to a journal or publisher.

All the changes in the text were made at sentence level with some reformulations at phrase level offered, as illustrated in Example 1 (see also *Methodological Tool 4*).

TH 4.2 Example 1

Changes made	Example	Author response
Definite/indefinite article	characterised by [the *inserted*] gradual or rapid onset of [the *deleted*] disorder	Accepted
	the purpose of this study is to present [a *deleted*] [the *inserted*] case of a child	Rejected
Punctuation	and behavio[u *deleted*]ral disturbances [, *inserted*] as well as inthe aphasia	Accepted
	is verbal agnosia[, *inserted*] which may be so profound	Accepted
Spelling	Le[a *deleted*]d	Accepted
	Behavio[u *deleted*]ral	Accepted
Reformulations {Conjunction/syntax/ negation/concord}	She did not speak spontaneously, nor did [she *inserted*] understand [and *deleted*]or respond to spoken commands	Accepted
	Her [ability *moved to end of phrase*] [of *deleted*] oral expression	Revised by author as *her oral expression*
Reformulation	As [for *deleted*] [regards *inserted*] the written language	Rejected
Reformulation	School [notes *deleted*] [marks *inserted*]	Revised by author as *results*

In total some 110 suggestions were made in handwriting by the language broker on a 3,270 word text, most of which the author accepted, as evident from the version she submitted to the journal. Four suggestions were not accepted by the author and three suggestions by the broker were further modified by the author, as illustrated in Example 1. In addition to the suggestions made by the language broker, four further sentence-level corrections were made by the author (on definite articles and plural forms) prior to submission.

The main author was quite happy with the work done by the language professional. This is in no small part due to the fact that what the broker does – focus on sentence-level corrections and reformulations – is what the author expects him to do. But the author's satisfaction is also due to the process in which she engages with this broker on a regular basis: in addition to corrections written on the text by the broker, the author and broker also usually meet face to face to work through and discuss the suggestions. This is obviously more time consuming for both but gives the author a greater sense of control and negotiation over her text, opening up opportunities for clarification and debate over suggestions. This is a clear example of successful brokering from the author's perspective, in that corrections are made and the paper is submitted and published. However, as we discuss later in this chapter, whether this kind of brokering alone would be sufficient to ensure publication success in other targeted publications, such as English-medium 'international' journals, is questionable.

TH 4.3: An informal language broker

Informal brokering of texts involves friends and family who are considered to have a good enough knowledge of English for the authors to call upon them to check or 'polish' the language of the text. This usually takes place in the pre-submission stage of a text – that is, before the text is submitted for publication, for the first or subsequent times to different journals. This broker can be a family member, as in the case of one scholar whose mother was a first language speaker of English.

TH 4.3 Example 1

> I have a mum (laughs). My ma had edited a couple of them [papers] – less often lately. But when I first wrote my first papers, she would do a lot of editing. I would go to her and she would teach me. In terms of 'Oh, I've been a teacher of English in college and typically these things – like for example, in English you write in short sentences, in Spanish they, Spanish academics are into long sentences.' So my ma said 'try and be short'. So okay, I try and think of short sentences when I write in English.

(Discussion)

And the same scholar calls on members of his extended family to check phrasing that he knows is not right, as in the example of the title change below.

TH 4.3: Example 2

Scholar's first version	After discussion with informal broker
Children's Storyteller's Ideologies of the Audience	Storytellers of children's literature: ideologies of the audience

While this scholar calls on family members, it is more common for scholars to involve Anglophone friends, usually to 'check the grammar'. Emphasis in informal language brokers' responses is usually on sentence-level corrections, with the following features commonly identified: the use of definite and indefinite articles, inclusion/exclusion of personal pronouns, spelling corrections and verb concord. However, it is difficult to track the impact of informal brokers as their comments are often made orally and fleetingly (by phone or casual meeting), which scholars act on at a later moment, or because revisions are made by authors while working at their keyboards; so the textual evidence of informal brokers' impact is erased. Overall, there is far greater mention by scholars of the role played by informal brokers than it is possible to trace in texts.

For scholars, the advantage of calling on an informal language broker for help or advice on an English-medium text is that such help is not tied to formal scheduling but rather called upon as and when the scholar gets the opportunity to communicate with the broker; and it does not usually cost anything, or involves a small gift, such as a bottle of whisky – given by one scholar to a friend (as reported by one scholar). This is an important issue given the material constraints scholars often work within. (See Figure 4.1 for example of costs of translation and author editing.)

Scholar Profile 7: Carla, Psychology, Spain

Carla, 47, is an associate professor who has been an academic for 19 years. She works in an interdisciplinary field using experimental methods that result in both theoretical and applied publications. In one research line she has collaborated long term with a colleague in a nearby city as well as with her former dissertation director and, on a short-term basis, with a British scholar. She served as her department's director of graduate studies, until health issues forced her to reduce her commitments.

Carla's first language is one of the languages of the autonomous communities in Spain, which is used as an official medium of teaching and learning at her university; she is bilingual in this and Castilian. She has also studied German and English as an adult. She is very comfortable with reading and conversation in English but writing in English presents more of a challenge. Carla has regularly paid her son's English teacher and more recently an American living locally for help editing her texts. Carla has been publishing in high status English-medium journals for about 15 years. Her primary line of research is not commonly studied in her local national context and Carla feels there are currently no national journals interested in her theoretical work; thus publishing in English is crucial not only for responding to institutional rewards and pressures but also to reach a knowledgeable audience. *The journals which are important are American journals, or English*; they also have an impact factor, which gives them higher status in her institution regardless of the actual impact factor number.

The lack of grant funding to pursue more theoretical research raises a number of important issues for Carla. First, she needs funding to build a laboratory and equip it with appropriate instruments but she has not yet obtained the kinds of grant that would position her to secure these resources for her research: *My objective is to work in this more theoretical research but at the same time it's more difficult for me because I need better labs and resources.* Without local collaborators, including those with seniority to support grant applications, Carla's hands are tied: *It is very difficult for people who have never had a grant before, it's always the same people who are always obtaining the same grants.* Recently Carla began participating with colleagues at her university in a new project that has greater potential for grant funding than her main research topic and offers a welcome change from working in relative isolation. So far a number of Spanish and English publications have resulted from this collaboration.

The impact of academic brokers on texts

Brokering is a significant activity in English-medium academic text production overall. However, it is important to note that brokering is not an evenly distributed activity, in relation to the category of brokering, target community or text type. So far we have focused on language brokering activity which centres predominantly on sentence-level language corrections and modifications. But it is clear – even if the same label is used – that other kinds of brokering activity are involved in text production, often directly linked to the target audience/publication:

> If the text is only for conference proceedings, I will write the text and don't care about proofreading because it's all dependent on time and I don't have it. But if there is a competition, a selection, in that case I prefer a *native speaker* proofreading to, to the *translator* [EAL]. Because my purpose is to get more the native 'knack', and I know the responsibility for the special talk, special discourse of the discipline is on myself. So sometimes I do not accept the recommendations of the native speaker. If it is for an international journal, then we try to have a *professional* [academic] native speaker like S or R.
>
> (Discussion: *italics* = our emphasis)

This scholar points to the different brokering activity he considers necessary in writing texts for different target audiences. In making decisions (within the constraints of time and resources available to him) he points to a hierarchy of brokering according to type of publications: from no literacy brokering at all (authored by himself) for non-competitive conference proceedings; to the involvement of a translator or preferably a 'native speaker' if the submission is to go through a selection process; to the involvement of a 'native English speaking' academic literacy broker if he is aiming at an 'international' journal publication. By explicitly mentioning 'international' outlets this scholar is signalling the distinction often made between English-medium national and English-medium international texts (see Chapters 2 and 6).

The involvement of different kinds of brokers deemed necessary by this scholar in writing for different target publications is borne out in patterns across the 284 Text Histories collected and illustrated in Table 4.1. Of all brokers documented as being involved in text production, 72% were involved in journal article production, 86% of these were *academic* brokers. Furthermore, of all brokering in journal article production, the vast majority relates to 'international', rather than national, English-medium journals – 88% of brokers are involved in the production of texts for 'international' journals, as compared with 12% of brokers involved in article production for English-medium national journals.

Thus, far more brokering activity is going on in journal articles; more brokering is going in texts written for English-medium 'international' journals than for English-medium national journals; and, as we explore below, a large amount of this brokering is being carried out by academics, many of whom are Anglophone-centre scholars who, while they do make sentence level corrections, orient to issues well

Table 4.1 Brokers, textual orientations and target publications

Category of broker	Text extract	Broker comment/action	Textual orientation	Target publication
ACADEMIC				
Example 1: General academic	We could say that the target group participants are more middle-class than the random sample participants.	*Query by broker* Isn't this a bit problematic. What do you mean by middle class?	Knowledge content	English-medium 'international' publications – book chapters, journals
Example 2: Discipline specialist	We used correlation analysis to examine the relationship between mental rotation ability and intelligence subtests (Table 2 and 3). The result indicated an **interference** between verbal abilities and performance time of mental rotations.	*Reformulations made to text by broker* Correlational analysis **was used** to examine the relationship between mental rotation ability and the intelligence subtests (Table 2 and 3). The result indicated a **negative correlation** between verbal abilities and performance time of mental rotations.	Target journal conversations	
Example 3: Subfield specialist	The evaluation of the X methodology is discussed and recommendations for intervention activities are proposed.	*Section deleted by broker*	Disciplinary conversations	
LANGUAGE Example 4:	**at** first grade.	*Correction to preposition made by broker* **in the** first grade.	Specialist discourse	English-medium national journals conference proceedings Conference abstracts
Example 5:	Research was undertaken on 5 locations.	*Correction to preposition made by broker.* Research was undertaken **in** 5 locations.	Sentence level changes/corrections	

beyond language. It is perhaps not surprising that so much brokering is going on towards the production of English-medium 'international' journal articles and of course some aspects of this brokering activity are well known – that is, the involvement of editors and reviewers once papers are submitted. But the nature of such brokering is often hidden, and given the high stakes 'goods' that published texts constitute in the global academic market place, it is an important phenomenon to explore in more detail, particularly in tracking what happens to texts as they move from the 'periphery' to the 'centre'. We begin this exploration with a focus on the trajectories of several Text Histories, and continue this discussion in Chapters 5 and 6.

Academic literacy brokers and the construction of knowledge in English-medium 'international' journals

> Despite an objective 'empiricist' repertoire, we are far away from a world in which power, allegiance and self-esteem play no part, however much they may seem absent from the frigid surface of RA [Research Article] discourse. And yet we find the research article, this key product of the knowledge-manufacture industry, to be a remarkable phenomenon, so cunningly engineered by rhetorical machining that it somehow still gives an impression of being but a simple description of relatively untransmuted raw material.
>
> (Swales 1990: 125)

A focus on literacy brokering activity takes us beneath the 'frigid surface' of the 'international' research article and helps illuminate the geolinguistic and geopolitical dimensions to academic text production in a global context. The Text Histories discussed in this section are drawn from the four distinct national contexts of our study. The theoretical approaches in the psychology THs (4.4, 4.5, 4.6) reflect the range of key paradigms in psychology, from experimental to social psychology; the education TH (4.7) reflects some of paradigmatic tensions of education as a scholarly field (Nisbet 2005).

The lead writers in each Text History are not 'novices' either to the academy or in academic publishing. As can be seen from Table 4.2, all scholars have considerable experience in academia and success in writing for academic publication. In addition, they all work at prestigious institutions in their countries and have been using English for work-related activities (e.g. relating to conferences, email exchanges, reading and writing academic papers) for at least ten years.

TH 4.4: Picking the most attractive point

This Text History illustrates the potential impact of academic brokering pre-submission to a journal. The authors are two Central-Eastern European psychologists who have been researching and writing together for ten years. Four brokers were reported to have been involved in the text production: one language professional (a copyeditor post-submission), one informal language broker (a friend on a pre-submission draft) and two Anglophone-centre academic professionals, (one pre- and one post-submission). The broker most influentially involved was an

Table 4.2 Scholars' professional academic experience and publication records

	Lead author – qualifications, position, experience	*Publication record*
TH 4.4	PhD Professor 25 years in academia Psychology	LNL = 21 articles, 1 book chapter English = 7 articles, 4 book chapters
TH 4.5	PhD Associate professor 14 years in academia Psychology	LNL = 1 book, 3 book chapters, 11 articles English = 3 book chapters, 3 articles
TH 4.6	PhD Associate professor 17 years in academia Psychology	LNL = 6 articles English = 4 articles
TH 4.7	PhD Professor Education	LNL = 57 articles, 2 book chapters, 5 books English = 15 articles

Note: LNL = local national language.

academic professional pre-submission and the impact of this involvement is the main focus here.

The main author, who had *established initial contact with the broker following the fall of the communist dictatorship in the early 1990s* (Discussion), sought comments from this broker particularly on the 'English'. Yet the broker clearly contributed to the text's trajectory in more important ways: by identifying an appropriate centre target journal and, as is illustrated below, playing a major part in the shape and content of the final article.

Using the text heuristic (see *Methodological Tool 4*), significant changes were identified in Draft 2 when the academic broker was involved. Changes made here stayed through to submitted and published versions, indicating that the reviewers and editor agreed with revisions suggested by this broker. The most salient change relates to the way methodology is positioned within the article. The first significant change to the place of methodology in the article is made by the pre-submission broker in Draft 2, where the methodology is deleted from the moves in the abstract, shown in Example 1.

TH 4.4 Example 1

Draft 1 Abstract	*Draft 2 Abstract (and maintained in publication)*
Presented results outline the procedure that was used for conducting the [X] methodology and description of the structural, social and cultural context in the [X]. The evaluation of the [X] methodology are discussed and recommendations for intervention activities are proposed.	Deleted

Further deletions of references to methodology were carried out by the academic broker, pre-submission, and a 400-word section on the evaluation of the methodology was deleted by the editor post-submission. The editor's response confirms that the pre-submission broker's decision to reduce the centrality of methodology in the article was in line with the target journal's interests. Methodology makes its way to the final published draft but only as a brief description of the research process, not as a significant focus.

Other salient changes made by the academic literacy broker pre-submission are in the Results section, illustrated in the changes in subheadings shown in Example 2 below. Thematic labelling of subheadings is used in both drafts but, as can be seen, the broker makes several important changes: reducing the number of subheadings, and backgrounding the distinction between the kinds of substances – tobacco, alcohol, illegal substances – which become subsumed under one noun, 'substance'. The effect of these reformulations is to reduce the emphasis on distinct substances and to create one overarching focus, that is, a link between substance use and sexual behaviour, as shown in Example 2.

TH 4.4 Example 2

Draft 1 Results	Draft 2 Results (and maintained in submitted and published text)
Subheadings	Subheadings
Structural, Cultural and Social context of [X] environment:	Structural. Cultural and Social context of X environment:
Sexuality during [X]	1 The context of sexuality
Health consequences	2 The context of psychoactive substance use
Risks:	
Psychoactive substances use	3 Substance use and sexual behavior
Tobacco	
Alcohol	
Illegal substances	

This textual 'marshalling' (after Newell 1984) of distinct elements towards one main focus or argument is sustained through further cuts and reformulations made by the same broker in the Results and Discussion sections, two significant examples of which are shown in Examples 3 and 4.

TH 4.4 Example 3

Draft 1 – Results	Draft 2 – Results (maintained in submitted and published text)
[the] explosion of the problems with drug abuse in [X] expected for a long time (by the majority of the [X] medical experts) has not yet taken place as yet and opinions in its justification differ	Deleted

TH 4.4 Example 4

Draft 1 – Discussion	Draft 2 – Discussion (maintained in submitted and published text)
It can be characterized by the idea that there is **male sex drive** that requires insistent satisfaction whenever access to opportunity (usually women) is allowed. (our emphasis)	It can be characterized by an, at least implicit, **promotion of alcohol** consumption in connection with casual sex practices.

The effect of these deletions and reformulations is to avoid what might be considered 'dangerous digressions' (after Knorr-Cetina 1981), in that Example 3 potentially undermines the importance of the contribution of the paper by suggesting that (some) substance use is not as significant as might have been anticipated; Example 4 raises an issue which is not discussed elsewhere in the paper. The comment in Example 4 might also be dangerous in that its biological-evolutionary discourse is unlikely to be in keeping with the more socially oriented paradigm of the target journal.

The main author was extremely appreciative of the support offered by the centre academic professional and both authors were delighted at what was their first success in publishing in an English-medium 'international' journal. The main author's attitude towards the involvement of the broker reflected the broker's account: the broker was actively committed to supporting the writing of scholars in this subfield as a way of supporting the intellectual endeavours of Central-Eastern European scholars, who have historically been isolated from the Western academy.

But what of the changes made to the text, as illustrated here? Commenting on the shift away from: 1) methodology as a key focus in the article, and 2) the deletion of several 'digressions', the author states that the effect of the revisions is that the text *doesn't offer a kaleidoscope* – [the broker] *picks the most attractive point* (Discussion). However, given the value of publishing in English-medium 'international' journals, the author for the most part was pleased at the outcome.

TH 4.5: From contrast to confirmation

This Text History concerns a paper produced by a close-knit group of Central European researchers who have researched and co-authored for some eight years. The group consisted of three experienced scholars: the most senior scholar has been involved in academic work for some 40 years and is world renowned in her specialist subfield; the most junior in the group – the lead author – has some 14 years' experience in academia and some 20 academic publications (see Table 4.2). She is named as lead author of the paper because she was considered by the team to be the originator of the key ideas. No brokers external to the group were involved before submission of the article. After submission, the authors received a response from the editor of the Anglophone-centre journal who, following reviews, stated his interest in the paper, but proposed the involvement of an additional scholar, a statistician, whose involvement the editor subsequently organized. Here we focus on the involvement of these professional academic brokers, the editor and the additional scholar, both of whom are Anglophone-centre academic professionals.

The most salient change from submission to publication is a shift in the main knowledge claim. In the version submitted to the journal, emphasis is on signalling the difference between the findings of the study reported and a key previous study. In the published version the claim to difference is replaced with claims to confirmation; that is, the study in the paper is reported as confirming the findings of the previous study. This shift is exemplified in text extracts in Example 1.

TH 4.5 Example 1

Submitted text – Argument *Examples of emphasis on claiming* *contrast/difference*	*Published text – Argument* *Examples of emphasis on claiming* *confirmation*
Another difference from the Z et al study is that in our procedure – (I)*	The results (see Table 1) **are consistent** with those of Z et al. in that … (R and D)
The difference between the strongest factor of Z (author) **and ours** – (I)	These results **appear to be supported** in a different linguistic and cultural setting …
In our case this is accompanied by – **while in Z (author) study** …(D)	(R and D)
In our case the X factor explanatory value (among other factors) **was greater than in the case of Z et al** (D)	The X also **correlated significantly** with … (R and D)

Note: *I = introduction; D = discussion; R = results section.

In the published version, there are ten overt shifts from signalling difference towards signalling confirmation. The extent to which the reported study confirms the previous study is hedged at several points (see Example 2), but such hedging doesn't alter the overall shift towards confirmation.

TH 4.5 Example 2

These results also **appear to be** supported in a different linguistic and cultural setting (R and D published version)

and one ambiguous instance of hedging is included:

is quite similar (R and D published version)

It is difficult to pinpoint exactly who made the changes from contrast to confirmation and at what point in the redrafting process: although data for this Text History are considerable, several hard copy versions were no longer available (see

Methodological Tool 1: Text Histories). However, we can glimpse key aspects of the process surrounding these changes by drawing on data sources which signal the influential roles of the statistician and the journal editor.

In his response to the authors on their first submission, the editor said that a different statistical method was required. The main author said they would be happy to revisit the statistical method but that no one in her department, including the statisticians, was familiar with the particular method proposed. What is significant about the impact of the additional scholar is that he was involved not only in contributing to the statistical method but in the redrafting process of the whole article. Indeed, such is his status within the authoring process that later correspondence from the editor is directed to him, and not to the lead author. The changes towards confirmation begin to occur in the drafts when the statistician is involved, indicating that he played a significant part in developing such a shift. It is also clear that the editor favoured or indeed encouraged such a shift, stating in one correspondence that he valued the 'confirmatory aspect' of the study. The main author appreciated the involvement of both academic literacy brokers. She recognized that the editor had made considerable efforts towards publishing this paper: *I was happy to have his help*, referring to his approach and actions as akin to those of *a friendly grandfather* (Discussion).

The shift in the overall argument of the article was evident to the main author. She accepted it, acknowledging that it would be easier to publish *if we focus on the similarities rather than the differences*. However, she had mixed feelings. In considering the shift from contrast to confirmation, the author foregrounds the position of her national context as a peripheral location for academic production: *Saying something from Central Europe which is new is not good, not allowed. Of course it's absolutely their perspective to see Central Europeans as, I don't know, a tribe trying to do something scientific* (Discussion). She sees this publication, and the compromise it implied in terms of the shift in the main argument, as a necessary first step for researchers writing out of her national context who are marginal to, in her words, the 'mainstream'. In practical-epistemological terms, it provides her research group with an authorized citation to use to reference their work in future publications in English-medium international journals (for related research on citation practices, see Lillis *et al.* 2010; Hewings *et al.*, forthcoming).

TH 4.6: Responding from the 'periphery' to conflicting reviews

This Text History draws on eight drafts; the lead author's correspondence with two journals, the first of which rejected the article; and two interviews and email correspondence with the lead author. The lead author is an associate professor of psychology at a Southern European university. As indicated in Table 4.2 she had previously published four psychology articles in English-medium journals as well as six articles in journals in her national context. Her co-author for this Text History was an Anglophone-centre academic professional, whom she sought out for his expertise in an interdisciplinary subject area. The lead author spent six weeks at her co-author's laboratory to conduct experiments and write with him. However, he died unexpectedly after co-authoring two drafts of the article, which the lead author then finished and submitted to two English-medium 'international' journals chosen by her co-author. No literacy brokers were involved before submission. Post-submission brokers were academic professionals: the editor of the first journal was an Anglophone-centre academic professional, the editor of the second, a non-Anglophone-centre academic professional (the national/ linguistic backgrounds of the five reviewers are not known). We return to the question of anonymity of reviewers in Chapter 6.

The salient changes to the article were made by the lead author in response to reviews from the first journal asking for a stronger rationale and clarification, 'to focus more directly on supporting [the] main conclusions' (Written Review). One reviewer suggested not discussing 'every single data point from this large and complicated experiment individually' (Written Review). The author responded by cutting an entire section reporting the analyses of 17 stimuli, and, as TH 4.6 Example 1 shows, by foregrounding one type of stimulus. Also shown is that she provides a rationale for using this particular stimulus, primarily through adding citations, including one referring to her co-author's previous work:

TH 4.6 Example 1

Draft resubmitted after reviews (I): Reformulations, additions

[X] stimulus had been previously used in different experiments (three new references). The model developed by WB and M (1994) **also used [X] stimulus**. This motivated, in part, our use of this type of stimuli.

The lead author added three short paragraphs in the Discussion section that explicitly hypothesize results from using this specific stimulus, extracts of which are in Example 2.

TH 4.6 Example 2

Draft resubmitted after reviews (D): Additions of extracts from three new paragraphs

Such **a mechanism could be responsible** for the results of the present experiments ... But with A and B [types of stimuli] **there might be an additional effect** ...
This **could explain the differences** produced by A and B ... compared to C and D, although further work would be necessary to **confirm this hypothesis**.

Additionally, to bolster her conclusions the lead author followed one reviewer's suggestion and added 'post-hoc statistical analysis of the reported differences' in Results, as Example 3 shows:

TH 4.6 Example 3

Draft resubmitted after first reviews (R): Addition

Differences among the levels of the [durations of the application of stimuli] **by means of a Tukey test showed significant differences** between [four sets of durations of the application of stimulus C]. The differences between [two other durations of the application of stimulus C] **were not significant**.

After resubmission of the article, the reviewers were still dissatisfied; one felt it now only 'contains the description of a single experiment with a single interesting finding' (Written Review); another reviewer noted that the lead author's cover letter had included more discussion of her results than had her revision. In her third round of revisions, the author removed much of the post-hoc Tukey analysis and reinstated the report of the analysis of 18 experiments. Finally, as Example 4 shows, she strengthened her discussion by including strongly hedged claims from the cover letter she had written.

TH 4.6 Example 4

Draft submitted after second round of reviews (D): Addition

The **'enhancement effect' may be responsible** for the greater effects found in the A and B conditions. That is, [two sentences of explanation added].

However, two reviewers now felt the evidence did not support the lead author's claims. One reviewer who had previously recommended acceptance now rejected the article; another reviewer who had opted for rejection now wanted to accept it. The editor rejected the article.

The lead author next decided to submit to the second journal identified by her late co-author, an English-medium journal that was *not so prestigious* [as the first], *but it was the most important in Europe* (Discussion). She jettisoned most of her revisions for the first journal and returned to an early version of the article, but made several salient changes. First, she reformulated what had been a claim as a research question (see Example 5).

TH 4.6 Example 5

Draft rejected by first journal (I)	*Draft submitted to second journal (I): Reformulation*
[The Z process] **takes time** to build up.	We also **attempt to estimate the time course** of the Z process.

In the Discussion section, she added some explicitly stated hypotheses about this research question, as shown in Example 6.

TH 4.6 Example 6

Draft submitted to second journal (D): Addition

[I]t might be expected that [the Z process] would take time to build up leading to a gradual increase in recognition score with [A-D stimuli] whereas as soon as [A-D stimuli are] established as a separate [process,] **[X theory] predicts that the score will increase sharply**. The present experimental results support both hypotheses equally. [Provides a sentence of specific details of experimental results to support both hypotheses.]

The changes shown in Examples 5 and 6 helped shift the rhetorical framing from one of reporting experimental results to one of hypothesis testing, more consistent with current conventions of natural sciences journals (Bazerman 1988). The second journal accepted the article 'with minor revisions' such as putting statistical results in tables, shortening sections and describing experiments more precisely.

Although the main author was pleased to publish the article, she was frustrated with her *really tiring* experience with the first journal. Of course the death of her co-author contributed to her feelings of exhaustion, but other problems she identified included publishing *in a journal that is not the typical journal for psychologists – other customs, other processes for me, it has been different*. In addition, she noted, *I am not a* [specialist in her co-author's field], *I am a psychologist* (Discussion). To her, the crux of the problem was that the *three reviewers wanted different things, so if I modified the article according to the first reviewer for example, it was the opposite of what the second reviewer wanted*. The second journal's acceptance of the article in nearly its original form reinforced her view that the problem lay in the first set of reviewers: *Curiously, you can see that these* [second journal] *reviewers agreed with everything* (Discussion).

TH 4.7: Resisting the call to simplify

In this Text History we draw on three drafts, two sets of reviewers' comments and editorial overview and two interviews with the co-authors. The article was produced by two scholars who have been working together for some 40 years in Southern Europe in the field of education. They work within a specific theoretical paradigm, initially developed by a well known English scholar. The brokers involved in this TH are two reviewers from the journals to which the paper is submitted.

Both reviewers point to the complexity of the article about which they express significant concern. Reviewer 1's comments centre predominantly on this concern and suggest the authors re-think the focus and goal of the article.

TH 4.7 Example 1

Reviewer 1 - *Extracts from written comments*	Author comment (in discussion)
For an audience unfamiliar with this work [specific theoretical approach] it would be very difficult to understand. The abstract is very dense. This section is not clearly explained to a general reader.	It was clear to me that this person knows nothing of [x theorist].
I think the authors should reconsider exactly what the article is about.	[Reading Reviewer 1's comments aloud]: 'This is crazy you know [laughs]'.

Overall, Reviewer 1 argues for a more introductory approach to the theory and method being discussed, a proposal which the lead author flatly rejects: *It is a research paper so in fact, if we are totally honest, we must disregard what this man says* (Discussion). Whilst the author refers to 'this man', the reviewers were anonymized and there was no indication that the authors recognized the identity of the reviewers in this case. We return to the question of identification practices in reviewing in Chapter 6.

Reviewer 2 echoes Reviewer 1's call for a more introductory stance and to discuss the method in the paper in ways 'which are useful to teacher educators and teachers in action based research' (Written Review). Although the lead author is not so dismissive of Reviewer 2's authority in this field – not least because the reviewer indicates a familiarity with their work as discussed below – she refuses to accept the reviewer's push to introduce what they see as basic notions: *and there is no way in which we can go back now and write something which is, is the same, which repeats what we have said in other papers* (Discussion).

The authors' commitment to the version of the paper as submitted reflects a life-long commitment to developing theoretical tools and empirical methods in order to establish a paradigm that can engage with the complexity of education. The authors see the reviewers' recommendation that the paper be moved to a more introductory footing as a fundamental problem with the way the field of teacher education internationally shies away from engaging with complexity. Therefore, this is not a question of the authors targeting the wrong journal, or of writing the wrong paper for this journal, but of them explicitly trying to bring specific disciplinary and theoretical conversations to this particular journal and field. The authors are aware that the approach may not be acceptable to the journal editor:

> I'm not sure whether the editor read the paper – I mean they may not accept it, I'm not sure, mostly because, as this referee points out, this journal is about teacher education and teacher education is, very light. Usually, they publish articles which are conceptually very light, very weak, you know. And this is one of the problems about teacher education. Teacher education is not conceptualized.
>
> (Discussion)

The author decides to make two minor concessions in responding to the reviews. The first is to include an additional diagram, taking up half a page, and the second is to include an additional footnote. These additions are intended to clarify the definitions of key notions in the paper. Both additions occur in the second section of the six-part article, the *Theoretical Framework*. In making such minor revisions, thus ignoring the major concerns of both reviewers, the authors are adopting a potentially risky position in terms of securing publication. However, they take this risk, we suggest, for three reasons: 1) because of their philosophical commitment to bringing complexity to teacher educators, described above; 2) they are at a point in their careers where securing an international publication is not as high stakes as it is for more junior scholars; 3) because they have some confidence that one of the reviewers is supportive of their work.

In this TH the lead author was clear from the outset about exactly what she wanted to have published and the extent to which she was (not) willing to compromise. Having made two small concessions to the reviewers – the addition of the diagram and a three-line footnote – she was prepared to have the paper accepted or rejected by the editor. In the event, it was accepted and published and the authors were therefore satisfied with what they had set out to achieve.

Conclusion

Academic literacy brokering in academic text production is a familiar practice to many scholars in their (our) roles as writers or reviewers, but has been the object of little systematic empirical research. Literacy brokering merits considerably more attention than it has received to date, across all contexts of production, as it is a phenomenon that is highly consequential. Yet because of its ordinariness to academics (we all 'know' about it) and also a sense in which such brokering – particularly communication between gatekeepers and scholars – is viewed as 'private', it tends to remain invisible.

In our focus on brokering in the context of multilingual scholars' production of English-medium texts, literacy brokering activity varies considerably. We have emphasized two key types of brokers – language and academic brokers. For busy scholars writing outside the Anglophone centre, the use of language brokers as a key resource for text production – whether English-speaking friends and family, or translators and English language professionals – would seem to be an obvious way of sustaining publishing activity in English alongside publications in local and other languages. However, whereas authors are mainly satisfied with the suggestions made by language brokers – professional and informal – who orient to mainly sentence-level corrections – translation is overwhelmingly viewed as problematic on two main counts: cost and accuracy. Even where scholars are in a position to pay for translation, scholars tend to avoid using professional translators because they find that accuracy at content and discourse levels is very difficult to achieve for translators who are not part of their academic subfield specialism.

The usefulness of sentence-level corrections and comments on texts for English-medium publication is evident from scholars' satisfaction and the fact that their texts (often) get published. However, this type of brokering may only be successful for specific types of publication – those which in the global academic marketplace are usually considered lower status such as conference proceedings and English-medium national publications (see discussion of rewards systems in Chapter 2). That different types of brokering are needed for higher status publications is borne out by the fact that the different types of brokering are not evenly distributed across text production, but are stratified according to target publication: most clearly, the involvement of academic brokers is particularly high in the production of articles aimed at Anglophone-centre journals. Academic brokers here tend to be from the Anglophone centre, accessed by scholars via network activities (discussed in Chapter 3) and who broker text production in a number of ways and certainly beyond sentence level: making specific changes to the text (THs 4.1, 4.2), suggesting or requiring specific changes be made to texts (THs 4.4, 4.5) and identifying appropriate target journals (THs 4.5, 4.6). The value of these brokers' interventions is clearly not primarily at the level of linguistic medium: rather, they influence opportunities for gaining access to English-medium journal publication as well as significantly contributing to the shaping of textual knowledge. Their textual interventions can be considered with respect to the orientations we identified for this category of brokers: content, disciplinary conversations and target journal conversations. That such interventions in these Text Histories are successful is evidenced by the publication of these texts. All lead authors expressed appreciation and pleasure at achieving publication.

As indicated in other studies (e.g. Flowerdew 2001), such brokers offer considerable time and energy, as well as material resources (see Canagarajah 1996) such as access to journal issues, other people and research opportunities. However, brokering activity needs to be located within a broader discourse-oriented frame which takes account of two further dimensions to global text production: the privileging of English-centre literacy/rhetorical practices and the differential power relations between centre/periphery relations around knowledge production. These dimensions are signalled at different levels of explicitness by the scholars themselves, who expressed misgivings about the process and/or the changes resulting from brokers' interventions; whether articulating a sense that brokers' interventions may have reduced the complexity of the knowledge they were constructing or feeling the text was being shifted in relation to the perceived marginal position from which the authors made their contributions. Some key rhetorical changes instigated by brokers can be understood as Western Anglophone academic literacy practices, where specific notions of textual unity and, conversely, digressions, most evident in TH 4.4, are privileged (Golebiowski and Liddicoat 2002; Mauranen 1993; Scollon and Scollon 1981).That such rhetorical practices are dynamic even within centre disciplinary contexts (Bazerman 1988) may also be a dimension to TH 4.6, where there appear to be different approaches to the rhetorical treatment and function of experiments from the brokers for two English-medium 'international' journals.

That practices of literacy brokering and text production are affected by unequal power relations is evident, most obviously in the dependence in the Text

Histories on centre brokers' support. Power relations are also more subtly evident in what gets valued as knowledge, as is most suggestively illustrated in THs 4.4 and 4.7. In TH 4.4 the contribution is not suppressed – rejected for publication – but its value shifts from a 'new' contribution to knowledge, to a confirmation of existing knowledge through what we may call a process of 'exoticization'. The value of its contribution becomes its capacity to demonstrate that findings from the centre can be replicated in a 'different' (other, 'exotic') context. In TH 4.7 the contribution is challenged because it is viewed as too 'new' or unfamiliar to potential readers. We continue with this central question of academic novelty and what gets valued, where and by whom in trajectories towards publication in the following two chapters.

Suggestions for further reading

When first exploring the brokering activity involved in text production, the work of Judy Kalman (1999) and Mike Baynham (1993) reminded us very powerfully of the material significance of literacy mediation. In discussing this phenomenon we learned a great deal from colleagues who work in translation and editing including Karen Shashok (1992, 2001, 2008, 2009) and Mary Ellen Kerans (2000; Shashok and Kerans 2000). The work of Charles Bazerman (1988) and Paul Prior (1998, 2003) on disciplinarity as a historical process continues to signal for us the need to find ways of capturing the dynamism in text-as-knowledge construction, production and evaluation – a task which still needs much attention. The dynamism emphasized by Bazerman and Prior connects with: 1) at the text level, John Swales's (1990) useful notion of 'rhetorical machining' and Ken Hyland's considerable mapping of disciplinary registers (e.g. see Hyland 2000); and 2) at a broader sociodiscursive level with Jan Blommaert's clear articulation (2006) of the importance of exploring 'how well texts travel'.

5   Staying 'local', going 'global'?
Working at Enlightenment Science

Introduction

Local and *global*, and the related notions of *localism/ity* and *glob(c)alization/ism*, are highly contested as ways of describing and theorizing the ways in which we live and work in the twenty-first century. With regard to text and knowledge production, as we have already seen, the local and the global – and the relation between these – are often refracted through two other notions, *national* and *international*, which are powerfully bound up with evaluations of scholarly publishing activity. In this and the next chapter, we set out to explore the significance of these notions, foregrounding two quite distinct (yet often overlapping) perspectives on the politics of knowledge making in a global context: the first, which we explore in this chapter, reflects an Enlightenment ideology of Science as a global utopia; the second, which we explore in Chapter 6, represents a more dystopic vision of knowledge making within the global academic community, where boundaries are clearly set between Anglophone-centre and non-Anglophone scholars and their contexts of research. We begin the discussion of locality in this chapter by focusing on the significance scholars attach to the specific localities in which they routinely live and work. We then move on to consider the particular significance of locality in academic writing for publication.

This chapter:

- Explores the significance attached to specific localities by scholars and how this connects with their research and writing activity;
- Documents which kinds of knowledge are being distributed across national and transnational contexts and the extent to which certain types of knowledge are 'staying local' or 'going global';
- Considers how a functionalist framing of scholarly writing reflects and enacts an Enlightenment ideology of Science.

The importance of the 'local' in scholars' writing lives

Most scholars around the world literally stay geographically local, out of choice or constraint, and work and write in institutions in localities to which they have strong historical, personal, cultural and linguistic connections and in which they invest time and energy in order to sustain (see Sassen 2009).[1] This connection with locality in part accounts for the ongoing commitment by scholars to continue to publish in local national languages, even in the face of the growing status attributed to English as the linguistic medium of academic knowledge production, and institutional pressures to publish in English. Acknowledging the significance of locality may seem obvious but can often be underestimated in high profile discussions about globalization 'from above', which focus on more abstract notions of the 'global' and globalization processes – such as the impact of ICT highways, mobility structures and supranational strategies of powerful groupings and agencies (see discussions in Castells 2000; Dor 2004; Falk 1999), as well as on postmodernist discourses which emphasize diversifying/hybrid practices, often resulting from globalization viewed through the First World (see discussion in Baumann 1998).

Drawing on discussions 'from below', that is, scholars' accounts and practices, we can see that there are (at least) two core aspects to the importance attached to locality: what we refer to as *immediate locality* and *imagined locality*. By immediate locality, we mean the material locality where people live and work, who they work and communicate with on a day-to-day basis, which language(s) and cultural identities they daily experience and espouse, and the kind of resources they have access to depending on what is made available through locally structured funding systems and institutions. Immediate locality has a strong reality in scholars' research and writing lives, shaping both opportunities and constraints for research and writing, notwithstanding the ways in which scholars are connected through virtual technologies to scholars, institutions and resources in other parts of the world (see Chapter 3 for a discussion of the importance of local networks for research and text production). By imagined locality (after 'imagined communities' in Anderson 1983; Norton 2000), we refer to the meanings attached to a specific locality by scholars, often grounded in immediate local connections and relationships, but also the sense of locality which they (we) carry with us even as we move to a very different locality. People's scholarly – and scholarly writing – *habitus* (Bourdieu 1990) is powerfully informed by both their immediate and imagined sense of locality and has a strong pervading influence in their/our personal and working lives.

The importance attached to locality is illustrated in the following brief accounts of some scholars' decisions about staying local, that is, staying in a locality with which they have strong autobiographical, personal and work-based connections. The accounts also illustrate the pull of more resource-rich institutions, particularly in the Anglophone centre, and scholars' responses to such opportunities. The accounts illustrate the significance of such opportunities, how they arise at different historical moments in individual scholars' lives, and how scholars engage with them.

Account 1: Elizabeth, full professor, aged 70, Central Europe

Elizabeth was invited in the 1970s to be a visiting scholar at a prestigious university in the United States. Securing permission to leave her country and take up such a scholarship was far from easy during what was at the time a rigid communist state bureaucracy. Having had her application rejected three times, she decided to seek an interview with the relevant party official to demand a reason for this refusal. He told her of the concerns: 'Well, you got the best education here and we're anxious of your leaving the country because you [will] get fantastic possibilities in the United States.' She convinced the official that she would not be tempted to stay on in the United States, saying that she had strong loyal and emotional ties to people and the country. Eventually, she was given permission to take up the scholarship. While in the United States. she was invited to stay more permanently, an invitation she warmly appreciated but had no intention of taking up. Colleagues in the United States were surprised at her decision: 'Are you mad?' 'Why don't you stay here?' 'What a chance; you get a chance like this only once in your life.' While the material and intellectual conditions on offer were many, she was clear that she had a major commitment to her local national research and educational context:

> I could have got a lot of equipment, possibilities to exchange ideas and, and a lot of resources I could not get at home. But what I had told this man [the party official], it was right. I had and I still have that feeling of responsibility, perhaps because of my family background, that the country needs people like me, with not only education and knowledge but with moral standards.

> (Discussion)

Account 2: Vicente, associate professor, aged 35, Southern Europe

Vicente wanted to study for his PhD in the United States because he wanted to *work with two of the best guys in the field*. Having secured a scholarship he spent four years in the United States and on completion of his doctorate had every prospect of securing a position there. However, he returned home.

> This was the stupidest thing – to come back.

> (Discussion)

The reason for being so critical of his decision to return relates to the severe constraints under which he feels scholars are expected to do research. *There is no Science here. They are just playing at being scientists.* He considers that underfunding severely restricts opportunities for sustaining and encouraging serious scientific activity, particularly compared with the United States. In order to do any research in his national context he feels that *you have to have contacts, and even then, everything proceeds very slowly.* For family reasons, both close and extended, he decided to return home. This was a particularly difficult decision, given that he knew that he could have secured a place in a US university.

Account 3: Margarida, associate professor, aged 35, Southern Europe

Margarida has very strong links with a group of researchers in the United States with whom she collaborates on specific projects and writing for publication. She regularly spends periods of time at their US institution, where the material support for research is considerably greater than that provided in her home institution.

> There they have experimental subjects, here we don't. They have a lot of labs and everything, it's well equipped, we don't have here. There, we have all the journals we want and we don't have here. There we have everything.
>
> (Discussion)

Margarida is passionate about her research and aware of the gap in opportunities that such resource differentials entail between 'there' and 'here'. She is also clear that there would be job opportunities for her in the United States but it is not something she has ever seriously considered. *I have children and I do not want them to grow up American. My life is here.* Margarida is strongly committed to building the research community locally and edits a national journal as part of this goal.

Account 4: Julie, associate professor, aged 39, Central Europe

Julie was until recently an education scholar in a Central European university. She was always keenly interested in research and has published extensively in English. Julie consistently felt at the margins of her university's focus on teaching and not recognized for her research interests and output. A few years after her PhD she began to conduct and publish research in the local context; however, *the administration of grants was very cumbersome, it took more time to keep the administration of a project going than doing the research*. Recently, at the age of 39, she took a senior-level position in an Anglophone-centre university. She listed her principal reasons for this move as follows:

> The very hierarchical structure of higher education here where it does not really matter what you have published and how much you have achieved, but how old you are and who else you are friends with in the academia – this put serious obstacles for me in terms of promotion and winning grant opportunities. The lack of sufficient resources in terms of IT and access to library resources. I felt that I needed a challenge and that I wanted to learn from other people in the profession. There is also little teamwork.
>
> (Email)

The move to an Anglophone-centre institution has not led Julie to abandon her interest in research in her local national context, and – with colleagues from the local national site – she has recently applied for a European Research Council grant.

Account 5: Andrea, assistant professor, aged 30, Central Europe

Andrea studied for a postdgraduate degree in Rome after attending an Italian bilingual high school for her secondary education. Although later offered the opportunity to study her PhD in Italy, she decided against this for both personal and academic reasons: she was recently married and her husband was working in their country of origin; she was not interested in the specific paradigm being pursued in the department. She therefore undertook her PhD studies in a Central European institution, close to her extended family, working with a supervisor with whom she had strong intellectual and personal connections. Both during and after completeing her PhD, she secured a number of research and teaching positions within the same institution. Her involvement in a European research project gave her the opportunity to be *local and global at the same time*. Unfortunately, despite her ex-supervisor's best efforts, they have no 'international' projects at the moment. Such projects *mean money, it means prestige for the institution and it means fresh air – new people, new approaches, new places to see* (Email). Weary at times of what she considers often to be a 'provincial' research culture in her department, Andrea is attracted to research and study elsewhere – in particular the United Kingdom. Gaining access to resources that such a move would offer is only a minor part of the attraction for her; rather it is a matter of the research culture and subsequent opportunities for publication that would arise. However, for family reasons – not least having children and wanting to have a stable home life – she sees herself staying, and continuing to research in her local national context. On the positive side, staying local offers her the opportunity to develop local research networks and activity, particularly around issues of direct relevance to the current sociopolitical situation nationally and regionally, such as identity and change.

All these scholars are powerfully committed to their research and aware that the resources for carrying out such research are generally considerably greater in other parts of the world, notably in the United States and the United Kingdom. However, as the extracts indicate, even when they have opportunities to join Anglophone-centre institutions – whether in the past or currently – in most cases they do not do so. Clearly, making decisions around working, researching and knowledge making as part of life activity involves more than considerations about access to available resources for research and writing; as scholars' comments indicate, importance is attached to home, family and a sense of strong connection with and/or commitment to the locality in which they live and work. Even where scholars shift their physical location of research and writing, as in the case of Julie, the importance of their historical/cultural and linguistic locality remains strong. Scholars thus stay connected to both immediate and imagined locality in a profound sense. The complex relationship their specific locality has with other localities and the 'international' context is a significant dimension to scholars' research and writing activity, as we discuss in the rest of this and the following chapter.

But, of course, whether staying physically local or strongly connected to their specific imagined locality, scholars are not interested in generating knowledge that is kept within a specific bounded, local community. To the contrary, all the scholars also have a powerful global 'imagined community' of scientists with whom they want to communicate their understandings and findings, in order to develop their own thinking or to extend a specific field of enquiry. This is reflected in scholars' interest in communicating with other scholars in their disciplines from around the world (as discussed in Chapters 2 and 3), which extends beyond the mere desire to gain access to resources for carrying out research and publication. Rather, this desire to communicate locally and transnationally reflects the aspiration for a global academic utopia which is part of longstanding historical traditions of knowledge making. This utopia is writ large in scholars' accounts of writing for publication, at the same time as, and alongside, accounts and practices which foreground more dystopian aspects such as: Anglophone-centre or Western dominance; English-medium dominance; inequality and prejudice against those writing outside the Anglophone academic world. Both utopic and dystopic visions and understandings, while apparently contradictory, are often in play in scholars' accounts of the decisions they make about which contexts and audiences they are seeking to publish in/for.

In the following section, we explore how an Enlightenment academic utopia is sustained through a functionalist approach to knowledge production transnationally; in Chapter 6 we turn our attention to consider the more dystopian aspects. In both Chapters 5 and 6 we consider what a focus on scholars' practices, opportunities and experiences – refracted through either a functionalist or a critical lens – can tell us about the politics of knowledge production in a global context.

Everything in its place in the global academic utopia

Science as universal

The idea that knowledge has a universal value and should be generated and shared across the world is embedded in many scholarly, intellectual and religious traditions, ranging from medieval wandering scholars (Waddell 1932/2000), to current practices of conference attendance around the world (actual but sometimes virtual), to scholars who foreground 'travel' as being both of both material importance and a significant metaphor for developing the research imagination (Kenway and Fahey 2009; see also discussion in Chapter 7). This deep commitment to sharing and building knowledge or Science translocally can be considered 'universal' both as a phenomenon and as an ethical value which is echoed, albeit in particular ways, in the European Enlightenment tradition, specifically around knowledge production, a principal concern of this book. Here notions of *universalism* and *community* are particularly relevant, whereby universalism refers to the principle that 'in science all men [sic] have morally equal claims to the discovery and possession of rational knowledge' and 'community' refers to the community of scholars, emphasizing the importance of sharing where, given the value attached to sharing; 'secrecy becomes an immoral act' (Cronin 1984: 19). Other core values get codified alongside universalism and community within the European Enlightenment tradition to constitute a specific epistemology: these include, notably, rationality, absence of bias and disinterestedness (see Figure 5.1). Together, these principles or norms project a vision of both the nature of the scientist's role – to produce and to share – and the values by which this work will be judged – fairly and impartially.

Methodological Tool 5: Ways of viewing talk and communication around academic texts

There is a tendency in much (writing) research to treat writers' talk (discussions in this study) and comments (informal comments, emails) about their texts as transparently meaningful. However, it is important to treat such data in at least three ways and to: 1) acknowledge that these 3 dimensions are always in play; 2) recognize that the strength of such data lies in its potential to generate analytic understandings at these multiple levels.

Three dimensions to talk around text

1. *Transparent/referential.* Insider accounts/perspective on texts (part of a text), practices including information about the writer – for example, about the person – age, languages spoken, number of papers published, number of assignments written and so on.
2. *Discoursal/indexical.* As pointing to specific discourses about self, writing, academia and so on.
3. *Performative/relational.* Researcher and those being researched performing practices related to research, identity, power, specific at specific moment/place in time.

Example

Extract from discussion: *If it's research that I think adds at some point to the topic and will help scientific communities to understand better something or some process or something ... then I will try to publish outside* [the national context] *– If it's something that it doesn't bring nothing new – then I would publish it in Portuguese.*

Analytical comment

Transparent/Referential: Information about what a scholar publishes, where and why.
Discoursal/indexical: Discourses of Enlightenment Science; discourse of 'novelty' in academic knowledge production.
Performative/relational: Scholar sharing particular view at a particular moment in time: alternative perspective emerges at another moment in time.

Scholar Profile 8: Letitia, Psychology, Central Europe

Letitia is an associate professor in her fifties. She has held a permanent position in an academic institution for some 26 years and has regularly taught in other institutions, like other colleagues, for no payment. She has published in Slovak, English, French and Russian.

She is the only person in her department working on her specialism and works with medical practitioners in the local national context both for carrying out her research and in her writings, usually taking the leading role in writing even if she is not named as first author. Letitia has connections with colleagues in many parts of the world relating to her specific research interests. She works at least six days a week, seeing this as inevitable. *In my country*, she says with a smile, *Saturday is a work-free day. We are free to work as much as we want.*

She learned English on various courses, particularly after the Velvet Revolution in 1989 when considerable funding was made available in Central European countries for English language teaching through organizations such as the British Council. She is meticulous in her crafting of all her writing in English – from emails through to articles for journals. When making preparations for writing a paper in English, she works through papers on the same or similar topics written by 'native' English speakers, looking for specialist terms, their synonyms and frequency. This strategy *helps me to find more appropriate and more precise special terms and enlarge a variety of expressions*. She is disappointed when she finds errors in published papers – for example if editors allow mistakes in English to be published, or make grammatically incorrect revisions to her own texts – because she feels *a reader merits papers without errors*.

Letitia sees publishing as being important for the dissemination of academic research and ideas, and emphasizes that what is important is not the linguistic medium of a text, but whether the publication is regarded as being of high quality, as indicated by its inclusion in important indexes, such as the SCI. At the same time, she also considers that English-medium publications are important because of the increased visibility they make possible for her work, and she has made a conscious effort at writing for English-medium journals and books. However, more recently she took the decision to direct her energies towards writing in the local national language for Central European journals: writing in English requires considerably more time for her than writing in her local national language, so by writing for national and regional journals, she can expect more papers to be published each year.

Faith in rationality
Emotional neutrality
Universalism
Community
Disinterestedness
Impartiality
Suspension of judgement
Absence of bias
Group loyalty
Freedom

Figure 5.1 The norms of Enlightenment Science (after Mitroff 1974, in Cronin 1984).

While the *universalism* evident across all scholarly traditions can be viewed as a 'benign' phenomenon (after Tomlinson 1999), or, more positively, as an ethical principle and a scholarly aspiration to be welcomed (as discussed in Chapter 7), the universalist stance evident in the European-based Enlightenment tradition of Science has been much critiqued as an ideology in three fundamental ways that are directly relevant to our discussion here: first, as a specific epistemological tradition which seeks to mask its specificity and deny the value of alternative epistemological traditions (see discussions in Canagarajah 2002a, 2005; Lather 1991); second, for the way it denies the significance of the local in knowledge production and evaluation practices (emphasized in work such as Gilbert and Mulkay 1984; Knorr-Cetina 1981; Latour and Woolgar 1986); third, and of particular relevance to our focus on the linguistic medium of knowledge production, for the way in which the language for communicating knowledge is viewed as a transparent rather than discursive or constitutive medium (Bazerman 1988; Lillis and Turner 2001; Turner 1999, 2003). With regard to the transparency perspective, the question of which language should be the medium of global scientific communication is seen as irrelevant or, if considered at all, as a historical sleight of hand which is of no particular significance for knowledge making. In this way, English is viewed as simply 'happening' to be the global language of Science, in contrast to Latin or Arabic, and in the more recent past, French, German, Russian (Ammon 2001; Truchot 1994). The specific linguistic medium is viewed as irrelevant as long as core linguistic values are upheld: clarity and transparency, which encapsulate the notion of ideas being put into words, often referred to as the 'conduit metaphor' of language (Reddy 1979). Here, knowledge and language are construed as two completely distinguishable objects and language viewed simply 'the necessary adjunct' to knowledge (Lillis and Turner 2001: 63). The Enlightenment conduit metaphor of language emphasizes the carrier rather than the constitutive function of language:

> For Language being the great Conduit, whereby Men convey their discoveries, Reasonings and Knowledge, from one to another, he that makes an ill use of it, though he does not corrupt the Fountains of Knowledge, which are in Things themselves; yet he does, as much as in him lies, break or stop the Pipes, whereby it is distributed to the publick use and advantage of Mankind.
> (Locke 1689, quoted in Harris and Taylor 1997: 127)

This conduit functions at its best when 'plain', as Cottingham (1988: 32) indicates in his summary of the Cartesian method:

> Descartes insisted that no concept should be allowed in a philosophical or scientific explanation unless it is either transparently clear or capable of being reduced by analysis to elements that are clear.

Thus clarity of linguistic expression is wedded in a fundamental way with clarity and rationality of thinking (for further discussion, see Turner forthcoming b).

While the Enlightenment ideology of Science has been heavily critiqued on a number of academic fronts, not least in postmodernist discourses, feminist and post-colonial writings, and in the sociology of knowledge (see for example, Knorr-Cetina 2003, 2007; Lather 1991; Latour and Woolgar, 1986; Said 1993; Weedon 1997), what is significant to our discussion here is that it continues to exert a powerful influence over knowledge production and evaluation practices – even in those intellectual fields where this ideology is fundamentally challenged. Thus the belief that an objective evaluation of knowledge is both possible and desirable continues to be embedded in evaluation practices across all disciplines and epistemologies, notably through such practices as 'peer review'. Peer review (mostly 'anonymous', officially at least, but see Chapter 6) exists to ensure that fair evaluations of contributions to knowledge can take place for the greater good of the global community of scholars; the goal of building a universal knowledge base is assumed to override any personal prejudice or professional jealousy, institutional power, politics and differential funding (a position challenged in work by Lamont (2009), for example, analysing the process of reviewing grant applications). Furthermore, the transparency ideology of language embedded in Enlightenment thinking ensures that, for the most part, little attention is paid to the politics of language in academic text evaluation.

It is easy to understand why this particular utopian vision around knowledge production and evaluation practices continues to hold sway in Anglophone-centre contexts even while it is heavily critiqued. It is a vision which leaves the centre's powerful position intact and allows us (centre scholars) to ignore the more troubling aspects of knowledge production practices. Yet such a vision also continues to hold sway in non-Anglophone-centre contexts where multilingual scholars are confronted with the geolinguistic and geopolitical dimensions to writing for publication which challenge and disrupt fundamental beliefs about a neutral zone of knowledge production and evaluation. Most obviously this is played out in everyday research writing activity in two ways: first, in decisions surrounding whether and what to publish for which communities, in particular between what we refer to in our discussion below as '*local-national*' and '*global-international*' outlets, notably journals; second, in the geopolitical dimensions to scholars' attempts to get their work published in 'international' Anglophone-centre journals. The tensions surrounding both of these aspects signal a more dystopian version of knowledge making which we discuss more fully in Chapter 6. But first we focus on how the Enlightenment ideology of knowledge production, premised upon core notions such as universalism and objectivity, are sustained through what we identify as a functionalist framing of scholars' research writing activity.

Scholar Profile 9: Ernesto, Psychology, Spain

Ernesto, 57, is a full professor and until recently, served for five years as department chair. During this time, and before, he had also headed a large research group comprising colleagues from his and other departments, and graduate students. Ernesto is well known in his field and has a number of formal and informal collaborations with scholars in other European contexts – some forged through Special Interest Groups of European and 'international' associations. He was recently invited to contribute to a project from another national context which funded not only his travel to meetings but also some of his students to stay for a few months.

Ernesto's first language is Spanish (Castilian). He studied French at school and currently uses English regularly for work. Twice in the 1980s he spent four weeks in England, and since the 1990s he has visited various American states for two or three months at a time. He is confident in his English, both in writing and oral communication. He writes many drafts of English texts and has a positive attitude toward the use of English for academic publishing:

> the way that people use English in my opinion is more clear, more precise than the way Spanish people usually speak. Sometimes the way Spanish scholars express their ideas, at least in the field of education and psychology, denotes vagueness and confusion. Quite often they do not try to be precise and clear enough in their claims. And science is not confusion, it is clarity.
>
> (Discussion)

Indeed, Ernesto feels that writing in English has had a 'great influence' on his Spanish writing:

> not only my style of writing, but my style of thinking, so I'm convinced that writing reflects how you think quite clearly. You write clearly, precisely, your mind is clear, precise and this is probably the most important benefit I've obtained trying to write in English.
>
> (Discussion)

Ernesto has published extensively, often in highly prestigious journals in his field in both English and Spanish, but prefers English for wider distribution of his research as well as the material benefits of English as a *sign of good research*. He acknowledges the effort needed to publish in English, but invests such effort in order to aim for high impact factor journals.

Promotion to full professor has meant more freedom for Ernesto to make choices about where to publish, including disseminating his research in Spanish publications as well as writing applied materials, such as papers about the software his group has developed. He also sees Spanish-medium publishing as important for supporting the development of his graduate students' careers until they improve their English sufficiently to be able to co-author with him in English.

Functionalist distinctions

Psychology scholar Margarida summarizes how she decides where to target her writings for publications as follows:

> My decision [about where to aim to publish] is, if it's research that I think adds at some point to the topic and will help scientific communities to understand better something or some process or something, then I will try to publish outside [of the national context]. If it's something that doesn't bring anything new, it's a good research project and has good data and it's good for students and it's good because it shows how research can be done and everything, it's more educational, then I would publish it in Portuguese.
>
> (Discussion)

Publishing 'outside' here refers to Anglophone-centre journals, in contrast with the local national (Portuguese-medium) journals. What counts as 'locally' and 'globally' relevant knowledge is thus refracted through 'national' and 'international' publications, most commonly through 'national' and 'international' journals. A distinction is made in the different overall purpose and goal of such geographically and geolinguistically marked contexts of publication. In Margarida's case, two aspects are explicitly signalled – the target community and the nature of the contribution. Thus a distinction is made between the *scientific* communities, and bringing something *new*, as compared with the more educational purpose of informing people about research, *good for students*. The former involves aiming to publish in English-medium 'international journals', and the latter publishing in local national journals. The second distinction is made on the basis of what is 'new', with 'novelty' long since recognized as a key value in academic journals (see Kaufer and Geisler 1989; see also critique in Sassen 2009). If new (the study, data, theory), then Margarida is clear that her work should be in an 'international journal'; if not new, then it can usefully be presented in a local national journal.

This 'new versus overview' distinction between what should be, and often is, published locally and 'internationally' is found across scholars' accounts and practices, albeit with slight variations of emphasis. Ernesto, a Southern European psychologist with many high-status English-medium SSCI publications, distinguishes between possible communities for his publications along two axes: local national language versus English and academic versus applied. English-medium journals are the target for research articles and local national journals the target for papers on applied work. Applied writings for scholars in psychology and education are aimed at bringing relevant research findings to practitioners such as teachers, nurses, doctors and clinical psychologists. Like Ernesto, many scholars argue that applied writings should be published locally-nationally because they are more relevant to the local contexts, sometimes on the grounds that empirical datasets which are situated and generated locally are likely to be of immediate interest to local, rather than non-local, practitioners. In addition, scholars often see local practitioners – rather than practitioners from other contexts – as being within their overall remit of scholarly responsibility and commitment. One scholar states, *Our approach is to the Spanish audience of practitioners. This has been important also because most of them don't speak any English, don't have any English.*

A further distinction is made on the basis of scale of reach and readership. As discussed, English-medium publishing is viewed as necessary to reach a larger audience, in addition to the status that accrues to English-medium publications. Ernesto states:

> The first reason [for English-medium 'international' publishing] is that many more people have access to your publications if you write in English. The second reason is the value of your research. Obviously it's, well, a sign of good research when you publish not just in English, not only in English, but in good academic journals.
>
> (Discussion)

Ernesto, like Margarida and other scholars seeking to engage with the global academic community, has not abandoned publishing research in local national journals but for the most part his goal in writing for local national communities aligns with the kind of educational goal indicated by Margarida. More specifically in Ernesto's case, he has two main goals in publishing locally: to disseminate the locally generated knowledge of research methodologies that he is developing; and to support his graduate students in building their careers by co-authoring with them in local national languages: *My purpose writing these* [local national] *papers was to give local researchers information about our tool because probably most of them don't read this* [English-medium 'international'] *journal* (Discussion).

The distinction made between the different purposes of local-national versus 'internationally' or globally relevant publications, leads some scholars to radically rethink their publishing priorities. Olivia is a senior Central European psychologist who has participated in an EU-funded project and has published some English-medium papers. Her primary concern at this stage in her career, however, is not with increasing her English-medium research output for institutional evaluation but using research to improve local education. She publishes *more, not in the specialized way, but more general things, but useful for practical teaching and everyday life of people working here* (Discussion). In fact, she specifically shifted her research focus from a topic she describes as relevant to a small percentage of the school-aged population to a broader topic affecting more students:

> I have a little bit changed, from this specialized orientation to a wider and more practical approach, so this is something which is more interesting for people living here, working here, teaching here. And so I have changed my audience and the topic in this way.
>
> (Discussion)

Olivia sees one of her contributions as introducing current knowledge published in English into the local context at the university level, thus acting as a conduit of Anglophone-based knowledge to local scholars and students: *What I'm doing is maybe to forward to our educationally interested community so most of the topics I write on are in* [the local national language] (Discussion). She feels a responsibility to university students who are given *the same things in old ideas* in textbooks [in the local national language], so that one compelling reason for her to write is also *because of* [university] *students who don't read English, so it's writing something, articles, just*

Table 5.1 Refereed psychology and education journals

	Psychology	Education
Total listed in Ulrich's	816	1,318
Published in Hungary	2	4
Published in Slovakia	2	6
Published in Spain	16	23
Published in Portugal	5	2

Source: www.Ulrichsweb.com, accessed 22 June 2009.

for the students. As a senior scholar, Olivia's applied and educational commitments, rather than concerns about career advancement drive her publishing decisions.

We return to presumed readership and how this relates to the ideals of scholarship, in Chapters 6 and 7. Here we wish to point to the key distinctions that are made in the goals and purposes of the texts to be published locally and globally: new/review, local/global reach and academic/applied. Such distinctions are often justified by scholars in terms of 'appropriateness' where the 'international' publication is viewed as offering more 'appropriate' outlets and spaces for specific contributions to specific subfields than local publications. 'Appropriate' here relates in part to the sheer difference in numbers of specialist journals in Anglophone-centre locations than in most other parts of the world (See Table 5.1 for comparison of numbers of psychology and education journals in the four national contexts of the research sites). These journals stand in contrast to the comparatively fewer journals in many national contexts, which tend to be broader in paradigmatic scope, in contrast to highly specialist journals where tiny yet significant contributions to specific knowledge areas can be noted and evaluated. Within a functionalist framework, a matter-of-fact acceptance is often expressed by scholars that Anglo-American journals offer the best outlets for specialist research where, worldwide, the specific research community may be very small. This has been signalled in Chapter 2 where we noted how one scholar, Istvan, feels that international journals are the forum through which he can communicate globally with specialists in his field. And Carla, a Spanish psychologist, notes that she is one of a handful of researchers in the world working on her topic, which she feels is too specialized to interest local journals: *In Spain, there is no research in this field* (Discussion). Likewise, one Hungarian scholar states that there is no *real public* for her specialist research locally, in that the field is very small:

> there are two more persons in Hungary who are dealing with my area at this time and, and they read the international articles, so if they are interested they can contact us at any time and have the English version.

> (Discussion)

The 'real public' for her academic specialist research therefore consists of the few 'local' specialists, along with all those scholars working in her specialism worldwide.

Functional distinctions between local and global publishing and how these are refracted through the signifiers 'national' and 'international' can be mapped along

Linguistic medium	Knowledge: Local-national	Knowledge: Global-international
Local language	Overviews of existing knowledge Applied knowledge	
English	Overviews of existing knowledge Applied knowledge	New, innovative, knowledge

Figure 5.2 Functionalist distinctions between linguistic medium and knowledge for local and global outlets.

a number of lines, as outlined in Figures 5.2 and 5.3. And of course the number of such functional distinctions may increase for any individual scholar, depending on the number of disciplinary areas and specialist subfields in which he or she engages. But even where the number of target groups multiplies, the functional distinctions along local/international can be sustained, as indicated by Figure 5.3 where the distinctions made within one scholar's publishing activity are mapped against language and local versus 'international'. This scholar's main or primary academic area is psychology and although her work involves collaboration with doctors and researchers in the medical field, she does not aim to contribute to the academic field of medicine, which can be described here as her 'secondary' rather than her primary academic specialism. However, in addition to her primary specialism in psychology, she does aim to contribute to applied, practice and policy making both related to her primary specialism – the field of psychology – and her secondary specialism – medicine. The functionalist distinctions made are mapped in Figure 5.3, which shows that she makes contributions to her primary academic specialist field via English-medium 'international' journals, and to applied, practitioner fields, drawing on both her primary and secondary specialism, via local-national journals. This particular scholar does not write for English-medium national journals, so her local national publications are all in the local national language, Hungarian (see Chapter 2 for different target communities).

Of course, once scholars are working across a number of domains (which may be their primary or secondary academic specialisms and may be academic or

Linguistic medium	Knowledge: Local-national		Knowledge: Global-international	
	Psychology	Medicine	Psychology	Medicine
Local language	Applied knowledge	Applied knowledge		
English			Academic specialist	

Figure 5.3 One psychology scholar's functionalist distinctions between publications aimed at academics and practitioners in two academic fields.

applied) in a number of languages (at least two), difficult decisions have to be made about where to invest time and energy. A Central European psychologist who works across theoretical/applied and specialist domains considers that it is just not worth the investment of his time and effort to target English-medium international journals for his more clinically oriented research writings. Furthermore, he also doubts whether they would be interested in work about *the culture and the mental dynamic process of* [local] *psychology which is culturally not preferable to English journals* (Discussion).

Scholars clearly make distinctions between what they are aiming to publish where, predominantly on a 'local-national'/'global-international' basis. We have already noted that 'international' is a particularly pervasive sliding signifier and we return to this issue in Chapter 6. But a point we wish to stress here is that in many scholars' accounts, even though at other moments they signal the evaluative distinctions between national and 'international' publications, they often emphasize the 'appropriateness' of such distinctions, pointing to the importance of different kinds of function and purposes of different kinds of text – and hence knowledge – for different contexts of publication. The kinds of descriptive-functionalist categories attached to national and 'international' publications are summarized in Figure 5.4.

	LOCAL	GLOBAL
	National publications	*International publications*
Academic status	Appropriate to national context	Appropriate to international context
Geographical production	Published within national borders	Published within other national borders/across national borders
Geographical authorship	Authors predominantly from one national context	Authors from a number of national contexts
Geographical readers	Read predominantly within national context	Read in a number of national contexts
Geographical editorship	Predominantly national editorial board	Editorial board from number of national contexts
Scientific function	Overviews of existing work Applied/practitioner	New findings Academic/theoretical
Scientific value	Of value to the local community – 'review of knowledge'	Of value to global community – 'new' knowledge
Scientific language	Local national language English	English

Figure 5.4 Functionalist-normative mapping of 'local' and 'global' against 'national' and 'international' journals.

What is important about this functionalist approach to scientific publishing is that it enables an Enlightenment version of scientific knowledge making in a global academic utopia to remain alive and valid, while masking or downplaying the politics surrounding academic text production. The more critical framing of the distinctions made between local and global publication is discussed in Chapter 6.

An obvious point to note is that scholars' decisions around what to publish where – that is, the *geolinguistic* dimension which must be taken account of, in addition to the paradigmatic dimension that tends to be Anglophone scholars' sole concern – are clearly impacting on what kinds of knowledge are circulating in which geolinguistic contexts. Most clearly, the knowledge that scholars designate as 'new' seems to be being directed towards 'international' journals. This is not the only pattern of knowledge distribution, as we discuss in Chapter 7, but it is a key one.

An issue we wish to raise at this point in the discussion is that a functionalist distinction made between the kinds of knowledge that are 'appropriate' for local and 'international' contexts also presupposes that all scholars committed to the universalist endeavour in their discipline are able to engage in the global conversation that takes place via English-medium 'international' journals. In this way, it is assumed that writers and readers from whichever local context who are specialist in the specific subfield specialism can be part of their global disciplinary research community. However, even where scholars feel able to sustain and uphold the functionalist-normative division in their decisions around *writing* for publication, cracks in this framing are evident once the question of scholars-as-readers is brought into the picture, not least because of the medium of the global scientific conversation – English. Participating in the global conversation may not be so straightforward as the universalist paradigm neatly implies, and as the functionalist framing seems to reflect. This is evident in the additional reasons scholars give for the need to publish in local-national contexts, as indicated by Ernesto's comments above, where he states that *probably most of them* [local scholars] *don't read* [a specific English-medium journal]. Given this readership gap, scholars' writing in local national contexts functions as a bridge or conduit between 'international' disciplinary conversations (that many local scholars may not have access to) and local disciplinary conversations, mainly in local national languages. The extent to which this bridging is one-directional (Anglophone centre to non-Anglophone contexts) rather than multidirectional is raised further in Chapters 6 and 7.

Working toward equivalence

A less common way in which the Enlightenment ideology of knowledge production is sustained is through a notion of *equivalence*, whereby decisions surrounding what should be published where are replaced with the attempt to publish research and knowledge produced by a scholar (or team) in both local-national and global-international contexts. Translation (by others) would be the obvious means by which such equivalence could be (easily) achieved. But as discussed in Chapter 3, translation is not a straightforward option for many scholars, not least because of

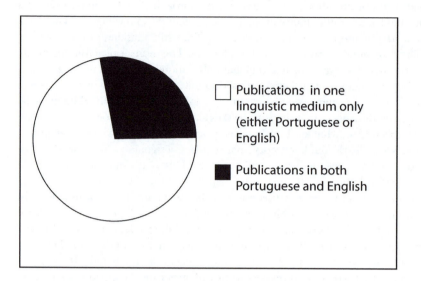

Figure 5.5 Working at equivalence in Portuguese and English-medium productions: publication record of one Portuguese research team.

costs and translators' often limited expertise in relevant subfields of knowledge. But some scholars, rather than maintaining the functionalist divisions, most starkly between *national-review* and *international-new*, aim to publish as much as possible of what they do both in English and in local national languages so that similar knowledge is made available in national and 'international' contexts. We refer to these as 'equivalent' versions rather than 'translations' as, while there is considerable overlap in such texts,[2] there are also significant differences. See Figure 5.5 for a mapping of the work by two scholars and their research team who have worked together for considerable time, writing in both Portuguese and English. Almost a third of their publications (of a total of 116) are available in both English and Portuguese, in different types of publication: journal articles, book chapters and conference proceedings. Of the publications available in both languages, 67% were written and published first in Portuguese and then in English; some 15% were written first in English and subsequently in Portuguese; and some 18% published in both languages at the same time (in the same year). The result is that a considerable amount of work produced by this team of scholars is available in two languages, which they feel connects their work to both local-national and global-international contexts.[3]

Such equivalence in knowledge production comes at the cost of incredible effort by these scholars, who not only carry out the research but also write (and translate) for publication in two languages (in addition to occasionally publishing in other languages). The impact of such equivalence on knowledge production and circulation practices merits further study.

Scholar Profile 10: Ornella, Psychology, Hungary

Ornella, 32, has been an assistant professor for five years at the institution where she earned her doctorate. As she was required to present or publish papers in both Hungarian and English before finishing her degree, from early on she presented research in English at conferences in Europe and Canada under the guidance of her PhD supervisor. She also co-authored some seven publications with him in both languages as well as other publications individually. During her doctoral study she had an ERASMUS scholarship for three months in Finland; later she spent six months in Spain on a Marie Curie Fellowship. At a conference, Ornella met one Spanish scholar who supervised her stay in Spain. This connection was the beginning of a network she established with scholars in Spain (with whom she has collaborated on projects independent from her work with her supervisor) as well as connections to scholars elsewhere.

Ornella uses Hungarian, Spanish and English for her academic work; she also speaks German and studied Russian at school. She began learning English at secondary school, but stopped at university. During her doctoral programme, she had one course in the specialized (English-medium) discourses of psychology. Her comprehension of English is strong and during research stays in Finland and Spain she considers she improved her oral and written English considerably: *I learned a lot* [in Spain] *and I got a possibility to write a book chapter in English and also I read a little in English so I think now I have a sense to know, no, but to feel how to write correctly in English.* Developing her English is important to Ornella, who is acutely aware of the role of high status English-medium publishing to her future success.

At the same time, these extended visits to other places have contributed to Ornella's growing appreciation for Hungary, which has influenced her thoughts on where to build her academic career:

> When I was a teenager I really wanted to leave my country because of the narrow opportunities and the Hungarian approach to a way of life but now I'm very, very proud after my travelling, I'm really proud of my country. So I really like to be Hungarian and to stay at home. Sometimes I feel that I needed to go abroad just to take another point of view and to get away from my group and my limitations but now I know that I'm not going to live abroad forever. My dream is, before I have children, to travel and make a short visit to different universities just to have some experiences to compare myself, my knowledge with the level of other researchers.

(Discussion)

Conclusion

Most scholars are staying local, with the local – most obviously understood as place, people and language – being centrally relevant to scholars' research and writing activity. Even when scholars are not staying geographically local, the local as immediate and imagined locality powerfully influences their research focus and interests and opportunities for research and writing.

The global research community is also part of the imagined research community with whom scholars wish to communicate and which connects with longstanding scholarly traditions in Science and knowledge making as a shared human endeavour. However, one particularly powerful ideology of Science continues to hold sway – that is an Enlightenment ideology of Science as a rationalist and objective project where all are free to contribute and knowledge production is evaluated according to established norms of justice and fairness. This ideology looms large in scholars' accounts and practices, even while, at the same time, they point to prejudice and lack of equality in opportunities for research and in evaluation practices in the global academic marketplace.

An Enlightenment ideology of Science is sustained through the functionalist framing evident in scholars' accounts and practices, whereby decisions are made about what should be published where – 'internationally' or ' locally' – on the basis of a series of distinctions: new versus overview (or review); academic versus applied; English versus local national language and/or English. Fewer scholars sustain an Enlightenment vision through a practice of equivalence rather than distinction – whereby they endeavour to make their most significant contributions to their field available in local national contexts and languages, as well as globally through English.

We have noted again the key sliding signifier in the discourse surrounding academic text production – 'international'. In the following chapter we continue to focus on this signifier but turn our attention to questions around the valuing of the 'local' in our discussion of the more dystopic vision of text and knowledge making within the global academic community.

Suggestions for further reading

The small book written by Blaise Cronin on citation practices in 1984 usefully reminds us that any discussion of systems of knowledge evaluation – in particular the increasing use of 'bibliometrics' across all disciplinary areas – needs to engage with ideologies of Science. Patti Lather's 1991 book offers a sharp articulation of key distinctions between epistemological/ideological frameworks, as does Joan Turner (for example, 1999, 2003), who furthermore provides a careful tracking of the relationship between epistemologies and ideologies of language. We found work by Richard Falk (1999) and Michael Burawoy (2000) to provide thoughtful arguments against the significance of grand theorizing on globalization for making sense of what's happening 'on the ground', and the need to stay close to scholars' accounts and text trajectories.

6 Boundaries and stratification in the global academic dystopia

Introduction

This chapter continues the focus on the politics of knowledge making but shifts the emphasis away from the functionalist framings sustaining an Enlightenment version of academic knowledge making towards the more dystopic aspects which frame multilingual scholars' opportunities for publishing, particularly in high status Anglophone-centre journals. Such aspects – which foreground the obstacles scholars face in attempts to publish in Anglophone-centre contexts – are strongly evident in scholars' accounts and practices, often alongside the more utopic accounts. A key focus in this chapter are the gatekeeping practices surrounding publication which powerfully influence which knowledges get to 'go global'. This is a theme that has been touched on across the book and which we pay specific attention to here, exploring the textual ideologies at work in such practices. Of particular significance is the way in which 'locality' is or is not valued in the research writings which scholars are seeking to publish in Anglophone-centre journals.

This chapter:

- Discusses the vertical relationship between 'local' and 'global' publications and the boundaries between these;
- Explores the ways in which locality is evaluated differentially within global academic knowledge production – as 'marked locality' (non-Anglophone contexts) and 'unmarked locality' (Anglophone contexts);
- Examines how Anglophone-centre-based gatekeeping activities structure the regulation of knowledge value internationally;
- Discusses the textual ideologies at work in evaluation practices.

Science as local: 'global' is a place called the 'US'

> The global is the self-presentation of the dominant particular. It is a way in which the dominant particular localizes and naturalizes itself.
>
> (Hall 1997: 67, discussed in Canagarajah 2005: 4)

The universalist ideal of a global Scientific community, sharing academic knowledge across localities (usually framed as national borders), continues to hold sway in scholars' ethical positions and intellectual aspirations. However, the politics of

Scholar Profile 11: Olivia, Psychology, Slovakia

Olivia, 53, an associate professor, has been based in one higher education institution for 28 years. She also teaches at a second local institution, and sometimes in a university in another city. Earlier in her career she conducted experimental research, but recently her interest has been in applied research, focusing on improving practice and contributing understandings from her specialist subfield.

> During my career I have a little bit changed my orientation from this specialized orientation to something wider and more practical. That means I'm working with something which is more interesting for people living here, working here, teaching here and so I have changed my audience and the topic in this way. It's better, not better but more meaningful, I would say. I feel better.

> (Discussion)

In addition to Slovak, Olivia mainly uses English although she studied Russian and German at school. She began to study English in secondary school, and continued at university and through her doctorate. She is confident and proficient in English for reading, listening, correspondence and conference presentations but feels writing is more problematic, depending on level and topic.

Olivia collaborates most frequently with colleagues at her second institution and their doctoral students. In 2002 she was invited to join a multicountry European Union project on developing an assessment instrument, but she has had few other transnational collaborations. Because Olivia sees her work as benefiting the local community, she is more concerned with publishing in the local national language than in English. She recognizes that *the international journal is most or more heavily valued, more valued than publishing in the* [local] *home journals*, but she does not feel strong pressure to publish in English. Also, she does not see 'international' research journals as interested in her work:

> The problem is that we are working in a region, I would say, really, and many journals we follow and read are at this regional level. This topic which I am dealing with, is, I would say, it's not the topic for the reader of these [international] journals nor of international character.

> (Discussion)

Furthermore, Olivia feels that 'international' journals are not read by the people she wants to reach. However, publishing in local – national and regional – journals, which are not 'Currented' (i.e., indexed in Current Contents), means that for institutional evaluation *you need to publish twice as much if you don't publish in a Currented journal.* Olivia's publications in English have focused on reporting developments in the local context and been produced as a contribution to an international association for which she has served as the local representative. To date no collaborative publications in English have resulted from the EU project, although researchers involved in the project, including Olivia, have published in local national languages.

location are also strongly evident in scholars' accounts and practices and signalled as thwarting the fulfilment of such an ideal.

We have already discussed some of the obstacles scholars writing outside the Anglophone centre face in their attempts to join in 'global' academic conversations: funding and resources, evaluation systems which privilege Anglophone-centre publications – including the privileging within such systems of English-medium over other linguistic-medium publications – and gaining access to research networks that support English-medium publishing. A further and significant problem are the gatekeeping practices surrounding the evaluation of what kinds of knowledge are relevant to the 'global' academic community and therefore what should, or should not, be published in centre journals. In contrast to the 'global' as an imagined universal community of scholars wishing to share their best research and understandings, 'global' and its proxy in academic publishing, 'international', become almost synonymous with the Anglophone centre, the prototype being the United States. The United States, through its considerable material resources, the large number of US-based high status journals and its key location in relation to knowledge evaluation (through powerful institutions such as the ISI), has considerable power in gatekeeping what counts as contribution to universal knowledge (for overview discussions, see Carli and Ammon 2007; Gnutzmann 2008).

Within this more dystopic version of the global academic community, the functionalist distinctions emphasized in Chapter 5 which offer a neutral and unproblematic account of what kinds of knowledge should be published where, disappear. These distinctions, rather, are reframed in hierarchical terms, with the *local* – refracted through *national* publications and being construed as non-Anglophone centre – having less value than the *global* – refracted through *international* publications and being (predominantly) construed as Anglophone centre (often as US). Within this critical rather than functionalist framing of academic knowledge production, the categories which are used as straightforward descriptions of outlets for scholarly publication (as set out in Chapter 5, Figure 5.2) take on a more ideologically loaded significance. As outlined in Figure 6.1, the vertical (hierarchical) relationship between the two contexts of publication stands in contrast to the horizontal framing emphasized in Chapter 5 and raises difficult questions about the *boundaries* rather than the *distinctions* between the two contexts, particularly in scholars' attempts to cross these.

Crossing boundaries (or attempts at 'scale-jumping')

That there are problematic boundaries, rather than functionally valid distinctions, between what counts as locally and globally relevant knowledge, becomes evident once scholars attempt to cross the boundaries between their local national context to the 'international' or Anglophone context, as we illustrate here by drawing on THs and accounts from scholars.

TH 6.1: Attempting to publish a new model

As discussed in Chapter 5, Margarida believes that Science is and should be a universal endeavour and that the 'international' journal is the appropriate place/space

	LOCAL	GLOBAL
	National publications	*International publications*
Academic status	Low (informally and formally though evaluation systems)	High (informally and formally through evaluation systems)
Geopolitical location	Published within national borders	Anglophone centre Indexed in ISI
Geographical authorship	Authors predominantly from local-national institutional affiliations	Authors from predominantly Anglophone-centre institutions
Geographical readership	Read predominantly within national/regional contexts	Read in a number of national contexts particularly Anglophone centre contexts
Scientific function	Overviews of existing work Applied/practitioner	New findings as refracted through Anglophone-centre control
Scientific value	Of value only to the local community	Of value to global community as refracted through Anglophone-centre control
Scientific language	Local national language English	English

Figure 6.1 Ideological distinctions to local and global publications in the global academic dystopia.

for contributing and sharing 'new' knowledge. She therefore strives to contribute to international conversations by publishing in high status US journals and has had some success, usually while co-authoring with US colleagues. However, problems occurred when she attempted to make a specific contribution to her specialist sub-field, presenting a theoretical model that she individually has pioneered. For 10 years she has been attempting to publish her model, developed from her PhD thesis, which aims to take forward an existing theoretical model in significant ways. She has submitted a paper outlining, theorizing and critically evaluating her model, four times to two US-based (SSCI-indexed) journals. She knows that some of the reviewers have been the same for both journals; in one review they signed their names. Following each review she made what she considered to be substantial revisions in response to reviewers' and editors' comments but she is still no nearer publication. She is disheartened not least because she is not convinced by the arguments given to account for the rejection:

> I always thought that to publish those studies [on her model] would help people clarify what is going on. And the other guys [reviewers] say 'We already know this. Why do we need another paper on exactly the same

thing?' So when I started to call attention to [X] they said 'Okay, but now you have to show this.' And I can't do that because I believe that [X] and [Y] really are the same thing. So we keep arguing. It's good to argue but the only problem is that they don't allow me to publish. I would love to continue this fighting but it might make it harder for me to publish at all so I am thinking of giving this up and starting another line of research.

(Discussion)

Margarida feels she is being prevented from publishing her model, but at the same time she is reluctant to accept the explanation for the continued rejection of her model that her locally based colleagues offer her:

We always guess and joke and say that there are always enemies every-where. Some people say this more seriously. 'You know that if [X] is a peer reviewer you know you will not be able to publish at all. You are challeng-ing what he is doing and so he has higher status and can stop you.' I never usually believe this. I love to talk with my enemies. When I say 'enemies', I mean enemies of ideas. And I never thought that people would say 'no' just because they want to maintain their status. But there is a lot of talk about this and there are some things that support that a little. You can notice who is citing who and you can see that some line of research try to ignore the other one which is really relevant … And you see that Germans cite Germans, people from Netherlands cite Netherlands, the Americans cite Americans, and you can't find the school. And I don't like this. This is not Science.[1]

(Discussion)

Margarida has a strong belief in an Enlightenment view of Science – with objectivity and universalism at its core. But almost in spite of this ideological posi-tion, she feels that her specific geopolitical status – indexed here through the reference to (other) nationalities – is impacting on her opportunities to get her spe-cific contribution published and thus contribute to advancing knowledge globally in her specific field.

Other scholars share Margarida's reluctance to explain rejection of papers submitted to high status journals in terms of Anglophone-centre discrimination, but at the same time they are more categorical about the significance of their geopolitical location as scholars and how this impacts on their opportunities for publishing.

TH 6.2: Attempting to make a significant contribution

Ruben and his two co-authors have been attempting to publish one particular paper for some six years in Anglophone-centre journals. It was first submitted to a European Anglophone journal and rejected. Following a reworking of the paper, the authors submitted it to a US journal as they were (are) convinced that the study and theoretical insights offered are significant for their field. Following reviews from this journal, they were invited to resubmit and did so a year later. The response from the editor was a request for further revision stating that he would accept a further resubmission, albeit with a clearly stated ambivalence about the potential publication of the paper.

At this stage, given the length of time that had been spent on this paper (six years), the number of rejections and requests for major revision, the authors might have been expected to give up. This lead author – like most scholars – sometimes gives up on papers, accepting that some are not publishable. However his persistence in this instance is a result of the authors' conviction that the paper makes an important contribution. The authors reworked and resubmitted the paper, and subsequently received a rejection. The lead author is not convinced of the validity of the rejection and unimpressed by what seems like a rhetorical move by the editor to preempt any complaints about the quality of the reviewing process:

> It is obvious that the three reviewers spent a substantial amount of time on your paper. These are three highly esteemed colleagues, each of whom provided extremely thoughtful and detailed critiques.
>
> (Written Letter, Editor)

The reassurance that such a comment on the ethos and personae of the reviewers was presumably intended to provide, failed to convince the authors (for ethos/personae discussion, see Cherry 1988; Ivanič 1998: 89–91). Ruben has a strong publishing record in high status journals – he is not a novice in his field or in publishing and is confident, having taken account of early criticism and acted on this, that the paper represents a significant contribution to his field and as such is important to publish. He also makes clear his explanation as to why the paper is facing such a difficult road towards publication: that journal editors and reviewers are not prepared to publish significant, innovative contributions from scholars from Southern Europe.

Ruben, like Margarida, is reluctant to offer a geopolitical explanation for failure – *I don't like this kind of explanation* – yet at the same time he is categorical in his conviction that this is a primary cause for continued rejection. He argues that being from Southern Europe and the global south more generally is incompatible with making a significant contribution to the field and is construed as potentially threatening to the status quo of the journal in some way.

The authors' comments in THs 6.1 and 6.2 stand in sharp contrast to the more utopic accounts in Chapter 5 where decisions around which knowledge to publish – nationally or 'internationally' – are represented as within the scholars' control, depending on notions of 'appropriateness' (for critical framing of this notion, see Fairclough 1992). A useful concept to help theorize what is going on here is that of 'scale' and in particular the notion of 'scale jumping'. 'Scale' is a way of connecting time and space – *Timespace* – and of exploring the significance of this dimension to our specific interest here, scholars from one geopolitical location attempting to publish in another – higher prestige – location. 'Phenomena that develop in TimeSpace are social phenomena' (Blommaert 2006: 4) and thus, like all social phenomena, involve issues of access and power, including the power to define which criteria need to be met in order to be recognized as being (or communicating) at a particular scale level. With regard to our focus here, the problematic surrounding scholars researching and writing from outside non-Anglophone centre contexts, yet seeking to publish in those contexts, can be conceptualized as a question of different scale levels, with the shift from local to 'international' involving an attempt at scale jumping which may or may not be successful. We return to the question of scale below.

What counts as 'new'? Locality, parochialism and exoticization

The examples above point to the significance attached by scholars – albeit reluctantly in some cases – to the politics of location and scale in the processes surrounding academic publishing. Most obviously, what is valued at one point on the scale (in the local context) is not valued at a higher point on the scale (in the Anglophone-centre context) and scholars are often struggling to cross from the former to the latter.

The politics of location are at work in other less obvious ways, impacting not only on what doesn't get published but on the terms governing what does get published. For, while the instances above emphasize work that is *not* getting published in Anglophone-centre journals, it is not the case that the doors of international publication are completely closed to non-Anglophone-centre authors. Evidence from this and other studies is that non-Anglophone scholars are getting published, even if the task is arduous and challenging (see Chapter 2, Chapter 4; see also Belcher 2007; Flowerdew 2000; Hewings 2006; Li 2006; Uzuner 2008). Perhaps more significant then is to consider the specific terms under which their contributions are getting published, that is, the conditions governing what counts as relevant knowledge in centre contexts of publication. And here 'locality' takes on a particularly tricky significance. In teasing out this significance, we have found it useful to distinguish between 'marked' and 'unmarked' locality in tracking trajectories towards (non-)publication. By marked locality, we mean localities which are explicitly non-Anglophone centre, which stand in contrast to unmarked locality, localities which are Anglophone centre. Marked locality is made visible in a number of obvious ways in the process towards submission for publication: in cover letters, through reference to author's affiliation and national context; and in submitted texts, through explicit mention of national/regional context usually with reference to the research site or data, such as *x participants from two Hungarian universities took part: analysis of Spanish vocabulary was carried out: the study took place between 2000 and 2002 in a large city in Slovakia*. Unmarked locality may be present textually – for example through reference to a study carried out in New York – but is treated as a 'default' locality within the global economy of signs (Blommaert 2005: Ch 1), and attributed a very different kind of status in gatekeeping practices surrounding publishing and therefore knowledge production and dissemination.

Scholars often express the view that their specific locality of research and writing presents a problem: in general, there is the concern that studies done outside the Anglophone world and data generated from such studies are not considered relevant to the Anglophone centre – they are marked in a specific (often negative) way and not 'misrecognized', to use Bourdieu's term (1991). As one Spanish education scholar's comments indicate, echoing Ruben's comments above, there is a perceived lack of interest by Anglophone scholars in anything non-Anglophone. *We are in the south and I am very conscious of being in the south of Europe, no one out there cares about what you can say* (Discussion).

This perspective is expressed across research paradigms – from experimental to qualitative. Another Spanish scholar, Mercedes, a psychologist, perceives a lack of interest from high status Anglo-American journals in locally generated Spanish qualitative data, even though a key tenet of the qualitative theoretical paradigm in which she works is the valuing of richly situated study and analysis. She questions whether this valuing of specific, contextualized study in qualitative research – which necessarily includes an emphasis on the 'local' – extends beyond Anglophone contexts, arguing that case studies are *okay for Americans* but not necessarily for Spaniards. Several THs provide empirical support for her concern that marked locality (marked as being outside the Anglophone centre) is viewed as problematic. Consider one example relating to a different Spanish psychology scholar presenting qualitative research, where a reviewer asked the following question of her work in the review:

> Please could they outline why Madrid was chosen as the place of study in the first place, and why indeed Spain might be a useful comparison with other previous work.
>
> (Written Review)

It is hard to imagine a similar comment requesting justification for a study being carried out in a capital city or whole country from an Anglophone-centre context, such as the United States or the United Kingdom.[2]

Such comments by centre journal gatekeepers are not unusual. Consider a reviewer's comment on a Hungarian paper submitted for publication:

> Why did the authors choose to study Hungarian students? The answer seems to be that the authors are from Hungary however, I wonder if there is anything particular about the Hungarian situation that would make it useful to study Hungarians, rather than, say, British students. I – and I suspect, many other American academics – know nothing about Hungary's educational system.
>
> (Written Review)

Writers are therefore sometimes explicitly called upon to justify the location of their research. But, at the same time, such mention of specific locality means that they run the risk of their work being accused of being bound to the 'local' – and being cast as 'parochial'. In one instance a Southern European experimental psychologist explained that an article, which focused on 'degraded' speech and its relevance to understanding about hearing loss, was rejected by a US-based journal specialist in this field because, they weren't *interested in Spanish data*. The reviewers/editors stated that they felt the results would not be generalizable from Spanish. The scholar points out that no matter what language is used in these types of experiment, because of phonetic differences across languages, such research can never be generalizable at this micro level, including research using English words. The same issue was raised by a reviewer of another of the same scholar's articles:

> The reviewer wanted to know if the result, well I think it was a silly, it was a silly thing but he wanted to know if the results in our article can be generalized to other languages, which is evident that not, so I had to explain [in her revision] the difference between Latin languages and English.
>
> (Discussion)

Her use of 'silly' here indicates the kind of resignation many scholars seem to feel about this process, pointing to a situation which is as absurd as it is consequential. We return below to the way in which marked locality in this scholar's work gets taken up differently by another Anglophone-centre journal, and some possible reasons why.

It is not just the locality of specific studies that may be challenged by reviewers but in some instances the location of an entire research base, as is illustrated in TH, 6.3.

TH 6.3: Citing non-Anglophone research

In this TH involving an article written by a group of Hungarian scholars, reviewers' comments on their submitted article signalled the problematic significance attached to the linguistic medium of some of the citations used in the paper.

TH 6.3 Example 1

Reviewer comment *(extract from Written Review)*	Lead author's comment *(extract from Discussion)*
As a general comment the style needs to be polished. In any instance sentences follow each other without logical connections and the **authors often refer to other publications that may not be available to the ordinary unilingual or even bilingual North American reader.** By themselves these two points make it difficult to evaluate the results or the comments passed (our emphasis).	And there were some very rude remarks, for instance, when we referred to a Hungarian reference and they said how can they mention Hungarian article? You know in this case we had to answer each of the remarks of the anonymous reviewers. And for instance we wrote that 'as far as we know, it's an international journal' [laughter]. Among the – I don't know – forty references there is one Hungarian, it's maybe ... So it was not at all a helping circumstance.

It's important to note not just the specific, single aspects that the reviewer identifies as problematic ('style', 'other publications') but how these cluster together to constitute the overall 'problem' and in which marked locality plays a significant part. We return to the issue of indexical clustering below.

It is instructive to take the reviewer's concern at face value in the first instance to consider whether the paper does in fact include citations of many works which are hard to access. In the final bibliography, there are, as the lead author mentions in her comments, 40 references. Of these 40, one is Hungarian-medium (an unpublished PhD thesis) with an English translation of the thesis title provided. Of the 39 English-medium references, 33 are from English-medium Anglophone-centre journals – United States, United Kingdom and Australia. The remaining six references are as follows: one US unpublished PhD thesis, three English-medium papers presented at Anglophone 'centre' conferences, two English-medium papers given at an English-medium non-Anglophone conference (Central Europe). The bibliographical reference list therefore is overwhelmingly a list of work from Anglophone-centre contexts of publication and therefore – particularly for the 'ordinary North American reader' – not difficult to access (for fuller discussion of this TH see Lillis *et al.* 2010).

Drawing on the notion of scale is again useful here, particularly the notion of 'outscaling' (after Uitermark (2002) in Blommaert 2005: 6): ' *"Outscaling"* is a frequent power tactic: lifting a particular issue to a scale-level which is inaccessible to the other'. A key way in which such outscaling occurs is by marking non-Anglophone contexts as 'local' while (implicitly) claiming Anglophone-centre localities as universally relevant and applicable. Moreover, as discussed in Chapter 5, it is not possible for non-Anglophone centre scholars to avoid locality – thus they can always potentially be outscaled in the ways we have seen above. This can be further illustrated by attempts by scholars to avoid or circumvent locality being marked, and thus avoid the kind of negative response by reviewers and editors discussed. For example, one scholar writing from a Spanish research base and institutional context, in one submitted paper framed the discussion at a regional level (Europe) rather than a national level (Spain). However, the paper is criticized for its 'decontextualised' framing. The reviewer states:

> It is oddly decontextualised – for example, their [*sic*] are references to the research community, as if [X] educational researchers across the globe take the same approach, have the same concerns, and work under the same conditions.
> (Written Review)

The paper was rejected. Here the scholar's attempt to scale-jump (from local to Anglophone-centre publication) by preempting criticisms of the locality of his contribution – from national to European level – was challenged for being too decontextualized.

What is clear from an analysis of THs and scholars' accounts is that marked locality is of particular significance in text trajectories towards possible publication in Anglophone-centre journals. Key points to note are: 1) marked locality stands in contrast to unmarked locality (Anglophone centre); 2) locality – including the

Location	ISI highly cited researchers (social sciences)*
United States	4,072
United Kingdom	62
Spain	23
Portugal	1
Hungary	7
Slovak Republic	0
* http://hcr3.isiknowledge.com/home.cgi, accessed 15 July 2009	

Figure 6.2 Location of most highly cited researchers, ISI 2009.

location and/or linguistic medium of the research and the authors' affiliation – outside non-Anglophone contexts is always marked; 3) marked locality cannot be avoided; 4) marked locality requires justification. Most obviously, research writings with marked locality may not be recognized as relevant globally and may be construed as locally bounded, that is, to local interests, and therefore 'parochial'. Locality therefore plays a significant role within the global currency of 'what counts' as a relevant and important contribution to global knowledge. Given some of the difficulties scholars face in making 'new' contributions to their specialist fields, it is perhaps not surprising that they do not figure as prominently as Anglophone-centre scholars in citations indexes or, as illustrated in Figure 6.2, in the lists of those most highly cited.

How locality gets valued in global knowledge making

While the previous section points to the problematic status attached to marked locality in Anglophone-centre gatekeeping practices, there is evidence of non-Anglophone locality being positively evaluated in some THs. This seems to occur in one of two ways: by serving as an exotic point of contrast and confirmation with Anglophone-centre research, or by being relocated in some way, as primarily 'centre'-based research.

Confirmation and exoticization

TH 6.4: Signalling of difference

In Chapter 4 we discussed a TH where in the trajectory towards publication there was a definite shift in the principal claim made from 'contrast' to 'confirmation'. In the same TH trajectory, another significant shift was made which illustrates how 'marked locality' gets to be valued within global knowledge making. In the submitted version of the paper, the national context of the study is mentioned three times through adjectives and nouns referring to the translation of a specific research tool. However, in subsequent drafts, there are 14 additional references to the national context of the study and moves to position it as a point of comparison with an earlier US-based study through phrases which signal marked locality as a point of contrast with the default Anglophone-centre context (unmarked locality). These are phrases such as, 'different linguistic and cultural settings', and 'cultural differences' (see example below) which are clearly intended to constitute a 'referential chain' (see Halliday 1994: 337) with the explicit mentions of nationality/the national and linguistic context of the study. This foregrounding of the specific national and linguistic context of the study – and the explicit signalling of this linguistic and national context as 'different' (from the earlier study) is a significant shift in the paper's trajectory towards eventual publication.

TH 6.4 Example 1: extracts from revised paper

Specifically we wished to assess whether the [X] ... would obtain *in a different linguistic and cultural setting*

Subjects ... responding from *a different linguistic and cultural background*

the present study was designed with the intention of replicating P *et al.*'s findings – and to determine if the results held across **another culture**

Subjects – responding *from a different linguistic and cultural background*

a different sample

a different linguistic version of all measures

As with the overall shift in the argument of the paper towards confirmation rather than contrast (discussed in Chapter 4), it is difficult to establish who made these revisions and additions or at which point in the production process. However, what is clear is that these additions were made following the involvement of the additional (US-based) scholar and the editor of the journal, who throughout took an active part; in correspondence with the lead author and the additional scholar, the editor refers to his 'refining' of the text and his hope that they – the lead author and the additional scholar – would not take offence at such considerable intervention. Of course, as this analysis indicates, marked locality cannot be separated from other elements in any paper, and in this TH we see the specific value of marked locality in contributing to knowledge in the field: it provides an explicit point of contrast with the US study and therefore has a specific value as 'other'. Thus marked locality comes to be valued as a confirmation of existing knowledge through what we may call a process of 'exoticization', whereby 'difference' is not denied or erased 'so long as difference is exoticised' (Bernasconi 2005: 241). Exoticization is signalled by the increased salience in the published draft of the 'local national context' but only in so much as it confirms existing Anglophone-centre-based knowledge. The value of its contribution becomes its capacity to demonstrate that findings from the centre can be replicated in a 'different' context.

If marked locality has a value as an exotic point of contrast with the centre, it is also clear that such value can only be sustained while it remains as 'other', as exotic. In order for marked locality to remain exotic within the broader economy of knowledge it can only figure sparingly. In practical terms, this means that publishing an article where a specific locality is marked, for example, Hungary can only happen every so often in centre journals. And as one Spanish scholar says, this is actually the opposite of a universalist vision of knowledge generating in a global context.

> If journals published research about Spain every year, readers would develop understanding about the Spanish context. But of course this would mean readers wanting to know about Spain for Spain's sake, not as counterpoint, contrast to UK or US.
>
> (Discussion)

Relocating within the centre

One way in which marked locality gets taken up and valued without being exoticized as a peripheral point of contrast with the centre, is when some aspect of that locality gets relocated (akin to recontextualized)[3] within the Anglophone-centre research context. This is exemplified in the case of the Spanish psychologist researching 'degraded' speech and hearing loss discussed above. While indeed some US-based journals rejected her papers on the grounds that findings based on the primary Spanish data were not generalizable, there is evidence of increasing interest by some other US journals in publishing research specifically using Spanish data because of the growing numbers of Spanish speakers in the United States. Of specific relevance to the research of this scholar is the growing elderly Spanish-speaking population, for whom hearing loss is an issue. The scholar states:

> Some journals are interested, for instance this one, because this journal belongs to the American Association of Hearing Disorders, and as the United States has a big population of Spanish-speaking people they are interested in these things.
>
> (Discussion)

She points out that some US journals would be happy to receive an article about the adaptation of a hearing test from English to Spanish that she and colleagues were working on:

> The editors are very concerned about preparing work about Spanish, testing Spanish language, because they, the Spanish population in the United States is very big. So they accept very well this type of publication, or test, or the evaluation for people, made for Spanish people.
>
> (Discussion)

Here then a specific aspect of marked locality – notably the linguistic medium of the data collected – gets valued because it is relocated as centrally relevant (literally) to the centre context.[4]

Scholar Profile 12: Fidel, Education, Spain

Fidel is a 42-year-old associate lecturer who has been working at university level in the field of education for some 16 years. He works predominantly with qualitative approaches and is a core member of a tightly knit local group of interdisciplinary researchers from across psychology, education and sociology. The core members of the group have worked together for some 10 years and together have been successful in attracting both national and European funding.

He uses Castilian and Catalan on an everyday basis for teaching, with colleagues for research purposes and also with family members. He has been learning English since he was eight years old and has spent several periods of up to four months in Anglophone-centre academic institutions. He also uses German with some colleagues when communicating about a shared international project as well as part of a long-term relationship with a group of scholars in Germany with whom he has formed strong ties over the years.

Fidel sees himself as atypical of his generation of academics in that his level of English is high, as is evident in both his written and spoken communication. Fidel feels that while his English is not 'perfect' he is confident enough to use it:

> My view with English has always been, well not always but for a few years now, that I should dare to say it, to speak or to write. I'm not fearful of making mistakes, but for me the important thing is to communicate and I don't mind if I say it wrong, or if I use a word which is not the best one, or if I use an idiom which is mistaken.

> (Discussion)

Although Fidel does not personally feel under pressure to publish in English he does want to secure grant funding and to participate with colleagues in European projects, which means that English publications are essential. Funding for such projects *allows you to hire people, and because no-one else in the department is interested my area, I have a chance to get people who are starting to do their PhD, to work for it.*

Fidel has published extensively in Spanish, for both an 'academic' and an applied audience (the latter including teachers and trainers, working with young people being a key motivating force for him). To a lesser extent he has published in English in book chapters and transnational English-medium journals. He considers his principal audience to be national, and thus that his work is most usefully reported and discussed in Spanish. Moreover, although writing about his research for publication in English-medium 'international' journals is a goal, he is not convinced that it would be positively reviewed, given its explicitly national research focus.

Textual ideologies in gatekeeping the boundaries between local and global

In the trajectory towards publication in 'international' Anglophone-centre journals, gatekeeping brokers most obviously play a particularly powerful role in evaluating whether texts should or should not be published. In order to ensure that such power and authority is used fairly, as discussed in Chapter 5, anonymous or 'blind' reviewing has developed as a common practice in journal gatekeeping, and is seen as central to ensuring the kind of objective evaluation crucial to the values of Enlightenment Science.[5] Given the emphasis on objectivity in the evaluation of knowledge production and the reviewing practices that have grown up to ensure that such values are sustained, how do the kinds of practice and ideology highlighted by scholars and evidenced in the discussion of some THs above get played out?

The first point to note of course is that it is because an objectivist ideology permeates text evaluation that the politics of language and location are made invisible, while powerfully shaping those same evaluation practices. The importance of making such ideologies explicit is an issue we return to in Chapter 7.

With regard to peer review practices, our central focus here, there are two key – interrelated – issues which merit our attention. The first relates to anonymity (of authors and reviewers) as a valued practice and the extent to which such anonymity can ever be secured. In small specialist subfields, scholars tend to be familiar with each others' work and thus even if no biographical information is provided and self-citations are deleted, reviewers often recognize the work, and by implication, the authors. Reviewers therefore may often know a lot about the authors – who they are, their institutional affiliation and by extension their geographical as well as their (sub)disciplinary location. And of course, even where author anonymity is attempted (by deleting for example authors' previous works in final references, their names and affiliations) editors certainly have access to scholars' identities, and editors play a powerful role in mediating reviewers' practices and decisions generally. Second, even if/where anonymity is secured, identification work continues to take place. Reviewers imagine or, as Tardy and Matsuda's (2009) study shows, attribute different aspects of writer identity to the academic authors they read, including gender, nationality, language background and ethnicity. Here then is another way in which imagined locality impacts on production practices: this time not the locality(ies) imagined by scholar-authors but the locality(ies) imagined by reviewer-readers.

In relation to our focus here on gatekeeping the boundaries between local and global, and the evaluation practices that determine what counts as globally relevant knowledge, two points are important: first that both 'real' (based on knowledge/information) and 'imagined' (based on assumptions, projections) identification work are always in play; and second, that aspects of identity (real and imagined) do not appear singly in the reviewers' mind and practices but rather constitute clusters which together impact on text evaluation. The two highest scoring aspects of writer identity that Tardy and Matsuda (2009) reported that reviewers 'read' off texts, were 1) the extent of the authors' experience in the field and 2) their disciplinary background. But it's important to acknowledge, as illustrated in reviewers' responses in the same study, that these aspects are not read off the text in isolation from others, whether other high scoring ones (such as 'signs of the author's language background') or lower scoring (such as 'use of citation style'). In so-called anonymized texts, 'real' textual indicators of marked locality are picked up alongside 'imagined' readings through an intricate relationship between textual/contextual markers in which the geopolitics of (mis)location powerfully influence how contributions to knowledge are evaluated and (mis)recognized (Bourdieu 1991). Traces of how these con/textual markers work in practice can be captured through the notions of *indexicality* and *orientation* (see *Methodological Tool 6*).

To illustrate the nature and significance of indexical clustering and the value of the analytic notions of indexicality and orientation, consider extracts from two examples drawn from writings by established scholars who have published in national languages and are experienced in writing and publishing in English. Both examples include extracts from texts submitted to English-medium 'international' journals and extracts from reviewers' comments which – while relating to the papers overall – directly link with the specific text extracts included here.

TH 6.5: Too Latin

TH 6.5 is part of a three-year Text History of a journal article which did not lead to publication. It was written by a Southern European scholar who on receipt of reviews – extracts from one of which are shown below – was particularly taken aback by the negative comments on her style and did not resubmit a revised version.

Extract from submitted text	*Reviewer comment*
This paper is situated at the cross-roads of the idea that international surveys serve valuable, although specific, comparison purposes, with the belief that these surveys can gain from incorporating questions based on previous detailed analyses of particular realities.	As regards the language the text also needs some revision. There are formulations that, in my view, are **a little bit over the top and too pretentious** (for instance 'This paper is situated at the cross-roads of the idea … with the belief …'; 'Theory that has a theoretical and empirical tradition … 'social transformations of our times.') **Maybe it is not the language, but it is just too Latin for a North-West European.** (our emphasis)

Methodological Tool 6: Indexicality, orientation and scales

Indexicality = the specific ways in which bits of discourse index, or point to aspects of social context

Orientation = how speakers/hearers, readers/writers orient to specific bits of discourse

Scales = metaphors such as 'scale-jumping' and 'out-scaling' help make visible hierarchies of norms and evaluations across time and space, *Timespace*

Discourse encapsulates = the what/how/who/where of language use: what is said/taken up, how it is said/taken up, who is (presumed to be) involved, where it is said/taken up

Why are *indexicality, orientation* and *scale* useful in academic writing research?

- They can help connect contextual understandings with textual analysis;
- They function as mediational and relational categories rather than referential categories, which means they can be used in addition to linguistic /rhetorical categories where relevant;
- They can help illuminate what is contextually significant and salient in academic texts and relations around academic texts and how these impact on specific trajectories towards publication;
- They can be used to empirically analyse texts in the immediate context of interaction but also to link these to larger social structures and patternings.

An example (for fuller discussion see page 152)

Journal reviewer response to submitted article: 'These papers do not want reading, they want translation. Poor writing doesn't encourage the reader to turn the page to read more about the ms. This comment is not about the authors' competence in scientific English. It is about thinking.'

Comment: A specific feature or series of features of the text index that the writer of the submitted article is not a 'native' user of English, which the reader responds to negatively and which colours his or her response overall. Thus a micro feature of the text becomes hugely significant in terms of how the text is read and evaluated. This response and evaluation reflect particular textual ideologies (not least here relating to 'native/non-native' varieties of English and transparency notions of language) but also signal and key into the scales in operation around academic publishing in a global context. Here the writer is being required to scale-jump from a (lesser valued) position of non-Anglophone-centre to a (higher valued) Anglophone-centre context and norms.

TH 6.6: Weasel words

TH 6.6 is part of a two-year Text History of a series of articles which finally led to publication. The papers were submitted as a group to a journal as part of plans for a special issue. Some of the reviewers' comments – as illustrated below – include comments they see as pertinent to a number of the papers, as well as specific comments on individual papers.

Extract from submitted text	*Reviewer comment on papers submitted by group of scholars*
Thereafter, we used the narrative of loss – revealing the most remarkable deviation as far as the relative frequency of negation is concerned – as a textual basis, and by then, by means of LINTAG, we compared the minimum (low-L, the relative frequency referring to negation is lower than 0.022) and the maximum (high-H, the relative frequency is higher than 0.046) quartiles of the frequency rates resulting from the negation module to the results of the Thematic Apperception Test (TAT) with the help of two-tailed t-tests.	**These papers do not want reading, they want translation. Poor writing** doesn't encourage the reader to turn the page to read more about the ms. **This comment is not about the authors' competence in scientific English. It is about thinking**. Using **weasel** words ('phenomena', 'approach', 'consideration') is useless to the reader. Their sole utility is to fill a void in the author's mind. One author – the one who's fond of 'phenomena' and 'approach' – Freudianly forgot to paginate his or her ms, while directly allowing himself or herself sentences 50-word long and more. And what about using weasel words 92 times (the word 'perspective') as one author allowed himself or herself to do (in the ms X). **Talking about long sentences, our prize goes to the ms with one sentence 83-word long**. (our emphasis)

In TH 6.5, the reviewer isn't criticizing the text in terms of what might be considered transactional values – the content – but explicitly (and negatively) comments on uses of language which s/he perceives to be inappropriate, or 'pretentious'. While the reviewer doesn't mention 'long sentences' as a problem, the fact that s/he quotes verbatim several long sentences, including the one in the extract, rather than shorter ones from the paper, suggests that sentence length may be part of the problem with language use that the reviewer defines as pretentiousness. What is unusual in the reviewer's comments here is that his/her final reflective comments offer an explicit articulation of where in fact the 'problem' may lie; not so much with the text but with what the text indexes – a particular tradition of scholarly writing which seems pretentious – and how s/he orients to that form – negatively. What is important here of course is that this orientation is located georhetorically. In making such comments, the reviewer indicates that hers/his is not an individualized response but can rather be located in terms of differing geocultural/rhetorical/ linguistic traditions. This is highly relevant to understanding what is at stake when scholars writing out of non-Anglophone traditions submit papers to 'centre' journals where literacy brokers are predominantly from the Anglophone centre, or, as we discuss in Chapter 7, orient to Anglophone-centre practices and ideologies.

In TH 6.6 the reviewer is commenting on a number of articles submitted from the same national context for a special issue of a journal and concludes with a comment on one specific paper which contains a number of long sentences. The text extract included in TH 6.6 comes from the latter paper. Once again style is clearly relevant to the reviewer's response; the reviewer reacts negatively to certain words used which are simply dismissed as 'weasel', rather than, for example, offering any serious paradigmatic or epistemological critique of the discourse used; the reviewer also has strongly negative views on 'long sentences'. Furthermore, the reviewer seems to connect 'weasel words' with syntax in the text in some fundamental way; towards the end of the extract, s/he states 'talking about long sentences' (even though s/he is talking about specific words at that point), and thus indicates that the previous comments on word usage cohere (for her/him) with her/his negative view on long sentences.

What is particularly significant in this reviewer's comments is his/her statement that s/he is specifically *not* concerned about the authors' 'competence in scientific English'. Rather s/he claims to be treating language as a transparent medium on the mind. Within this frame, the text indexes intellectual capacity and the reviewer orientates negatively to what s/he regards as the intellectual *content* of the text. But there is more going on here: while s/he states that style, or, 'competence in scientific English' is irrelevant, the fact that s/he mentions 'competence in *English*' and points to specific textual elements strongly suggest that the style is indeed significant to her/his orientation to the text; specific features in the text index 'non-Anglophone writer/scholar' (hence the reference to English) and may account for (at least in part) the reviewer's strongly emotive and negative orientation. This particular reviewer's orientation to the text illustrated in TH 6.6 seems to provide support for the concerns expressed by non-Anglophone scholars that if the style is judged to be inappropriate, it is not just the text that is negatively evaluated but scholars themselves and their intellectual activity. As Hungarian scholar Istvan reports,

> If the style or the form of the paper is not native or not current, reviewers think that 'this is a stupid man, this is not acceptable material'. They're not accepted for regional accent, for regional style, absolutely refusal, this is their attitude.
>
> (Curry and Lillis 2004: 678)

Both sets of reviewers' comments in THs 6.5 and 6.6 illustrate the kind of indexical clustering at work in evaluation practices, where specific language and rhetorical features are refracted through ideologies of location (geographical and geolinguistic). The comments also reflect and enact (albeit in different ways) the transparency ideology of language rooted in the European Enlightenment tradition of Science and academic culture, discussed in Chapter 5. The reviewers' comments indicate that the conduit ideology of language is alive and well in current evaluation practices.

Conclusion

The universalist ideology of Enlightenment Science masks locality by denying its relevance to knowledge production. There have been and continue to be considerable challenges to this modernist ideology, from many intellectual traditions As Canagarajah states, 'If modernist globalization tried to eradicate local knowledge, postmodern globalization incorporates it in its own terms' (2005: 8). The THs and accounts discussed indicate clearly that while Enlightenment ideology and vision have been strongly critiqued by Western scholars, they are alive and kicking in the evaluation systems surrounding contemporary knowledge production practices governed by the centre. The reviewers' comments illustrate furthermore how the politics of language and location – denied by a universalist notion of Science – are refracted through this ideology of language and are at play in evaluation systems in operation in our global 'neutral' zones of academic knowledge production.

As Hall (1997) states, everything is local (and some would argue global) but not all 'local/ity/tions' are equal. The specificity of more powerful 'local/ity/tions' tends to be made invisible while such 'local/ity/tions' are at the same time treated as the norm or default against which all other 'local/ity/tions' are evaluated. A powerful default location in academic knowledge production and evaluation is the Anglophone centre and locations in research writings emanating from outside this centre tend to get marked as problematic: the marking of something as 'local' is thus highly consequential. Locality plays a significant part in knowledge production and evaluation even though it is dismissed as irrelevant within a universalist-positivist notion of Science. Scholars are asked to account for locality in ways which are not expected of knowledge that is located and produced from the default centre. Marked locality gets valued in specific ways – we have exemplified two key ways; through confirmation and contrast, functioning as an exotic point of contrast with the default centre; and through a process whereby marked locality gets relocated within the Anglophone-centre research context. It is important to note therefore that locality is part not just of scholar-writers' imaginary but also of reviewer-readers' imaginary through which reviewer evaluations are refracted. Flowerdew noted that one of the criticisms made by centre journal editors of peripheral scholars is that they are too 'parochial' (2001: 134). The scholars' accounts and practices indicate that this is a position adopted on their work. Yet they also indicate another dimension, that the value attributed to peripheral work may often be its 'localness', as defined by the centre. Periphery and non-Anglophone-centre scholars may get caught in a double bind here: if they foreground the local, they may be accused of being parochial; if they background the local they may be denied claims to universal relevance or status because of their peripheral position in global relations of knowledge production. This latter point is articulated by many scholars who clearly echo Foucault's notion of the workings of 'enunciative modalities' in discourse (in Fairclough 1992: 43–45): that rights to occupy speaking positions are constrained, most saliently in the context of academic writing for publication, by geohistorical locations.

Suggestions for further reading

The work on locality by Suresh Canagarajah (2005) provides an accessible and thought-provoking account of the significance of the 'local' in reconceptualizing ELT (English language teaching). Jan Blommaert's (2005, 2006) foregrounding of the need to build vertical metaphors and frameworks in sociolinguistics, alongside the widely used horizontal frames, helped us to engage with and articulate scholars' multiple discourses around text production. His work on scales (with his colleagues Jim Collins and Stef Slembrouck 2005) helps make visible processes surrounding the symbolic and material boundaries drawn around 'local' and 'international'. Work by Lynn Mario T. Menezes de Souza (2008) drawing on work by Walter Mignolo (2000) foregrounds locality in knowledge-making practices, reminding us in particular of the geopolitics of knowledge making in our own field, literacy studies. A discussion paper by György Csepeli, Antal Örkény and Kim Lane Scheppele (1996) sharply articulates dissatisfaction with the different status attributed to scholars and their knowledge claims (in relation to 'West' versus 'East').

7 Decentring academic text production and evaluation practices

Introduction

Academic text production globally is powerfully shaped by the privileged status of English as the medium of publication as well as, increasingly, its codification into systems of evaluation. In this book we have explored some of the ways in which this privileged status specifically impacts on scholars working outside the non-Anglophone centre. Within the economy of knowledge production and exchange, multilingual scholars often have differential access to the global academic marketplace and the resources necessary for full participation in it. This concluding chapter revisits themes from across the book to raise questions about the current status of English as the global medium of academic text and knowledge production, distribution and evaluation. We consider some initiatives which seek to better support non-Anglophone-centre scholars' access to publishing in high status journals within current systems and practices. But we also argue for the need to decentre Anglophone-centre control and to reimagine the kind of knowledge production, evaluation and distribution practices currently governing scholars' practices and experiences. One way forward is to shift from a 'market' to a 'gift' economy (after Kenway *et al.* 2006), elements of which are strongly evident both in current practices and in scholars' desires, and reflected, in part, in the currently growing number of digitally supported 'open access' initiatives.

This chapter:

- Summarizes the key ways in which the privileged status of English as the medium of academic text production and systems of evaluation is impacting on the academic lives and practices of non-Anglophone-centre scholars;
- Outlines specific ways in which centre-based practices could be changed to better support scholars in their goals of publishing in English within the current academic marketplace;
- Argues for the need to decentre academic text production and evaluation practices in ways which will benefit scholars globally;
- Advocates the importance of reclaiming knowledge as a gift economy.

Academic text production within the current marketplace

In considering the ways in which the global status of English is impacting on the experiences and practices of scholars working in non-Anglophone-centre academic contexts, the following key issues have emerged:

- Powerful evaluation systems of academic knowledge production based in the Anglophone centre are both directly and indirectly supporting the privileging of English as the medium of academic texts for publication;
- Such increasingly supranational systems are impacting on formal and informal evaluation systems in non-Anglophone-centre contexts, at departmental, institutional and national levels to further privilege English in local systems of evaluation and rewards;
- English functions as a 'sliding signifier', being used both alongside and independently of other criteria (such as impact factor, rank in journal indexes) to signal 'high status' and 'high academic quality';
- 'International' is another key sliding signifier signalling high status and is often used alongside or instead of 'English' and vice versa;
- Different resources are available at national, local, institutional and departmental levels for research and academic text production (including English as a currently key resource) and these impact on the nature and quality of scholars' opportunities to engage in text production;
- Scholars from the non-Anglophone centre often rely on centre-based brokers to offer ways into publishing in Anglophone-centre journals;
- Multilingual scholars' ability to participate in research networks plays a role in their access to, and success with, opportunities to publish in Anglophone-centre journals;
- There is a routinized unidirectionality rather than multidirectionality to efforts around knowledge exchange; non-centre scholars are working to contribute to knowledge production within the Anglophone centre, as well as channelling centre-based knowledge to local contexts, but there is little indication that centre scholars are looking beyond the centre;
- Textual ideologies are in play in text evaluation practices, notably peer review, which often adversely affect scholars' publishing opportunities, particularly in attempts to claim 'new' contributions to knowledge.

We have illustrated some of the ways in which non-Anglophone-centre scholars are responding to the challenges, pressures and demands to produce in English, which include the following:

- Writing in English in addition to local national languages, and in some cases, also writing in other national languages;
- Working to sustain local research networks, including in some instances organizing and contributing to national journals that publish in local national languages and/or in English;

- Writing to bridge Anglophone-centre and locally produced research;
- Working in networks and/or drawing on network resources in order to mobilize the range of resources available for writing;
- Persisting in attempts to secure publication of knowledge/texts that they consider to be significant contributions to their fields – in some instances in the face of considerable rebuff.

Focusing on scholars' practices and experiences allows us to consider not only their responses to the growing (direct and indirect) pressure to publish in English, including some of the obstacles they face, but also to draw on their experiences to consider some ways in which they might be better supported to achieve English-medium publication success, while at the same time sustaining local national research and writing activity. In this respect a key issue to emerge is that of the significance of *brokering*, clearly an important aspect to text production and highly consequential for publication success. At the moment, brokering activity of all kinds in academic text production – whether by centre or non-centre scholars – goes largely unacknowledged, in part because of the textual ideologies at play in academic text production and evaluation, a point we return to below. By making brokering a visible and key dimension to academic text production in a global context, the spotlight can be put on what kinds of brokering can best support academic text production and who is best placed to offer this brokering and how. This is a challenge currently being taken up by some groups of professional *language brokers*, translators and authors' editors (see e.g. Kerans 2000) and evidenced in the work of professional groups such as Mediterranean Editors and Translators (www.metmeetings.org/) who, among a wide range of activities, are working to address issues around the quality of translation in specialist fields (a core concern of scholars in our study) and acting as mediators between authors, reviewers and editors. There is a growing body of professional expertise among 'word face professionals' (see Chesterman and Wagner 2002)[1] which, while grounded primarily in editing in the natural sciences and biomedical fields (not least because of greater funds available to scholars in these fields for these services), could be drawn on more widely in developing ways of supporting scholars' text production. There are of course costs to such brokering services and most scholars discussed in this book rarely have funds for such services. A notable example of free brokering currently growing in strength is *AuthorAID*, an initiative that offers volunteer editing programmes to support academic scholars in the 'south'.[2]

Even ignoring costs, brokering is not an unproblematic activity. A significant number of different types of brokering are going on which – when effective – support scholars' writing for publication. Scholars themselves indicate that in order to achieve success in high status English-medium journals, receiving specific types of brokering support is particularly helpful, if not essential: that is, the involvement of Anglophone-centre academics who provide information about conferences, journals and edited books, and directly impact on the texts being produced – often (implicitly) aligning them with centre disciplinary conversations, offering (again often implicitly) linguistic and rhetorical support. Some Text Histories discussed in this book indicate that some Anglophone-centre scholars are actively working

Scholar Profile 13: Larya, Psychology, Slovakia

Larya, 35, is an assistant professor, having earned her doctorate four years ago. She continues to work at the same institution where she was working previously as a research assistant. Her current position involves her working as a researcher half time while teaching full time at another institution in another city (14 hours per week). Her field is interdisciplinary and there are few local researchers working in it, either in her institution or in the country.

In addition to Slovak, Larya uses Czech, German and Russian, and for her academic work, English. Her study of English began at secondary school, continued at university and later at private academies. She is confident and proficient in English but would like to improve her writing *because there's not a lot of possibilities to meet English speakers so communication is through papers*. She has published in both Slovak and English, partly because she was required to publish three articles (in any language) before defending her PhD. She has more than met this requirement, although initially it:

> caused me some problems because at the beginning I didn't have a lot to write about, so I was forced from the surroundings, from my environment to publish and I'm not very satisfied with these [my early publications].
>
> (Discussion)

As there are only two Slovak journals in which Larya would consider publishing, she has wanted to seek out a wider audience, which also *increases the possibility to make some cross-cultural research*. By attending academic conferences in other European sites, Larya has been able to develop a transnational network that has afforded her various professional opportunities. Going to one small conference in her specialist subfield helped her to feel part of a larger research community. The experience was:

> very supportive for me because I realized that people in the West are doing almost the same research as we do, not higher statistics, not higher level, but the level that we do and they are almost the same. But I found more contacts and I'm not some 'big foreigner', but now in a community.
>
> (Discussion)

One contact Larya made at this conference developed into an invitation for her to do a research stay in Belgium as a PhD student, for which she got a government grant. Not only was she able to work with scholars in her area, but she also took advantage of the better library resources available, photocopying a stack of articles to bring home. Currently she is torn between enjoying teaching and being committed to research, as she has less support for research at the teaching institution where she currently works. Indeed, some of Larya's colleagues are surprised when she emphasizes the importance of publishing.

towards supporting some non-centre scholars in their attempt to 'scale jump' from 'national' to centre-based 'international' publishing, reflecting some awareness of the powerful position that Anglophone-centre scholars occupy. This awareness of the privileged position of Anglophone-centre scholars in the context of the global status of English is also evident in some (albeit only a few) centre gatekeeping brokers' comments, as in the reviewer comments below:

Reviewer comments: Example 1

Unfortunately, the writing is still unclear and difficult to follow in many sections of the manuscript. I truly sympathize with you because I suspect that English may be a second language. However, the lack of clarity and jumps in logic make it hard for the reader to understand the basic message. ... Below are a few suggestions that you might consider. I do not mean to be disrespectful by providing extremely specific comments. I realize that this is your paper and the words need to be your own. I only offer these suggestions to make the manuscript easier for the readers to understand. I think the findings are interesting but they get lost in the translation.

Reviewer comments: Example 2

The second potential problem is language. Because the authors are English second (probably third) language speakers, there are many non-standard usages, from curious word use (e.g. incorrections), to clumsy grammar, and prepositional infelicities. In fact, the entire paper would benefit from a thorough edit, probably best done by your journal. The paper would be worth it, and this is probably one of the costs of globalization that journals like yours will have to bear if it is serious about fishing in a seriously international intellectual pool. In particular, giving Anglophone readers access to Lusophone research of this quality would make it worth it.

While – unusually – both reviewers in these extracts hint at the politics of language as a resource for academic publishing, the second reviewer makes an explicit call to the journal to take some responsibility for (and thus funding of) language brokering as central to its stated commitment to internationalizing the 'intellectual pool' of contributors. And indeed there are some examples of editorial board initiatives – from both the centre and periphery – explicitly taking account of the importance of brokering, by drawing on their experience in receiving manuscripts or on research to find ways of building in a mentoring dimension to their procedures. The *Croatian Medical Journal* is well known for the explicit provision of what the editorial board calls *pre*-peer review support (for details of the model, see Mišak *et al.* 2005).

We work together with our authors on improving the presentation of their reports if we recognize them as worthy of extramural review and possible publishing. Close cooperation with authors also continues after the manuscript has been accepted for publication. This author-helpful policy has been followed since the journal was started.

(Mišak *et al.* 2005: 124)

In recognition of the challenges facing many multilingual scholars in non-Anglophone locations, some centre-based initiatives have also started to emerge. For instance, *TESOL Quarterly* launched a 'Mentoring Program' which pairs experienced academics with 'novice authors, whose work, after going through the full review process, did not meet the criteria for publication in *TQ*. As stated on its website:

> This program reflects *TQ*'s commitment to diversifying its research knowledge while continuing to publish quality scholarly work. It will enable the journal to include authors from diverse locations and nontraditional settings and junior scholars working in underrepresented contexts in the field.
>
> (www.tesol.org/s_tesol/seccss.asp?
> CID=632&DID=2461)

An example of a specific programme developed in the Anglophone centre in the field of international and comparative education comes from the journal *COMPARE*, which offers a mentoring programme for writers new to publishing in the journal. It starts with a one-day workshop and involves supporting scholars – with academic mentors from the editorial board – over a four-month period to the point of submission (for details of programme, see www.baice.ac.uk). Following submission, papers undergo the usual reviewing procedures of the journal.

Overall, however, such initiatives are few and far between[3] with the onus on scholars to mobilize the resources required to produce and submit acceptable texts in their final form. Equally, responsibility for providing such assistance often falls on the shoulders of volunteer 'brokers', in these cases, those who are already serving as reviewers and editors.[4] Thus initiatives which rest on the goodwill or interested actions of Anglophone-centre scholars acting as brokers, while clearly laudable, are at the same time highly dependent on individuals' willingness to offer their time and service.

In addition, while any initiatives aimed at increasing access and publication of non-Anglophone-centre scholars are to be welcomed and scholars' considerable energies and efforts at securing publication to be recognized, they leave the centre intact, as it were, with core textual ideologies – including the politics of location surrounding academic text production and evaluation – and the centripetal pull of such ideologies unchallenged. This *centripetal pull* of the Anglophone-centre systems – whereby practices and ideologies surrounding academic text production are drawn towards and influenced by existing powerful practices and discourses at the centre[5] – is evident in at least three ways. First and most obviously, the growing influence of bibliometric methods, such as impact factor which (directly and indirectly) privilege English in evaluating knowledge globally and across all disciplines. Second, the construction of bibliographic indexes in languages other than English, for example, the Chinese Science Citation Database (Jin and Wang 1999); in Japan, the J-EAST database;[6] in Spain, DICE, ISOC, IME and ICYT;[7] across Latin America, the Caribbean, Spain and Portugal, Latindex; in Brazil, SCIELO, the Scientific Electronic Library Online.[8] These indexes and databases are important because they make visible publications in languages other than English and thus help make research published in languages other than English recognized and institutionally acknowledged. Yet in practice they tend to orbit the ISI indexes and their symbolic shadow (English is what counts), thus leaving the global hierarchy of indexes (and publications) intact. Indeed, despite the existence of alternative indexes, being included in particular Anglophone-centre indexes continues to confer more status on the few journals published in other languages (albeit with English abstracts) that are included in ISI (see Chapter 1). Furthermore, the growing number of locally generated indexes are premised upon the same values as ISI, and as such are criticized by multilingual and non-centre scholars alike for the reasons outlined in Chapter 1. Such indexes – albeit in different linguistic media – reflect and share a perspective on knowledge production as a competitive marketplace. Third, and more crucially perhaps, the centripetal pull towards the dominant practices and ideologies in the Anglophone centre ensures that fundamental issues of what counts as relevant knowledge and who has the right to determine what counts as relevant knowledge remain with(in) the centre. Within this frame, Anglophone-centre localities lay claim to universality, while all other localities are positioned as 'other', with scales between such localities in knowledge making remaining intact. In the remainder of this chapter, we consider some ways in which this centripetal pull of the Anglophone centre can be disrupted.

Making visible ideologies of text production and evaluation systems

We have seen that the Enlightenment vision of Science continues to exert a powerful influence over knowledge production and evaluation practices through evaluation systems, such as the use of bibliometrics and, in particular, impact factor. The politics of text production and evaluation and specific ideologies – including those about language, location, authoring – are often rendered invisible, most evidently in text brokering and reviewing practices. One important way of resisting the centripetal pull of the Anglophone centre is to make such ideologies visible – so that the powerfully alive internationalist ideal of knowledge sharing, production and evaluation across regional and national linguistic and geographical borders can be sustained – rather than masked by a universalist ideology where actually only one locality is privileged. Examples of the kinds of question that would help make visible those ideologies which directly impact on text production and evaluation practices are listed in Figure 7.1. These questions can be taken up at different levels – individual engagement (by reviewers, editors, translators), publication boards (notably, journal editorial boards), and research institutions operating nationally and supranationally to evaluate academic work. There are not necessarily straightforward answers to these questions, but they need to be

Ideological orientations towards:	Questions to ask about how texts are evaluated:
Language	What ideology of language is being played out here? Language as transparent medium? Language as a culturally saturated resource? (transparent or constitutive of knowledge)
Languages	What languages are being valued as media of knowledge production? What ideologies are underpinning assumptions about specific languages and their speakers?
English(es)	What view of English is being sustained/ played out here? That there is one (or several Anglophone-centre) standard varieties? Or many?
Rhetorical practices	What assumptions are being made about what count as appropriate rhetorical practices?
Codification and control	What view of users and of authority over languages and rhetorical practices is being played out here? Is, for example, a 'native' authority over codification and control of English presumed? Who has the right to determine acceptable rhetorical varieties?
Enunciative modalities	What assumptions are being made about who has the right to say what, from where? What assumptions are being made about who can lay claim to new knowledge?
Locally and globally relevant knowledge	How are decisions made and by whom about what counts as 'locally' relevant knowledge and 'globally relevant' knowledge? What recourse do scholars have to contest these decisions?
Authoring and text production	What assumptions are being made about the nature of 'authoring' in academic text production? What assumptions are being made about who should be involved in text production, when, why and how?
Knowledge exchange(r)s	What assumptions are being made about the directionality of knowledge exchange? (e.g. Anglophone centre to non-Anglophone). What efforts are being made towards recognition and exchange transnationally? (e.g. Anglophone-centre scholars seeking out research from non-centre contexts).

Figure 7.1 Making textual ideologies visible.

asked, impacting as they do on all micro engagement with texts and being highly consequential.

We need therefore to add this layer of ideological orientations onto the brokering orientations outlined in Chapter 4 (see Table 4.1, 'Brokers, orientations and target publications') in order to make visible the underlying ideologies at work in interactions and interventions around texts. As Figure 7.2 indicates, each engagement with each micro detail of the text is refracted (albeit often implicitly) through ideologies around a number of key dimensions: language, rhetoric, English(es), enunciative modalities, locality, authoring and globality of knowledge, and authoring.

Asking questions about textual ideologies, and how such ideologies get played out at the level of the tiny details of specific texts, is important because it shifts the emphasis away from straightforward divisions – between Anglophone centre and Anglophone non-centre, between centre and 'periphery', between monolingual and multilingual – and indicates that there are choices to be made by all of us involved in academic text production and evaluation. Our aim in this book has been to emphasize the specific experiences of non-Anglophone-centre scholars in order to make visible key issues they face, yet we are of course also very conscious of the need to muddy the waters between any seemingly straightforward divisions for a number of reasons. First, within both non-Anglophone-centre and periphery contexts there are scholars with more or less privilege and access to (English-medium-based) resources, including distinctions between scholars who have spent time in Anglophone-centre contexts and those who have not (see discussions in Salager-Meyer 2008). Second, there are clearly peripheral contexts and students/scholars within the Anglophone 'centre', much commented on in relation to student writing

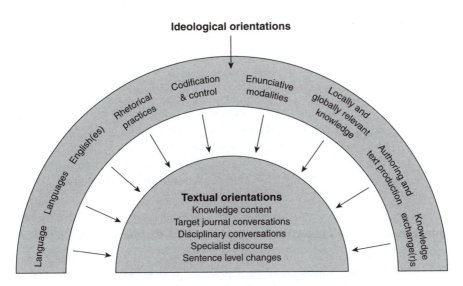

Figure 7.2 Ideological orientations in academic text production and evaluation.

(Curry 2001; Harklau *et al.* 1999; Horner and Lu 1999; Jones *et al.* 1999; Lillis 2001), less so with regard to professional scholarly writing. One example of the latter is evidenced in research carried out some time ago on reviewing practices in psychology in the United States, which showed how reviewers negatively evaluated papers by scholars they assumed to be from 'low status' as compared with 'high status' centre institutions (Peters and Ceci 1982).[9] Third, the textual ideologies summarized in Figures 7.1 and 7.2 and evident in the Text Histories and accounts discussed across the book, are enacted by scholars and institutions from many parts of the world; they are not restricted to Anglophone-centre scholars and institutions. Clear evidence of this is in the way in which the status of English-medium publications is being codified (formally and informally) as higher status in departments and universities around the world, regardless of other indicators of quality. At the level of individual scholars in their/our capacities as editors and reviewers, our study provides some evidence of what we might call 'hypercorrection' by non-Anglophone scholars: that is, a tendency towards a highly conservative stance on what count as 'appropriate' English language and rhetorical norms, and considerable intolerance of what are considered to be non-standard or less prestigious forms. Given the official anonymity of most of the reviewer comments shared with us in this study, it is difficult to reach firm conclusions. But based on scholars' accounts, some of the harsh comments about style, for example, appear to have been made by non-Anglophone scholars (see also Belcher 2007; Hewings 2006). Thus, while the privileged position of Anglophone-centre scholars needs to be acknowledged, making textual ideologies visible is relevant to all scholars working in academic text production and evaluation.[10] Whether removing the convention of anonymity surrounding reviewing practices would further help to challenge ideologies at work in text evaluation is a question worthy of serious debate. Whatever the merits or otherwise, it is the current evaluation systems which are ensuring that this convention of anonymity continues. Belcher (2007: 19) points to the external pressures applied by the compilers of prestigious citation indexes (e.g. ISI):

> Journal editors ... have begun to discuss the merits of discontinuing double-blind reviewing, i.e. insistence on author/reviewer anonymity. Revealing identities could enable authors to contact reviewers for further guidance during the revision process. The requirement of double-blind reviewing for inclusion in prestigious citation indexes, however, does not encourage journals to move in this direction, especially considering the rating systems now in place at many institutions worldwide that reward faculty only for publication in highly ranked 'indexed' journals.

Sustaining local research languages and publications

The assumption that one's knowledge is of sole universal relevance does not encourage conversation. It is possible to develop a pluralistic mode of thinking where we celebrate different cultures and identities, and yet engage in projects common to our shared humanity. Breaking away from the history of constructing a globalized totality with uniform knowledge and hierarchical community, we should envision building networks of multiple centers that develop diversity as a universal project and encourage an actively negotiated epistemological tradition.

(Canagarajah 2005: 20)

Sustaining local research and recognizing its value, as Canagarajah argues, is not the same as narrow localism or uncritical approaches to locality but rather involves acknowledging the existence and importance of a diversity of localities for knowledge making. Much of the scholars' activity discussed in this book indicates that their goal is to take part in global disciplinary conversations, and that for this to happen, such disciplinary conversations need to be maintained and developed at a local level, through local languages. There is no evidence therefore of what might be described as a retreat to localism.

However, *locality* is a key issue in academic publishing. Most obviously, a series of dichotomies have emerged as being in play in knowledge production which position non-Anglophone-centre 'local knowledge' as being of a different order – secondary, parochial, exotic – to that of the Anglophone centre. Anglophone-centre 'locality' seems to go unmarked and is granted a universal status in global knowledge making, most obviously in high status English-medium 'international' journals. While our study focuses on only a small part of the world – four countries in Central and Southern Europe – concerns about the ways in which the non-Anglophone 'local' is valued are raised in studies from other parts of the world (e.g. Canagarajah 2002d; Gnutzmann 2008) and merit further exploration.[11] There is clearly a view in powerful centre evaluation systems – notably ISI/Thomson Reuters and multinational publishers – that English is and should be the language of academic knowledge globally and that vernacular languages and research bases have at best a subsidiary part to play. This view is also evident to some extent in scholars' accounts where they point to functional distinctions they make between what should be usefully published nationally and 'internationally'. But we have also seen that this functionalist divide breaks down in at least two important ways: 1) scholars acknowledge that not everyone reads or writes in English, and therefore cannot take part in global disciplinary conversations, thus disciplinary conversations in local national languages are essential; and 2) scholars point to the existence of difficulties surrounding their attempts to join in such global conversations, to scale jump from the national to the 'international' publishing contexts.

Of direct relevance to the first point, which signals the importance of local research and writing, is the latest UNESCO Forum on Higher Education, Research and Knowledge (2001–2009) which documents the 'strong feeling' expressed about the importance of conducting research and publishing 'in languages other than the mainstream languages of scientific communication and publication' (UNESCO Forum: 197). While the Forum includes no explicit discussion of the systems governing the status of English in research publications, it directly challenges any assumption that research capacity should be restricted to only a few, richer countries, making the following statement of principles:

The right of each and every nation to build its own solid research community should be reaffirmed and their important benefits reiterated such as:

- Contacts with international research.
- Provision of local analysis and advice.
- Identification of relevant research agendas.
- Critical thinking in higher education.
- Evidence-based criticism and debate for policy-making.
- Capacity to train future generations of researchers.
- Stimulation of national innovation systems.

(UNESCO Forum: 20)

Sustaining a local research base, including in local national languages, is seen as essential to countries' overall development, and some commitment has been made to increase GERD (Gross Expenditures on Research and Development) towards meeting that goal.[12]

In order to address the second point above, that of the obstacles faced by scholars in 'scale jumping', engaging in explicit discussion about textual ideologies governing current practices is essential, as already discussed. A further question arises that merits more attention than we can give here, which is the extent to which assumptions made about the dichotomy between national and international publishing and contributions to knowledge – along new/review lines – is valid. Is it the case that scholars aim to publish 'their best in the west' (Swales 1997: 378), leaving a vacuum in local scholarship? Concerns are indeed expressed about the status of national journals, for example – in local national languages and in English – including the quality of the intellectual content and about readership, but it would be a mistake to accept a simple dichotomy at face value. For at the level of knowledge generation there is evidence, as we illustrate below, that the new ('international')/review ('local') distinction does not hold up in practice, not least because of the specific (and often alternative) kinds of opportunity that local national publishing opens up. Rather than the 'poor relation', then, local national publishing outlets, in local national languages and/or English, are creating intellectual spaces not necessarily available in Anglophone-centre outlets. We have seen how the complexity and density of some research ideas were viewed as problematic by some centre reviewers (Chapter 4) and how the call to simplify was resisted by the authors on the grounds that complexity was precisely what was needed in their specific field of education. This call to simplify was not a one-off occurrence in these scholars' writing for publication; and whereas the TH discussed in Chapter 4 finally resulted in a publication, this was not the case with other papers. In one instance, when once again confronted with the editor's and reviewers' comments that the paper would be very difficult for their journal readers to understand, the same authors decided against revising a manuscript and thus forfeited publication. Of course 'difficulty' and 'complexity' mask other dimensions here: a key issue with regard to the scholars and these specific THs is that in their work they were (are) setting out to challenge a specific and dominant (in this instance, psychological) paradigm in their field and to offer an alternative (in this instance, sociological) paradigm. The merit of each particular paradigm is not our concern here, but rather the fact that the constraints that the Anglophone-centre journal outlets were (are) imposing in this case stand in contrast to the opportunities afforded by the local national journal outlets which are broader in scope in terms of object of study and paradigm/epistemology. Thus, ironically, given the value attached to the 'new' in journal publishing, the Anglophone-centre journals viewed the papers written by these authors as a challenge too far, as too 'new' for its readers. In contrast, their papers are being published in national journals which are able and willing to engage with a newer paradigm, not only because of their broader paradigmatic remit, but because potential readers are (in contrast with the transnational readers) familiar with the local national research programme and the complex theories that the authors have been developing over a long period of time. One of the scholars in the research team signals the contrasting situation – between readers in the Anglophone-centre and local national journals – as follows:

> The papers are used by our students or ex-students, you know. That is to say they are used by people who are already inside, or even not just in master's courses, but our undergraduates you know, so they at least have a perspective which is not the usual perspective in the discussions in our field of education.
> (Discussion)

The broader paradigmatic framing along with the familiarity that local readers, predominantly students in this instance, have means that papers published in these journals can advance the thinking in this field further than is allowed in 'international' journals.

A similar example illustrates the value of an English-medium national journal for knowledge generation. One scholar gives an example of how a Central European English-medium journal, with an explicitly transdisciplinary framing, provided an intellectual home for a psychological paper he was writing which he considered highly innovative.

> The topic covered something that I was digging into concerning sexuality, concerning intimacy, concerning these issues which are quite, quite new concepts.
> (Discussion)

The main reason he gave for submitting this 'new' contribution to a local national (English-medium) journal was that in general *there is no market for this type of writing* and therefore this particular journal provided a space for the kind of discussion he wanted to have. This was not viewed as a poor option but in contrast:

> I felt, well, this will be great. I used some of this, before in that book and in some articles but it was never sort of comprehensive or let's say complex or closed. So I had it in my brain. I was really very eager to do something more with this issue.
> (Discussion)

Scholar Profile 14: Aurelia, Education, Southern Europe

Aurelia is 70 years old and an emeritus professor in the field of education. With a close colleague of over 30 years, she leads a strong and highly successful local research centre, made up of mostly postgraduate students, which has regularly received national funding. Their work draws on and aims to take forward, theories developed by an eminent (and often controversially viewed) Anglophone educational theorist with whom Aurelia studied for her PhD and whose influence radically transformed Aurelia's perspective, amounting to *a change of life*. The empirical and theoretical achievement of her work is acknowledged by specialist scholars nationally and transnationally – and indeed by the eminent foundational scholar himself in his own publications. Yet on occasions, in conferences, Aurelia and her team have been aggressively challenged by junior Anglophone scholars who treated them as if they didn't understand core concepts *because of our English*. At the same time, and although it took a long time for their contribution to be acknowledged, it is now highly regarded all over the world, from Australia and South Africa, to Germany, Canada and Brazil.

Aurelia uses Portuguese, and on a regular basis uses English for academic work, in email correspondence, for example, as well as writing for publication. She learned English for three years at school and only began to use English when studying in England for a year as part of her PhD work. She views reading and publishing academic articles in English as crucial, as a way of being part of a larger scientific community. But she and her colleagues always aim to ensure that what is published in English is also published in Portuguese because they see this as central to developing the field nationally and, at a more immediate level, to supporting their students, many of whom do not use English. In English, and more so in Portuguese, she aims to publish both Scientific and applied papers aimed at teachers, not least because Aurelia is committed to influencing local national policy and practices in education about which she has serious concerns.

More recently, she has become disillusioned with academic work in education nationally and transnationally, seeing it as often being *conceptually very light* and increasingly frustrated at the failure of educational policy makers at national levels to take educational research seriously. In part she blames the latter on the former and has responded to this situation by writing a number of articles for the 'serious' national newspapers. At this stage in her career her two priorities are to work with her local research group on developing research and to challenge the media's critical and impoverished view of what educational research(ers) can offer.

While the journal is published in the medium of English, a direct result of the status of English globally, it is also the case that this particular journal provides an intellectual space not available in either local national languages or English-medium Anglophone-centre journals. The nature and impact of the growing phenomenon of English-medium publications in the social sciences needs to be further explored, but here such a journal seems to be generating a 'third space' (Bhabha 1994)[13] providing evidence for a point signalled by Duszak in her discussion of academic writing for publication in Poland: 'Globalisation has released social forces that are working towards the generation of stronger (local) centres of power' (2006: 42).

The importance of building and sustaining local national journals and publications may be viewed as one such example of a local response to globalizing forces and the attempt to retain local control over research agendas and advancements. We have seen in Chapter 3 how local networks sustain local research and publishing activity. The establishment of local national journals – in national languages and/or English – is one key strategy towards this end which scholars are strongly committed to. In the case of one Central European scholar his establishment and editorship of an innovative transdisciplinary field is one of many strategies towards sustaining local research and ensuring it is recognized in a global context. Evidence of his success can be listed as follows: 1) the editorship of this local national journal has now been taken over by a scholar from outside the local national context with a significant shift towards internationalizing the editorial board and the contributors; 2) the local research team is growing in academic strength and confidence, including successfully publishing in local national as well as centre journals; 3) the scholar has recently had his overview of the specialist field in which he works published in his local language as well as in a mainstream UK-based English publisher – 'the first psychologist from his local national context to have been published by this publishing house' (Email). The point about such research and publishing success is that it has been sustained and nourished at local level – in local national languages as well as in English and other languages – and has made a contribution internationally.

In the above examples, the local national research context and media of publication (local national language and/or English) together provide a 'home' for scholars' intellectual creativity which can be explored and tested through local contexts – sometimes, as indicated, with more critical and engaged readership than 'internationally'. Having the opportunity for engaged dialogue with local readership is important for sustaining and nourishing individual researchers:

> Scientific knowledge advances through dialogue and exchange of views. This will not happen if the local scientific community is not large … This means that the scientist will not be able to subject his or her ideas, hypotheses or research results to informal peer review through regular contacts with his or her colleagues. The result is that the capacity of the individual to do research withers away.
>
> (Massaquoi 2008: 62)

Internationality rather than 'international'

Throughout this book we have emphasized that 'international' functions as a particularly slippery signifier which, along with English, is used both formally and informally to denote high quality academic texts. 'International' is a powerful signifier, because it has become codified (however vaguely) in evaluation systems while at the same time continuing to connect with quite fundamental scholarly aspirational ideals of international exchange in pursuit of knowledge. One way of opening up debate would be to put the spotlight on what is specifically being claimed in the use of the term 'international'. This is a challenge taken up by some researchers in bibliometric studies: Wormell (1998) sets out to analyse exactly what makes an 'international' journal. Likewise, Buela-Casal *et al.* (2006) highlight the ambiguity surrounding the use of 'international' in relation to academic journals and are particularly critical of key indicators currently used to define what counts as an 'international' journal, echoing many of the points discussed in Chapter 1. While critiquing current flawed notions and measures of what constitutes an 'international' journal, Buela-Casal *et al.* argue for the potential value of a term which seeks to measure transnational cooperation in some way and propose the use of 'internationality'. They suggest four criteria that could be used to begin to generate a valid and robust measure of internationality: multinational collaboration patterns; multinational distribution of editorial boards; multinational distribution of associate editors; multinational distribution of authors.[14] The primary concern of Buela-Casal and others is to develop a robust way of measuring the international nature of journals. However, their problematization of any straightforward understandings about the classification of 'international', and their argument that internationality is an important value in scientific work which needs more attention, is of relevance more widely. In developing principled criteria for claims about internationality, additional criteria by which journals could be judged based on discussions in this book are: the inclusion of citations to works outside the Anglophone centre and/or in languages other than English; evidence of engagement with research carried out in a range of localities; involvement of editors and reviewers from across all geographic locations; explicit discussion at editorial level about varieties of English and the politics of style.

All of these criteria imply a radical reorientation by Anglophone-centre scholars to their (our) positioning in global knowledge-making practices, requiring us to engage with the questions thrown up in Figure 7.1 and, in a more general sense, challenging us to adopt the kind of effort after knowledge exchange reflected in scholars' accounts in this book; most obviously to work at engaging with knowledge-based localities outside the centre.

Concluding comments: from knowledge economy to knowledge as a gift economy

Most academics believe that higher education and research has to contribute to technological progress, economic growth, societal well-being and cultural enhancement. The increasing expectation, in the context of a 'knowledge society' or 'knowledge economy', of relevant results of higher education is widely viewed as an opportunity for growth and for quality enhancement. However, fears are widespread that undue pressures for visible utility might undermine a creative environment in higher education and research, and might consider certain stakeholders, certain purposes and certain directions of innovation while neglecting others.

(UNESCO Forum: 108)

Within the current competitive market model, the specific use of bibliometrics in evaluation systems plays a crucial part. They have become not only a powerful way of evaluating written knowledge production but a central driver in university practices and values. Hazelkorn (2009) outlines the way in which bibliometrics are used to generate 'universal' university rankings such as the Worldwide Shanghai Jiao Tong *Academic Ranking of World Universities*. Commenting on the impact of ranking systems shifts in higher education at global levels, she states:

> The biggest changes are apparent in rebalancing teaching/research and undergraduate/postgraduate activity, and re-focusing resource allocation towards those fields which are likely to be (controversially) more productive, better performers, and indicator sensitive/responsive. The arts, humanities and social sciences feel especially vulnerable, particularly in institutions with a strong presence in the bio-medical and other sciences – but this may also apply to other non-medical health professions.
>
> (2009: 2)

Bibliometric data seems to be fast becoming not only a criterion for evaluation of academic work but a determinant of the goal of academic work/academia itself, crucial to the market model of production and consumption. Apart from the important fact that such a model excludes those who cannot pay – or cannot pay as much as others in both research and writing production or consumption as others – (as seen in the GERD input/publishing output relationship in Chapter 1) it also masks the fact, as pointed out by Kenway *et al.* (2006: 67), that such knowledge is currently being paid for in at least three ways:[15] to produce it (most obviously, the use of public funds for the production of knowledge, whether in public or private (or public/privately sourced) universities;[16] to review it (scholars review papers without payment); and then to purchase it (universities and libraries have to purchase hard copy or electronic journals and individuals can purchase articles online at high rates per article). This triple payment is a point also noted by Over *et al.* (2005: 11), who offer a possible response:

> This leads to the paradoxical situation in which publications that could not have been produced without public money have to be paid for a second time with state funds; at the same time the costs of buying and providing scientific literature in university libraries and other institutions have been rising rapidly over the last ten years. In response to this paradox, which can be observed

worldwide and which has led to the cancellation of journal subscriptions and the purchase of fewer monographs by libraries, scientists have coined the slogan 'Science back to the scientists', which sums up the ideological background of the open access movement.

The call here is for a shift away from knowledge production as a competitive market economy, and pointing to 'open access' as a possible way forward for knowledge production and dissemination, we would suggest, signals a shift towards what Kenway *et al.* have referred to as a 'gift economy'.[17] While knowledge is converted into goods in a market economy, and evident in discourses around the 'knowledge society', knowledge stands in sharp contrast to other kinds of goods in that it is 'an inexhaustible resource that is actually enhanced through use or consumption' (Kenway *et al.* 2006: 55). Drawing on Mauss's (1954/2000) conceptualization of gift giving and receiving which emphasizes the principle of reciprocity between people, Kenway *et al.* argue that there is a longstanding tradition of reciprocity in scholarly activity which in itself contributes to the furthering of knowledge and understanding. The notion of knowledge as a gift to be shared between people connects with the aspirations of many academics – Anglophone centre and non-centre and periphery – who resist the marketization and commodification of knowledge, and at the same time taps into the kind of utopian ideals that are promised yet undelivered(able) through an Enlightenment ideology of Science.

In sharp contrast to the use of digital technology to further sustain and develop a market model – whereby currently big publishing houses are buying up journals and controlling not only costs but also opportunities for downloading and exchanging materials – open access and public repositories provide clear examples of how digital technology can be used to enact knowledge as a gift economy. Open access (OA) was first defined by the Budapest Open Access Initiative (2002):

> By 'open access' we mean free availability [of research literature] on the public internet, permitting any users to read, download, copy, distribute, print, search, or link to the full texts of these articles, trawl them for indexing, pass them as data to software, or use them for any other lawful purpose, without financial, legal, or technical barriers other than those inseparable from gaining access to the internet itself. The only constraint on reproduction and distribution, and the only role for copyright in this domain, should be to give authors control over the integrity of their work and the right to be properly acknowledged and cited.
>
> (Open Society Institute 2002)

Other digitally mediated initiatives include a growing number of public repositories supported by national governments and transnational organisations and research institutions, as well as research networks explicitly seeking to challenge differences in resources and opportunities for scholars in different regions of the world, some examples of which are listed in Box on page 174.[18]

The existence of the open access network can enable scholars to create and sustain locally generated journals, and if they choose, to publish and review in several languages according to the linguistic resources available to them. Thus one Spanish psychologist, working at the request of his university department, recently set up an open access psychology journal, which receives submissions and publishes in five languages – Spanish, English, Portuguese, Catalan and Galician. The five working languages of the journal reflect the languages that members of the editorial board and reviewers are happy to read and offer reviews on. (To date 15 articles have been published in three languages.) The scholar leading this initiative considers it a success: it has both increased the department's visibility in a specific field and papers are regularly being submitted, reviewed and published. In terms of how he would like to see the journal develop, he sees two priorities: first, he would like it to be broader in scope (paradigmatically and in terms of phenomena studied) than it is currently: the mission statement is broad but *it would be nice if it were broader* (Discussion); second, while the department is happy with the level of activity to date, he personally would like to see more submissions and publications.

That other types of ICT resources are being taken up in scholarly contexts is illustrated by one Hungarian psychology scholar, who has launched a wikispace which offers more than traditional websites:

> We wanted all members of the site to be able to create/edit their own profiles and the news section. Its main aims were to
>
> (1)   present the organisation and its members;
> (2)   to offer news about conferences, research projects;
> (3)   to offer a home for a related e-journal.
>
> (Email)

The list of affordances of this wiki site illustrates the potential use of Web 2.0 technology environments, by offering users a means of participating directly in the construction of the interface and its features. Such innovations are dependent on resources, however, and the wiki described above was not functioning at the time of writing. The scholar who established the wiki reported difficulties in sustaining it:

> We're in the process of changing servers and it will take us maybe a week or two to get back online. Also, the previous server had a virus attack and they've lost parts of our database ... so we might need to re-write the wiki. This process took longer than anticipated (by at least a couple of months), in part because everyone was on summer vacation and we couldn't find a web expert to sort it out.
>
> (Email)

Access to knowledgeable staff to maintain or repair technology, of course, represents another instance of resource issues involved in pursuing such innovative technologies.

Digital initiatives supporting knowledge as a gift economy

Open access journals. There are currently 4,250 open access journals from 101 countries and 17 academic fields in more than 50 languages. English is the language most represented, standing at 3,674, in contrast to other large language groups, Spanish, at 939, and Portuguese at 515. The top provider is the United States, with 930 listed, followed by Brazil with 388 (www.doaj.org/, accessed 4 August 2009).

Public Repositories. This is a growing practice particularly by governmental and institutional funders of research who request (or mandate) that funded researchers archive their research papers in a public open repository. Examples include DSpace at the Massachusetts Institute of Technology (where institutional repositories were initiated); UK research councils such as the Economic and Social Research Council, Arts and Humanities Research Council; Centre national de la recherche scientifique (CNRS, France); Deutsche Forschungsgemeinschaft (DFG, Germany). The Eprints project maintains an information database of public repositories; it currently lists 1,523 open repositories from over 80 countries (www.eprints.org/, accessed 3 August 2009).

Globelics (Global Network for Economics of Learning, Innovation and Competence Building Systems). The aim is to develop a network of 'researchers without borders' and has developed largely in response to the gap between the 'North' and 'the Southern and Eastern Hemispheres'. The goal of this network is stated as:

> establishing a world wide network, connected through regular meetings (annual conferences and PhD courses) and through an ICT-infrastructure (home-page, electronic publishing and ICT based fora on specific topics). The aim is to bring in all major institutions around the world that pursue high quality and research training.

(www.globelics.org/, accessed 5 November 2009;
see also discussions in Teichler and Gağci 2009)

Academic Blogging. This is a means of publishing academic ideas, reports, papers and debates directly by users. The number of academic blogs is unclear but growing weekly. References are made to the 'thousands of academic and educational blogs' in existence (www.academicinfo.net/blog/mike-madin/2009/01/16/academic-blogs, accessed 5 November 2009). Some 235 are listed on www.blogscholar.com as compared with 470 in humanities alone on http://academicblogs.org, accessed 5 November 2009. The newly created site academicblogs.org (September 2009) lists academic blogs in six languages – English, Dutch, French, German, Spanish and Swedish. Blogging is explicitly referred to within terms of a 'gift economy' given its potential for knowledge distribution to all those who have access to the web. Blogging 'does not pay directly or extrinsically. It's the effective practice of giver's gain, enlightened self-interest, or community maintenance. The rewards are intrinsic and indirect' (Haskins 2007).

Initiatives such as open access and the use of some ICTs seem to offer one way in which 'an academic community can continue to flourish along the lines of a gift community' (Kenway *et al.* 2006: 68) by removing most of the costs associated with conventional academic publishing, such as subscriptions, licensing fees, copyright and permission. Although some OA journals ask authors to pay for their articles to be included, these fees generally help cover production costs rather than create profit for journals or publishers. Furthermore, the question of which linguistic medium should be used, as illustrated above, then becomes an issue of a pooled resource rather than a presumption that English should be the (sole) medium. Furthermore, open access means that additional spaces are available for the range of outlets that many multilingual and non-Anglophone-centre scholars are seeking to engage with and thus opens up the opportunity for this range to be sustained rather than restricted (a similar point is made by Ren and Rousseau (2004) with regard to English-medium Chinese publications). Nonetheless, a certain degree of resistance remains from many enmeshed in the current system of evaluation and rewards, including not surprisingly early career scholars who need to have sanctioned publications for advancement, at least until reward structures might shift to weight their criteria away from inclusion in indexes and more heavily in favour of other criteria. Although currently the number of OA journals is small – of the 61,666 total journals included in Ulrich's Periodicals Directory in 2009 (see Chapter 1), only 2,492 were open access – less than 4% (Ulrich's 2009a)[19] – the number is growing. And the recent history of how Thomson Reuters ISI has treated OA journals may signal the growing acceptance and incorporation of OA journals into systems of evaluation. In June 2004 Thomson Reuters/ISI identified 239 OA journals that were included its indexes (Pringle, 2004). Five years later, it unofficially counted about 600 OA journals in its indexes and provided links to about 1,000 OA journals (personal communication, 8 October 2009).[20]

We are pointing to open access initiatives here as examples of a major shift away from the tightly controlled evaluation systems which work towards privileging researchers in particular parts of the world, working towards a particular version of knowledge production, dissemination and evaluation. Open access is a technologically mediated continuation of a long tradition of knowledge as a gift economy. And of course at the heart of any such initiatives, whether small, large, face-to-face or electronically mediated, are enhancing relationships between people around knowledge.

In closing this book we wish to signal the importance of relationships around text and knowledge production – locally and transnationally – and also give the last words to the scholars who clearly enacted knowledge as a gift economy by so generously giving of their time to our discussions about their writing, some for as many as eight years. Throughout this book we have pointed to the tensions and obstacles scholars working outside of the Anglophone centre face, not least because we think there needs to be greater awareness among all of us involved in academic work of the conditions governing our participation, the control and centripetal pull of the Anglophone centre, including the impact of the status attributed to English on opportunities for knowledge production, distribution and evaluation. There is considerably more work and thinking to be done in this area but we hope to have made some contribution.

And while this book foregrounds the difficulties that scholars face, what most stands out to us from our long period of research is scholars' commitment to academic research and writing, including the joy and pleasure involved in academic endeavours, brief moments of which we have been privileged to share. In observing and participating in small ways in scholars' lives over the course of the study, we have witnessed their passion and commitment for engaging with particular questions and participating through their work in various academic and social communities.

> And for me, it was very pleasant in fact to be able to have someone who reflects on your paper saying things like 'I don't like this, I like that.' 'Let's change it.' 'Please put it here' or she put it somewhere else. This kind of work is something that I like, really working in a sort of team even if I have the responsibility for the final output. When it's like this, it really is fun for me.
>
> (Discussion)

> He became so enthusiastic immediately and it was actually it was the library, a room like this, and we had a lab and he said 'well why don't you look at that paper and we will think about the idea?' The whole experience was a kind of a miracle.
>
> (Discussion)

> My dream is to be able to discuss my ideas with people from around the world.
>
> (Discussion)

Suggestions for further reading

In a book which focuses largely on the inequalities surrounding knowledge production, dissemination and evaluation, it is important to foreground the commitment of some scholars and 'brokers' towards changing dominant practices – a particularly useful example is the longstanding work of the *Croatian Medical Journal* (see Mišak *et al.* 2005) and thinkers who open up alternative ways of conceptualizing knowledge sharing globally (see collection edited by Kenway and Fahey 2009). Publications which emphasize the success of multilingual scholars offer important narratives which serve as an inspiration to us all, such as the collections edited by Diane Belcher and Ulla Connor (2001); Christine Casanave (2002); Christine Casanave and Stephanie Vandrick (2003); and Eileen Carnell, Jacqui MacDonald, Bet McCallum and Mary Scott (2008).

Notes

1 English and the politics of academic knowledge production

1 Figures are taken from the International Association of Universities 2008/09; Morris 2007; Ware 2006.

2 Science with a capital 'S' is used throughout the book with its Latin-based meaning *scientia*, as knowledge making in general, rather than the natural sciences only, and as currently used in many parts of the non-Anglophone world. Where we wish to signal natural sciences as compared with social sciences, we use lower case 's', science.

3 For the historical position of English in Central and Eastern Europe, see Medgyes and Kaplan 1992; Petzold and Berns 2000. For Spain, see Morales-Galvez *et al.* 2000. For Portugal, see Kayman 2000; Naysmith and Palma 1997. For current figures on numbers of speakers of English in European Union countries, see European Union Education and Training at http://europa.eu.int/comm/education/policies/lang/.

4 More recently, there is evidence that the 'Bologna process' is impacting significantly differently across EU contexts on the use of English as the medium of instruction in higher education. For discussion, see Räisanen and Fortanet-Gomez 2008.

5 For useful discussion of difference within the 'periphery' see Ramanathan 1999. Of course there is a dynamism within centre/periphery and intra-regional relations. Most obviously in our study, Slovakia and Hungary were outside the EU when we started our research, becoming full members in 2004.

6 Similar definitions are provided by Collins Cobuild (2009) based on usage.

    1. of or involving two or more nations,
    2. controlling or legislating for several nations, an international court,
    3. available for use by all nations, international waters.

7 The senior scholar is Professor Wendy Stainton-Rogers, the Open University, to whom we express our warm appreciation.

8 Ulrich's Periodicals Directory is named after its author and founder, Carolyn Ulrich. For details of her career as a librarian and her work on the directory in the 1940s, see www.ulrichsweb.com/ulrichsweb/carolynUlrich.asp, accessed 10 August 2009.

9 For useful discussion on the difficulties of establishing figures on academic output and the range of different sources, see *The UK's share of world research output. An investigation of different data sources and time trends.* A report by the Research Information Network. June 2009. Available online at www.rin.ac.uk/uk_presence_research, accessed 15 July 2009.

10 The OECD (Organization for Economic Cooperation and Development) has 30 members, 27 from 'high income economies', see www.oecd.org. The G8's members are

Canada, France, Germany, Italy, Japan, Russia, the United Kingdom and the United States (the European Commission is also represented at summits).

11 The Asia 10 comprises East Asia (Japan, China, South Korea, Singapore and Taiwan) plus India, Indonesia, Malaysia, Philippines and Thailand. The figures we include here are based on available data sources covering the share of global publications output which tend to concentrate on science and technology publications as a return on research investment (GERD) by governments and industry. There appears to be relatively little interest in mapping out the global share of social science and humanities publications.

12 Of course there are also intra-national differences. See for example Gómez *et al.* 2006 for a brief discussion of differences in research and development expenditures and academic output in Spain.

13 Key works in NLS include Barton and Hamilton 1998; Gee 2007; Heath 1983; Ivanič *et al.* 2009; New London Group 1996; Street 1984, 2005.

14 We are using 'academic literacy/ies' (rather than the singular or plural form alone) to signal the epistemological and ideological approach towards literacy and academic writing outlined here, that is, a social practice approach. For full discussion of the use of the term and contested meanings, see Lillis and Scott 2007.

15 The largest publication base on student academic writing emanates from the United States, where there are several key journals – *College Composition and Communication, College English, Journal of Basic Writing, WAC Journal* and *Written Communication*. The existence of such journals reflects in part the considerable historical institutional provision for writing in higher education in the United States.

16 Here we are indicating a need to develop meditational categories which connect text analysis with context-sensitive understandings which existing textualist frameworks (including those with a social orientation) do not facilitate.

17 For cautions against inflated claims for the transformative power of IT in relation to education, see discussion in Goodfellow and Lea 2007.

2 Writing for publication in a globalized world: interests, regulations and rewards

1 Our transcriptions of scholars' talk use a standard orthography and repetitions and hesitancies of speech are cut. Brackets [ ] provide contextual information and cues not evident from the talk itself. Throughout we have been aware of debates surrounding the politics of representation (Mehan 1993 discussed in Roberts 1997; see also Bucholtz 2000). We have attempted to navigate a position between one which offers accuracy and a flavour of scholars' expression in English, while avoiding representations which might stigmatize them in any way, for example, as 'non-native' users of English. Taking care with how we represent scholars' speech is important on a number of levels, not least given our focus here on writing, to prevent any conclusions reached about scholars' writing on the basis of their represented speech. We have found the five maxims set out by Celia Roberts very helpful (1997: 170):

> *1. Where appropriate, use standard orthography even when the speaker is using nonstandard varieties to avoid stigmatisation and to evoke the naturalness of their speech, and never use eye dialect* [that is, an attempt to represent varieties of spoken language (regional, national, socially marked) by spelling words in nonstandard ways]. *2. Work as closely as possible with the informants to gain agreement on how they wish the features of their speech to be represented. 3. Think about some experimental ways in which speakers' voices can be contextualised/evoked, but*

do not underestimate the value of robust design principles for maintaining consistency and accuracy. 4. Use a layered approach to transcription, offering different versions and different levels – some relatively more ethnographic, some using fine-grained widely accepted transcription systems to give different readings. 5. Be more reflexive about the whole process of transcribing.

2 The original source of this phrase is under debate. The phrase is used in *The Academic Man: A Study in the Sociology of a Profession*, p. 197, a 1942 book by Logan Wilson. The book – focusing as it does on documenting the practices of the 'academic man' – is an interesting example of early work in the sociology of knowledge.

3 Academic titles around the globe are not always easily equated to titles in other systems. Here we use the American terms of assistant, associate and full professor – rising in category from the former to the latter – as approximations to the titles and categories used in scholars' contexts. When describing in English their status/position, scholars often used the US terms.

4 A useful site for information on different academic structures in EU countries is www.eui.eu/ProgrammesandFellowships/AcademicCareersObservatory/AcademicCareersbyCountry/Index.aspx.

5 ERASMUS = The European Region Action Scheme for the Mobility of University Students.

6 See discussions in Morales-Galvez *et al.* 2000 for languages used in different regions of Spain for academic output.

7 Swales (1998) offers a revised definition of discourse community, distinguishing between 'place' and 'focus' discourse communities. While this distinction is useful in exploring relations between local and more distant research contexts, it is still problematic for our purposes in that it seems to be premised upon a continued distinction between rhetorical and sociolinguistic needs and interests.

3 Mobilizing resources for text production: academic research networks

1 This research by Newman on networks is based on mapping out citations in journal publications rather than – as in our study here – on scholars' accounts and mapping of their network activity.

2 ICTs constitute an important medium of exchange and dissemination translocally. To the extent that they facilitate scholarly exchange and contact, ICTs are clearly an important part in scholarly text production – most obviously scholars in regions of the world where connectivity is low face considerable disadvantage. As such this area merits more discussion than we offer in this book. The main point for our purposes here is that ICTs do not of themselves transform the politics of text production, but as we discuss in Chapter 7 with regard to Open Access resources, offer the affordances by which some transformations can take place.

3 We draw on a range of data to illustrate network types and scholars' participation: 1) scholars' CVs, to map out collaborations across local and transnational network dimensions and over time; 2) sociograms created by scholars that depict their networks; 3) ethnographic data, including observations and interviews; and 4) specific Text Histories in relation to scholars' network participation. These data sources were used by us to generate the diagrams in Figures 3.3–3.6 – in contrast to the diagrams drawn by scholars already discussed.

4 Throughout the book, we use bold in text extracts to draw the reader's attention to significant changes in drafts.

4 Texts and literacy brokers

1 Recent work indicates a growing interest in what constitutes 'proofreading', particularly in relation to users of English as an additional language. See Harwood 2009; Harwood *et al.* 2009, forthcoming; Turner 2008, 2009, forthcoming a, forthcoming b; Turner and Scott 2007, 2008.

2 Brandt (2001) uses the word 'sponsors' to refer to institutions and individuals that foster the acquisition of various types of literacy; Burrough-Boenisch (2003) uses the term 'shapers' to discuss the work of 'authors' editors', professionals who are typically hired to make a manuscript conform to the requirements of publishing outlets, such as scholarly journals. Dysthe 2002 the term 'mediators' to refer to teachers' engagement with students' writing practices.

3 Knorr-Cetina's important study uses two categories which foreground content – deletion (deleting sections of text) and reshuffling (reorganising sections of text). A third, more obviously discourse-marked, category is modality (strength of claims and attitude towards claims). Gosden extended Knorr-Cetina's two more content-oriented categories to three – deletion, addition and reshuffling – and added a fourth discourse category, 'rhetorical machining', after Swales (1990). Rhetorical machining is made up of three discourse-marked categories – *discourse structure* (the ways in which links are made across the text through such markers as 'in addition'), *claims* (Knorr-Cetina's modality is key here, 'it can be seen that', etc.) and *purpose* (closely linked to claims, but signalled through such markers as 'therefore'). A fifth category mentioned by Gosden but not included in his analysis is *polishing*, which concerns sentence-level changes. Our heuristic was influenced by additional considerations. First, we added several categories of change which seemed significant following preliminary analyses: *argument, positioning* and *visuals*. Second, we avoided making a straightforward dichotomy between content/knowledge and form/rhetoric (as implied in Gosden's 1995 (after Swales) category 'rhetorical machining'), preferring to consider any change as being of rhetorical significance in any Text History. Third, we sought to treat texts holistically and characterize the most salient type of change. Salience here is a relational notion, related to specific trajectories and publication Text Histories. Fourth, given our interest in the practices surrounding academic writing for publication, we also wanted to consider the instigators of textual changes and, where possible, how authors responded to or made such changes. A final but important consideration in developing our framework was to use categories which, while robust, would be relatively accessible to participants and other non-linguists who might analyse sections of the texts.

4 Here we can only signal a crucial area that merits significant research activity. Translation of scholarly articles is a mainly hidden activity in academic text production globally. Translation is also far more common in the natural than the social sciences. For useful discussions, see Bennett (2007a, 2007b); Kerans (2000); and Shashok (1992, 2001, 2008).

5 Staying 'local', going 'global'?: working at Enlightenment Science

1 There is much valid concern about 'brain drain', particularly of expertise from the south to the north, although more recently there has been a focus on 'brain circulation', the ways in which knowledge is circulated back to 'home' countries and regions. The picture surrounding scholarly mobility (scholars and students) is complex, with indications of

both increased mobility, static mobility and reduced mobility. Few global statistics are available. See Meek *et al.* 2009.

2 Comparative analysis is not included in this book but is part of our ongoing work. See Fløttum *et al.* 2006 for example of comparative focus.

3 Scholars usually seek permission from journals when they wish to publish a version of an existing paper in another language. Some journals resist dual publication, but as Wen and Gao (2007) argue, the acceptance of 'dual publication' is a means to redress the inequality perpetuated by strict interpretations of the notion of 'first' or 'prior' publication for scholars with restricted access to the global academic marketplace.

6 Boundaries and stratification in the global academic dystopia

1 The issue of citations of work from outside Anglophone contexts is discussed in Lillis *et al.* 2010.

2 Although – as we stress throughout this book – there is little research on gatekeeping and brokering for Anglophone-centre scholars writing for publication.

3 For a useful discussion of recontextualization, see Blommaert 2005: 45 ff.

4 This example of academic interest in diversity within the Anglophone centre, resulting from changing demographics and patterns of migration and mobility – specifically here the increasing numbers of Spanish-speaking populations – may (potentially) provide a stimulus for challenging existing evaluation practices.

5 Not all journals subscribe to the practice of anonymous peer review and this is indeed being challenged by some Open Access journals. See Chapter 7 for further discussion.

7 Decentring academic text production and evaluation practices

1 The phrase 'wordface professionals' is in current usage by translators and authors' editors in Europe who work with researchers writing in English as an additional language. For examples see www.metmeetings.org.

2 Details can be found at www.authoraid.info/ and Shashok 2009. For other examples, see Scientists without Borders at http://scientistswithoutborders.nyas.org; SciEdit, funded by a group of US universities and the National Science Foundation, *Science Magazine* and others, which offers 'students in developing countries' the services of 'a group of elite university students with successful publication track-records in submitting to top peer-reviewed science journals including *Nature* and *Science* [who] will edit your manuscript and provide constructive feedback specific to your goals' (www.jyi. org/sciedit/, accessed 3 September 2009).

3 Such initiatives are also difficult to sustain. Teun A. van Dijk, editor of *Discourse and Society*, stated in an editorial in 1997 'this journal will increasingly try to set an example by evaluating papers in terms of the linguistic diversity of its examples and its references'. However, in 2009 he noted that this is not easy to implement.

4 Why such volunteers may offer an additional uncompensated service may be explained in part by Bourdieu's (1998; Chapter 4) notion of (dis)interest as occurring in fields of cultural production such as the scholastic. When monetary compensation, or economic capital, is not available, the interest or profit to be obtained takes the form of symbolic capital. As evidenced in Chapter 4, some brokers devote considerable time and effort to supporting the research and writing of multilingual scholars outside Anglophone contexts. In these cases the symbolic capital on offer may range from, on perhaps the

most public extreme, named co-authorship of journal articles or book chapters, to a more private receipt of gratitude from the scholar with whom the broker works. On the most private extreme, the sense of having 'given back' or made a contribution to a field/discipline/scholarly/political enterprise entails what Bourdieu refers to as a type of *noblesse oblige*.

5 We are using centripetal here in contrast to centrifugal, after Bakhtin (1981) whereby centripetal refers to official languages, discourses or socially powerful genres and centrifugal signals contrasting unofficial languages, discourses or genres usually with lower social status or prestige.

6 In partnership with the Chinese Academy of Science, Thomson Reuters is now hosting the Chinese Science Citation Database (see www.thompsonreuters.com). For J-EAST see (http://sciencelinks.jp/j-east/about/). Another index of English-medium publications from outside the Anglophone centre exists, the Asian Science Citation Index (www.ASCInet.org), but is also oriented to the SCI.

7 DICE – Difusión y Calidad Editorial de las Revistas Españolas de Humanidades y Ciencias Sociales y Jurídicas (http://dice.cindoc.csic.es); ISOC – Indice Español de Ciencias Sociales y Humanidades; IME – Indice Médico Español; and ICYT – Indice Español de Ciencia y Tecnología. For a useful overview of research output and evaluation in Spain, see the edited collection by Sebastián and Muñoz 2006.

8 For Latindex see www.latindex.unam.mx; for SCIELO see www.scielo.br.

9 This is a study exploring reviewing practices in psychology using psychological frames of reference. What makes the study even more interesting is that it is published alongside responses to the paper by other psychologists writing from their specific disciplinary perspectives.

10 A different, albeit related, concern about anonymity is expressed by some researchers about the peer review process. This centres on how reviewers' anonymity can become licence for crossing from legitimate critique to rudeness or 'crass' behaviour (Braine 2003: 88; see also Gosden 2003; Kourilova 1998).

11 This issue comes to the fore in explorations of citation practices where the push towards English-medium publication seems to be having a major impact on what is citable, which in turn raises questions about the sustainability of local research sites outside the Anglophone centre. See Lillis *et al.* (2010) with regard to citability in the contexts studied here; see Ren and Rousseau 2004, who raise similar issues in relation to Chinese publications.

12 With regard to the European Union, at the Lisbon Declaration (2000) the heads of governments called for an increase in the proportion of GNP to be spent on research. However, the Declaration leaves open the extent to which this aim should be achieved through increased public research expenditures or through increased private investments in R&D.

13 Third space is picked up and used in a number of ways with regard to meaning making, resources for meaning making and identity and knowledge construction. For examples, see Gutierrez *et al.* 1995; Wilson 2000.

14 Having established criteria they see as valid, they use these criteria to evaluate the internationality of four psychology journals – two Spanish and two US based. The US-based journals were 'two of the most prestigious journals' in the field (using existing criteria such as inclusion in indices and multinational readership); in contrast the two Spanish journals (which publish in English and Spanish and/or Portuguese), although they have 'international' in the title, are widely considered as 'non-international'. When using their 'internationality' criteria two interesting findings emerge: the two US journals have a

smaller share of international articles (defined as having at least two authors from two different countries); no one journal has an overall high score on the four criteria they use.

15 An argument also made in a recent report to the UK Research Councils – 'Open Access to Research Outputs Final Report to RCUK 2008', available at www.rcuk.ac. uk/cmsweb/downloads/rcuk/news/oareport.pdf, accessed 11 November 2009.

16 The situation is even more complicated in practice around the world where universities and grant funding bodies may involve both public and private funding sources. For example, in the United States the federal government is one of the largest sources of research funds in many fields, for example, from the National Science Foundation, National Institutes of Health. Researchers at private universities are equally eligible for these grants as are researchers at public (state-funded) universities. However, some granting agencies may restrict funds for specific programmes to researchers in particular types of institution, private or public. For a fuller discussion see Geiger 2004; Chapter 4.

17 See also discussions in Mauss 1954/2000 on gift economies.

18 The transnational body, the EU, explicitly supports open access: 'Universities and EUA [European University Association], through its Working Group on Open Access, will continue to work towards realising "open access" principles in relation to the dissemination of research results' (Lisbon Declaration 2007).

19 The number given by the Directory of Open Access is 4,250.

20 Whether OA journals are listed in these indexes is relevant both to scholars publishing in them and to those interested in issues of global knowledge production and bibliometrics. Bjork *et al.* 2009: 1, for example, note that 'ISI-indexed journals publish far more articles per year (111) than non-ISI indexed journals (26)'.

References

Ajayi, A. (2004) 'Impact factor misleading, citing all references', *Journal of the National Medical Association*, 96(1): 1,374.

Allison, D. (1996) 'Pragmatic discourse and English for academic purposes', *English for Specific Purposes*, 15(2): 85–103.

Ammon, U. (2001) *The Dominance of English as a Language of Science* (Editor's preface: v–x), Berlin: Mouton de Gruyter.

Anderson, B. (1983) *Imagined Communities: reflections on the origin and spread of nationalism*, London: Verso.

Appadurai, A. (1996) *Modernity at Large: cultural dimensions of globalization*, Minneapolis: University of Minnesota Press.

Apple, M. (2004, 3rd edn) *Ideology and Curriculum*, New York: Routledge.

Bahri, D. (1997) 'Marginally off-center: postcolonialism in the teaching machine', *College English*, 59: 277–288.

Bakhtin, M. (1981) 'Discourse in the novel', in M. Holquist (ed.), *The Dialogic Imagination: four essays by M. Bakhtin*, trans. C. Emerson and M. Holquist, Austin: University of Texas Press (259–422).

Baldauf, R. and Jernudd, B. (1987) 'Academic communication in a foreign language: the example of Scandinavian psychology', *ARAL*, 10(1): 98–117.

Barton, D. and Hamilton, M. (1998) *Local Literacies: reading and writing in one community*, London: Routledge.

Barton, D. and Tusting, K. (eds) (2005) *Beyond Communities of Practice: language, power, and social context*, New York: Cambridge University Press.

Barton, D., Hamilton, M. and Ivanič, R. (eds) (2000) *Situated Literacies: reading and writing in context*, London: Routledge.

Baumann, Z. (1998) *Globalization: the human consequences*, Cambridge: Polity Press.

Baynham, M. (1993) 'Code switching and mode switching: community interpreters and mediators of literacy', in B. V. Street (ed.), *Cross-Cultural Approaches to Literacy*, Cambridge: Cambridge University Press (294–314).

Baynham, M. and Maybin, J. (1996) 'Literacy Practices in English', in J. Maybin and N. Mercer (eds), *Using English: from conversation to canon*, Milton Keynes, UK: Open University Press (42–63).

Bazerman, C. (1988) *Shaping Written Knowledge: the genre and activity of the experimental article in science*, Madison: University of Wisconsin Press.

Becher, T. (1994) 'The significance of disciplinary differences', *Studies in Higher Education*, 14(3): 263–278.

Begley, S. (2006, 5 June) 'Science journals artfully try to boost their rankings', *Wall Street Journal*: B1.

Belcher, D. (1994) 'The apprenticeship approach to advanced academic literacy: graduate students and their mentors', *English for Specific Purposes*, 13: 23–34.

—— (2007) 'Seeking acceptance in an English-only research world', *Journal of Second Language Writing*, 16(1): 1–22.

Belcher, D. and Connor, U. (eds) (2001) *Reflections on Multiliterate Lives*, Clevedon, UK: Multilingual Matters.

Bell, A. (2007) 'Text, time and technology in news English', in S. Goodman, D. Graddol and T. Lillis (eds), *Redesigning English*, London: Routledge/Open University (79–105).

Benesch, S. (2001) *Critical English for Academic Purposes: theory, politics, practice*, Mahwah, NJ: Lawrence Erlbaum.

Bennett, K. (2007a) 'Epistimicide! The tale of a predatory discourse', *The Translator*, 13(2): 151–169.

—— (2007b) 'Galileo's revenge: ways of construing knowledge and translation strategies in the era of globalization', *Social Semiotics*, 17(2): 171–193.

Berkenkotter, C. and Huckin, T. N. (1995) *Genre Knowledge in Disciplinary Communication: cognition/culture/power*, Hillsdale, NJ: Lawrence Erlbaum.

Bernasconi, R. (2005) 'Levy-Bruhl among the phenomenologists: exoticisation and the logic of "the primitive"', *Social Identities*, 11(3): 229–245.

Berns, M. (1990) *Contexts of Competence: social and cultural considerations in communicative language teaching*, New York: Plenum.

—— (2005) 'Expanding on the expanding circle: where do we go from here?', *World Englishes*, 24(1): 85–93.

Bhabha, H. (1994) *The Location of Culture*, London: Routledge.

Bizzell, P. (1992) *Academic Discourse and Critical Consciousness*, Pittsburgh, PA: University of Pittsburgh Press.

Bjork, B-C., Roos, A. and Lauri, M. (2009) 'Scientific journal publishing: yearly volumen and open access availability', *Information Research*, 14(1), 1–14. Available at http://informationr.net/ir14-1/paper391.html, accessed 30 September 2009.

Blommaert, J. (2005) *Discourse: a critical introduction*, Cambridge: Cambridge University Press.

—— (2006) 'Sociolinguistic Scales', *Working Papers in Urban Language and Literacies*, Institute of Education, University of London and Ghent University.

Blommaert, J., Collins, J. and Slembrouck, S. (2005) 'Spaces of multilingualism', *Language and Communication*, 25: 197–216.

Boissevain, S. (1987) 'Social networks', *Sociolinguistics: an international handbook of the science of language and society*, 1: 64–69.

Boletín Oficial de las Cortes Generales (2001, December) *V11 Legislatura: 121/000045 Ley Orgánica de Universidades*, Madrid: Congreso de los Diputados.

Bourdieu, P. (1985) 'The forms of capital', in J. G. Richardson (ed.), *Handbook of Theory and Research for the Sociology of Education*, New York: Greenwood (241–258).

—— (1990) *The Logic of Practice*, trans. R. Nice, Stanford, CA: Stanford University Press.

—— (1991) *Language and Symbolic Power*, trans. G. Raymond and M. Adamson, Cambridge, MA: Harvard University Press.

—— (1998) *Practical Reason: on the theory of action*, Stanford, CA: Stanford University Press.

Braine, G. (2003) 'Negotiating the Gatekeepers: the journey of an academic article', in C. P. Casanave and S. Vandrick (eds), *Writing for Scholarly Publication: behind the scenes in language education*, Mahwah, NJ: Lawrence Erlbaum (73–90).

Brammer, C. (2002) 'Linguistic cultural capital and basic writers', *Journal of Basic Writing*, 21(1):16–36.

Brandt, D. (2001) *Literacy in American Lives*, New York: Cambridge University Press.

Brock-Utne, B. (2001) 'The growth of English in academic communication in the Nordic countries', *International Review of Education*, 47(3–4): 221–233.

Bucholtz, M. (2000) 'The politics of transcription', *Journal of Pragmatics*, 32(10): 1439–1465.

Buela-Casal, G., Perakakis, P., Taylor, M. and Checa, P. (2006) 'Measuring internationality: reflections and perspectives on academic journals', *Scientometrics*, 67(1): 45–65.

Burawoy, M. (2000) 'Introduction: reaching for the global', in M. Burawoy, J. A. Blum, S. George, Z. Gille, T. Gowan, L. Haney, M. Klawiter, S. H. Lopez, S. O'Raian and L. Thayer (eds), *Global Ethnography*, London: University of California Press (1–40).

—— (2003) 'Revisits: an outline of a theory of reflexive ethnography', *American Sociological Review*, 68(5): 645–679.

Burrough-Boenisch, J. (2003) 'Shapers of published NNS research articles', *Journal of Second Language Writing*, 12(3): 223–243.

Cameron, B. (2005) 'Trends in the usage of ISI bibliometric data: uses, abuses, and implications', *Portal: Libraries and the Academy*, 5(1): 105–125.

Canagarajah, A. S. (1996) 'Nondiscursive requirements in academic publishing, material resources of periphery scholars, and the politics of knowledge production', *Written Communication*, 13(4): 435–472.

—— (2001) 'Addressing issues of power and difference in ESL academic writing', in J. Flowerdew and J. Peacock (eds), *Research Perspectives on English for Academic Purposes*, Cambridge: Cambridge University Press (117–131).

—— (2002a) *A Geopolitics of Academic Writing*, Pittsburgh, PA: University of Pittsburgh Press.

—— (2002b) *Critical Academic Writing and Multilingual Students*, Ann Arbor: University of Michigan Press.

—— (2002c) 'Multilingual writers and the academic community: towards a critical relationship', *Journal of English for Academic Purposes*, 1: 29–44.

—— (2002d) 'Reconstructing local knowledge', *Journal of Language, Identity, and Education*, 1(4): 243–259.

—— (2005) 'Reconstructing local knowledge, reconfiguring language studies', in A. S. Canagarajah (ed.), *Reclaiming the Local in Language Policy and Practice*, Mahwah, NJ: Lawrence Erlbaum (3–24).

Candlin, C. N. and Hyland, K. (eds) (1999) *Writing: texts, processes, and practices*, London: Longman.

Carli, A. and Ammon, U. (2007) 'Introduction to the Topic: linguistic inequality in scientific communication today', *AILA Review*, 20: 1–3.

Carnell, E., MacDonald, J., McCallum, B. and Scott, M. (eds) (2008) *Passion and Politics: academics reflect on writing for publication*, London: Institute of Education.

Carter, A., Lillis, T. and Parker, S. (eds) (2009) *Why Writing Matters: issues of access and identity in writing research and pedagogy*, Amsterdam: John Benjamins.

Casanave, C. P. (1998) 'Transitions: the balancing act of bilingual academics', *Journal of Second Language Writing*, 12(1): 175–203.

—— (2002) *Writing Games: multicultural case studies of academic literacy practices in higher education*, Mahwah, NJ: Lawrence Erlbaum.

—— (2008) 'The stigmatizing effect of Goffman's stigma label: a response to John Flowerdew', *Journal of English for Academic Purposes*, 7: 264–267.

Casanave, C. P. and Vandrick, S. (2003) *Writing for Scholarly Publication: behind the scenes in language education*, Mahwah, NJ: Lawrence Erlbaum.

Castells, M. (2000, 2nd edn) *The Rise of the Network Society. The information age: economy, society, and culture, Vol. 1*, Oxford: Blackwell.

Cherry, R. (1988) 'Ethos v persona: self representation in written discourse', *Written Communication*, 5: 251–276.

Chesterman, A. and Wagner, E. (2002) *Can Theory Help Translators? A dialogue between the ivory tower and the wordface*, Manchester: St Jerome.

Chimbganda, A. B. (2000) 'Communication strategies used in the writing of answers in biology by ESL first year science students in the University of Botswana', *English for Specific Purposes*, 19: 305–329.

Ching, L. (2002) 'Strategy and self-regulation instruction as contributors to improving students' cognitive models in an ESL program', *English for Specific Purposes*, 21(3): 261–289.

Chomsky, N. (1957) *Syntactic Structures*, The Hague: Mouton.

—— (1965) *Aspects of the Theory of Syntax*, Cambridge, MA: MIT Press.

Collins Cobuild Dictionary (2009) available at www.Collinslanguage.com, accessed 27 August 2009.

Concise Oxford English Dictionary Online, available at www.askoxford.com/concise-oed, accessed 23 July 2009.

Cottingham, J. (1988) *The Rationalists*, Oxford: Oxford University Press.

—— (1998) *Philosophy and the Good Life: reason and the passions in Greek, Cartesian, and psychoanalytic ethics*, New York: Cambridge University Press.

Crane, D. (1972) *Invisible Colleges: diffusion of knowledge in scientific communities*, Chicago, IL: University of Chicago Press.

Crespi, G. A. and Geuna, A. (2008) 'An empirical study of scientific production: a cross country analysis, 1981–2002', *Research Policy*, 37: 565–579.

Cronin, B. (1984) *The Citation Process: the role and significance of citations in scientific communication*, Oxford: Taylor Graham.

Crystal, D. (2003, 2nd edn) *English as a Global Language*, Cambridge: Cambridge University Press.

Csepeli, G., Örkény, A. and Scheppele, K. L. (1996) 'Response to our critics (and our supporters)', *Replika*, 6: 21–22.

Curry, M. J. (2001) 'Preparing to be privatized: the hidden curriculum of a community college ESL writing class', in E. Margolis (ed.), *The Hidden Curriculum in Higher Education*, New York: Routledge (175–192).

—— (2002) 'Cultural models in the US writing classroom: matches and mismatches', in M. Graal and R. Clark (eds), *Writing Development in Higher Education: changing contexts for teaching and learning*, Leicester: University of Leicester (45–61).

—— (2003) 'Skills, access, and "basic writing": a community college case study from the United States', *Studies in the Education of Adults*, 35(1): 5–18.

—— (2007) 'A "head start and a credit": analyzing cultural capital in the basic writing/ESOL classroom', in J. Albright and A. Luke (eds), *Pierre Bourdieu and Literacy Education*, Mahwah, NJ: Lawrence Erlbaum (275–295).

Curry, M. J. and Lillis, T. M. (2004) 'Multilingual scholars and the imperative to publish in English: Negotiating interests, demands, and rewards', *TESOL Quarterly*, 38(4): 663–688.

Dor, D. (2004) 'From Englishization to imposed multilingualism: globalization, the Internet, and the political economy of the linguistic code', *Public Culture*, 16(1): 97–119.

Duszak, A. (ed.) (1997) *Culture and Styles of Academic Discourse*, Berlin: Mouton de Gruyter.

—— (2006) 'Looking globally, seeing locally: exploring some myths of globalization in academia', *Revista Canaria de Estudios Ingleses*, 53: 35–45.

Dysthe, O. (2002) 'Professors as mediators of academic text cultures: an interview study with advisors and master's degree students in three disciplines in a Norwegian university', *Written Communication*, 19(4): 493–544.

EurActiv (2006) *OECD: China's R and D spending 'stunning'*, available at www.euractiv.com, accessed 6 April 2009.

European University Institute (2009) Max Weber Postdoctoral Programme, Academic Careers Observatory, available at www.eui.eu/ProgrammesandFellowships/Academ CareersObservatory/CareerComparisons/SalaryComparisons.aspx, accessed 1 March 2010.

Fairclough, N. (1992) *Discourse and Social Change*, Cambridge: Polity Press.

—— (2006) *Language and Globalization*, London: Routledge.

Falk, R. (1999) *Predatory Globalization: a critique*, Malden, MA: Blackwell.

Faulstich Orellana, M., Meza, M. and Pietsch, K. (2002) 'Mexican immigrant networks and home–school connections', *Practicing Anthropology*, 24(3): 4–8.

Ferenz, O. (2005) 'EFL writers' social networks: impact on advanced academic literacy development', *Journal of English for Academic Purposes*, 4(4): 339–351.

Firth, A. and Wagner, J. (2003) 'On discourse, communication, and (some) fundamental concepts in SLA research', in B. Seidlhofer (ed.), *Controversies in Applied Linguistics*, Oxford: Oxford University Press (173–198).

Fløttum, K., Dahl, T. and Kinn, T. (2006) *Academic Voices: across languages and disciplines*, Amsterdam: John Benjamins.

Flowerdew, J. (1999a) 'Writing for scholarly publication in English: the case of Hong Kong', *Journal of Second Language Writing*, 8(2): 123–145.

—— (1999b) 'Problems in writing for scholarly publication in English: the case of Hong Kong', *Journal of Second Language Writing*, 8(3): 243–264.

—— (2000) 'Discourse community, legitimate peripheral participation, and the nonnative-English-speaking scholar', *TESOL Quarterly*, 34(1): 127–150.

—— (2001) 'Attitudes of journal editors to nonnative speaker contributions', *TESOL Quarterly*, 35(1): 121–150.

—— (2008) 'Scholarly writers who use English as an Additional Language: what can Goffman's "Stigma" tell us?', *Journal of English for Academic Purposes*, 7(2): 77–86.

Foucault, M. (1972) *The Archaeology of Knowledge*, London: Tavistock.

Freeman, L. (2000) 'Visualizing social networks', *Journal of Social Structure*, 1, available at www.cmu.edu/joss, accessed 5 June 2009.

Garfield, E. (1972) 'Citation analysis as a tool in journal evaluation', *Science*, 178: 471–479.

—— (1997) 'A statistically valid definition of bias is needed to determine whether the *Science Citation Index*® discriminates against third world journals', *Current Science*, 73(8): 639–641.

Gee, J. P. (1992) *The Social Mind: language, ideology, and social practice*, New York: Bergin and Garvey.

—— (2001) 'Identity as an analytic lens for research in education', in W. G. Secada (ed.), *Review of Research in Education*, 25, Washington, DC: American Educational Research Association (99–126).

—— (2007, 3rd edn) *Sociolinguistics and Literacies*, London: Taylor & Francis.

Geertz, C. (1973) *The Interpretation of Cultures: selected essays*, New York: Basic Books.

Geiger, R. L. (2004) *Knowledge and Money: research universities and the paradox of the marketplace*, Stanford, CA: Stanford University Press.

Gibbs, W. W. (1995a, May) 'Information have-nots: a vicious circle isolates many Third World scientists', *Scientific American*, 8–9.

—— (1995b, August) 'Lost science in the Third World', *Scientific American*, 76–83.

Gilbert, G. N. and Mulkay, M. (1984) *Opening Pandora's Box: a sociological analysis of scientific discourse*, Cambridge: Cambridge University Press.

Gnutzmann, C. (2008) 'Fighting or fostering the dominance of English in academia', in C. Gnutzmann (ed.), *English in Academia: catalyst or barrier?*, Tübingen: Gunter Narr Verlag (73–91).

Golebiowski, Z. and Liddicoat, A. J. (2002) 'The interaction of discipline and culture in academic writing', *Australian Review of Applied Linguistics*, 25(2): 59–71.

Gómez, I., Sancho, R., Bordons, M. and Fernández, M. T. (2006) 'La I + D en España a través de publicaciones y patentes', in J. Sebastián and E. Muñoz (eds), *Radiografía de la investigación publica en España*, Madrid: Biblioteca Nueva (122–146).

Goodfellow, R. and Lea, M. (2007) *Challenging E-learning in the University: a literacies perspective*, Maidenhead, UK/New York: McGraw Hill/Society for Research into Higher Education/Open University Press.

Gosden, H. (1995) 'Success in research article writing and revision: a social constructionist perspective', *English for Specific Purposes*, 14(1): 37–57.

—— (2003) 'Why not give us the full story?': functions of referees' comments in peer reviews of scientific research papers', *Journal of English for Academic Purposes*, 2: 87–101.

Graddol, D. (1997) *The Future of English*, London: British Council.

—— (2006) *English Next: why global English may mean the end of 'English as a Foreign Language'*, London: British Council.

—— (2007) 'Global English, global culture?', in S. Goodman, D. Graddol and T. Lillis (eds), *Re-designing English*, London: Routledge (243–279).

Granovetter, M. (1973) 'The strength of weak ties', *The American Journal of Sociology*, 78(6): 1360–1380.

—— (1983) 'The strength of weak ties: a network theory revisited', *Sociological Theory*, 1: 203–223.

Gutierrez, K., Rymes, B. and Larson, J. (1995) 'Script, counterscript, and underlife in the classroom: James Brown *versus* Brown v. Board of Education', *Harvard Educational Review*, 65(3): 445–471.

Halasek, K. (1999) *A Pedagogy of Possibility: Bakhtinian perspectives on composition studies*, Carbondale: Southern Illinois University Press.

Hall, J. K. and Eggington, W. G. (2000) *The Sociopolitics of English Language Teaching*, Clevedon, UK: Multilingual Matters.

Hall, S. (1997) 'Old and new identities, old and new ethnicities', in A. D. King (ed.), *Culture, Globalization and the World System*, Minneapolis: University of Minnesota Press (41–68).

Halliday, M. A. K. (1994) *An Introduction to Functional Grammar*, London: Edward Arnold.

Halliday, M. A. K. and Martin, J. (1993) *Writing Science: literacy and discursive power*, London: Routledge.

Harklau, L., Losey, K. and Siegel, M. (1999) *Generation 1.5 Meets College Composition: issues in the teaching of writing to US-educated learners of ESL*, Mahwah, NJ: Lawrence Erlbaum.

Harris, R. and Taylor, T. J. (1997) *The Western Tradition from Socrates to Saussure*, New York: Routledge.

Harwood, N. (2009) 'An interview-based study of the functions of citations in academic writing across two disciplines', *Journal of Pragmatics*, 41(3): 497–518.

Harwood, N., Austin, L. and Macaulay, R. (2009) 'Proofreading in a UK university: proofreaders' beliefs, practices, and experiences', *Journal of Second Language Writing*, 18: 166–190.

——— (forthcoming) 'Ethics and integrity in proofreading: findings from an interview-based study', *English for Specific Purposes*.

Haskins, T. (2007) 'Blogging as a gift economy', available at http://growchangelearn. blogspot.com/2007/01/blogging-as-gift-economy.html, accessed 22 September 2009.

Haythornthwaite, C. (1996) 'Social network analysis: an approach and technique for the study of information exchange', *Library and Information Science Review*, 18: 323–342.

Hazelkorn, E. (2009) *The Impact of Global Rankings on Higher Education Research and the Production of Knowledge*, Paris: UNESCO Forum Occasional Paper Series; Paper No. 15.

Heath, S. B. (1983) *Ways with Words: language, life, and work in communities and classrooms*, New York: Cambridge University Press.

Heath, S. B., and Street, B. V. (2008). *On Ethnography: approaches to language and literacy research*, London: Routledge.

Hewings, M. (2006) 'English Language Standards in Academic Articles: attitudes of peer reviewers', *Revista Canaria de Estudios Ingleses*, 53: 47–62.

Hewings, A., Lillis, T. and Vladimirou, D. (forthcoming) 'Who's citing whose writings? A corpus based study of citations as interpersonal resource in English medium national and English medium international journals', *Journal of English for Academic Purposes*.

Hicks, D. (2004) 'The four literatures of social science', in H. Moed, W. Glanzel and U. Schmoch (eds), *Handbook of Quantitative Science and Technology Research*, Dordrecht, The Netherlands: Kluwer (1–17).

Horner, B. (1999) 'The "birth" of "basic writing"', in B. Horner and M.Lu, *Representing the 'Other': basic writers and the teaching of basic writing*, Urbana, IL: National Council of Teachers of English (3–29).

Horner, B. and Lu, M. (1999) *Representing the 'Other': basic writers and the teaching of basic writing*, Urbana, IL: National Council of Teachers of English.

Huttner, J. (2008) 'The genre(s) of student writing: developing writing models', *International Journal of Applied Linguistics*, 18(2): 146–165.

Hyland, K. (1999) 'Academic attribution: citation and the construction of disciplinary knowledge', *Applied Linguistics*, 20(3): 341–367.

——— (2000) *Disciplinary Discourses: social interactions in academic writing*, London: Pearson Education.

——— (2006) *English for Academic Purposes: an advanced resource book*, London: Routledge.

Hymes, D. (1968) 'The ethnography of speaking', in J. A. Fishman (ed.), *The Ethnography of Communication*, The Hague: Mouton (99–138).

——— (1971) 'Competence and performance in linguistic theory', in R. Huxley and E. Ingram (eds), *Language Acquisition: models and methods*, New York: Academic Press.

——— (1974) *Foundations in Sociolinguistics: an ethnographic approach*, Philadelphia: University of Pennsylvania Press.

International Association of Universities (2008/09) *The International Handbook of Universities*, London: Palgrave Macmillan.

Ivanič, R. (1998) *Writing and Identity: the discoursal construction of identity in academic writing*, Amsterdam: John Benjamins.

Ivanič, R., Edwards, R., Barton, D., Martin-Jones, M., Fowler, Z., Hughes B., Mannion, G., Miller, K., Satchwell, C. and Smith, J. (2009) *Improving Learning in College: rethinking literacies across the curriculum*, London: Routledge.

Jacoby, S. and McNamara, T. (1999) 'Locating competence', *English for Specific Purposes*, 18(3): 213–241.

Jenkins, J. (2007) *English as a Lingua Franca: attitude and identity*, Oxford: Oxford University Press.

Jenkins, S. and Parra, I. (2003) 'Multiple layers of meaning in an oral proficiency test: the complementary roles of nonverbal, paralinguistic, and verbal behaviors in assessment decisions', *The Modern Language Journal*, 87(1): 90–107.

Jin, B. and Wang, B. (1999) 'Chinese Science Citation Database: its construction and application', *Scientometrics*, 45(2): 325–332.

Johns, A. (1997) *Text, Role and Context: developing academic literacies*, Cambridge: Cambridge University Press.

Jones, C., Turner J. and Street, B. (eds) (1999) *Students Writing in the University: cultural and epistemological issues*, Amsterdam: John Benjamins.

Kachru, B. (ed.) (1992) *The Other Tongue: English across cultures*, Urbana: University of Illinois Press.

—— (2001) 'World Englishes', in R. Mesthrie (ed.), *Concise Encyclopedia of Sociolinguistics*, New York: Elsevier (519–524).

Kalman, J. (1999) *Writing on the Plaza: mediated literacy practice among scribes and clients in Mexico City*, Creskill, NJ: Hampton Press.

Katz, J. S. (1999) *Bibliometric indicators and the social sciences*, Brighton, UK: SPRU, University of Sussex. Report to the Economic and Social Research Council.

Kaufer, D. and Geisler, C. (1989) 'Novelty in academic writing', *Written Communication*, 6(3): 286–311.

Kayman, M. A. (2000) 'A very old alliance? An introduction to English in Portugal', in B. Engler and R. Haas (eds), *European English Studies: contributions towards the history of a discipline*, Leicester, UK: English Association, for European Society for the Study of English (13–32).

Kenway, J. and Fahey, J. (2009) *Globalizing the Research Imagination*, London: Routledge.

Kenway, J., Bullen, E., Fahey, J. and Robb, S. (2006) *Haunting the Knowledge Economy*, New York: Routledge.

Kerans, M. (2000) 'Eliciting revision of manuscripts for peer review through process-oriented conferences with Spanish scientists', *XVIII Congrés de la Asociación Española de Lingüística Aplicada: Actes*, Barcelona: Universitat de Barcelona (339–347).

Knorr-Cetina, K. (1981) *The Manufacture of Knowledge: an essay on the constructivist and contextual nature of science*, Oxford: Pergamon Press.

—— (2003) *Epistemic Cultures: how the sciences make knowledge*, Cambridge, MA: Harvard University Press.

—— (2007) 'Culture in global knowledge societies: knowledge cultures and epistemic cultures', *Interdisciplinary Science Reviews*, 32(4): 361–375.

Kourilova, M. (1998) 'Communicative characteristics of reviews of scientific papers written by non-native users of English', *Endocrine Regulations*, 32: 107–114.

Labrie, N. and Quell, C. (1997) 'Your language, my language, or English? The potential language choice in communication among nationals of the European Union', *World Englishes*, 16(1): 3–26.

Lamont, M. (2009) *How Professors Think: inside the curious world of academic judgment*, Cambridge, MA: Harvard University Press.

Lather, P. (1991) *Getting Smart: feminist research and pedagogy with/in the postmodern*, New York: Routledge.

Latour, B. and Woolgar, S. (1986, 2nd edn) *Laboratory Life: the social construction of scientific facts*, Princeton, NJ: Princeton University Press.

Lea, M. R. and Street, B.V. (1998) 'Student writing in higher education: an academic literacies approach', *Studies in Higher Education*, 23(2): 157–172.

Leung, C. (2005) 'Convivial communication: recontextualizing communicative competence', *International Journal of Applied Linguistics*, 15(2): 119–143.

Li, Y. (2006) 'A doctoral student of physics writing for publication: a sociopolitically oriented case study', *English for Specific Purposes*, 25: 456–478.

Lillis, T. M. (1997) 'New voices in academia? The regulative nature of academic writing conventions', *Language and Education*, 11(3): 182–199.

—— (2001) *Student Writing: access, regulation, desire*, London: Routledge.

—— (2003) 'An "academic literacies" approach to student writing in higher education: drawing on Bakhtin to move from critique to design', *Language and Education*, 17(3): 192–207.

—— (2008) 'Ethnography as method, methodology, and "deep theorizing": closing the gap between text and context in academic writing research', *Written Communication*, 25(3): 353–388.

Lillis, T. M. and Curry, M. J. (2006a) 'Professional academic writing by multilingual scholars: interactions with literacy brokers in the production of English-medium texts', *Written Communication*, 23(1): 3–35.

—— (2006b) 'Reframing notions of competence in scholarly writing: from individual to networked activity', *Revista Canaria de Estudios Ingleses*, 53: 63–78.

Lillis, T. and Scott, M. (2007) 'Defining academic literacies research: issues of epistemology, ideology and strategy', Special issue – New Directions in Academic Literacies, *Journal of Applied Linguistics*, 4(1): 5–32.

Lillis, T. and Turner, J. (2001) 'Student writing in higher education: contemporary confusion, traditional concerns', *Teaching in Higher Education*, 6(1): 57–68.

Lillis, T., Hewings, A., Vladimirou, D. and Curry, M. J. (2010) 'The geolinguistics of English as an academic lingua franca: citation practices across English medium national and English medium international journals', *International Journal of Applied Linguistics*, 20(1): 111–135.

Lin, N. (2001) 'Building a network theory of social capital', in N. Lin, K. Cook and R. S. Burt (eds), *Social Capital: theory and research*, New York: Aldine De Gruyter (3–29).

Lisbon Declaration (2007) 'European University Assocation', available at www.eua.be, accessed 4 September 2009.

Locke, J. (1689*) An Essay Concerning Human Understanding*, Book III, Chapter 11, Section 5.

Lu, M. (1987) 'From silence to words: writing as struggle', *College English*, 49: 437–448.

—— (1994) 'Professing multiculturalism: the politics of style in the contact zone', *College Composition and Communication*, 45(4): 442–458.

Mabe, M. (2003) 'The growth and number of journals', *Serials*, 16(2): 191–197.

MacDonald, S. P. (1994) *Professional Academic Writing in the Humanities and Social Sciences*, Carbondale: Southern Illinois University Press.

Malinowski, B. (1923) 'The problem of meaning in primitive languages', in C. K. Ogden and I. A. Richards (eds), *The Meaning of Meaning*, London: Kegan Paul (296–336).

Massaquoi, J. (2008) 'Science and technology human resource capacity building in Africa – the role of regional cooperation', in U. Teichler and H. Vessuri (eds), *Universities as Centres of Research and Knowledge Creation: an endangered species?*, Rotterdam: Sense Publishers (59–70).

Mauranen, A. (1993) *Cultural Differences in Academic Rhetoric*, Frankfurt: Peter Lang.

Mauss, M. (1954/2000) *The Gift: the form and reason for exchange in archaic societies*, New York: W.W. Norton.

Maybin, J. (1994) 'Children's voices: talk, knowledge and identity', in D. Graddol, J. Maybin and B. Stierer (eds), *Researching Language and Literacy in Social Context*, Clevedon, UK: Multilingual Matters (131–150).

Medgyes, P. and Kaplan, R. B. (1992) 'Discourse in a foreign language: the example of Hungarian scholars', *International Journal of the Sociology of Language*, 98: 67–100.

Medgyes, P. and Laszlo, M. (2001) 'The foreign language competence of Hungarian scholars: ten years later', in U. Ammon (ed.), *The Dominance of English as a Language of Science*, Berlin: Mouton de Gruyter (67–100).

Meek, V. L., Teichler, U. and Kearney, M. L. (eds) (2009) 'Higher education, research and innovation: changing dynamics', *Report on the UNESCO forum on higher education, research and knowledge 2001–2009*, International Centre for Higher Education Research: Kassel.

Mehan, H. (1993) 'Beneath the skin and between the ears: a case study in the politics of representation', in S. Chaiklin and J. Lave (eds), *Understanding Practice*, Cambridge: Cambridge University Press (241–268).

Menezes de Souza, L. M. T. (2008) 'Beyond "here's a culture, here's a literacy": vision in Amerindian literacies', in M. Prinsloo and M. Baynham (eds), *Literacies, Global and Local*, Amsterdam: Benjamins (193–213).

Mignolo, W. (2000) *Local Histories/Global Designs: coloniality, subaltern knowledges and border thinking*, Princeton, NJ: Princeton University Press.

Milroy, L. and Milroy, J. (1992) 'Social network and social class: toward an integrated sociolinguistic model', *Language in Society*, 21: 1–26.

Mišak, A., Marušić, M. and Marušić, A. (2005) 'Manuscript editing as a way of teaching academic writing: experience from a small scientific journal', *Journal of Second Language Writing*, 14: 122–131.

Mitchell, J. C. (1986) 'Network procedures', in D. Frick (ed.), *The Quality of Urban Life*, Berlin: Walter de Gruyter (73–90).

Mitroff, I. I. (1974) *The Subjective Side of Science*, New York: Elsevier.

Monastersky, R. (2005, 14 October) 'The number that's devouring science', *The Chronicle of Higher Education*, 58(8): A12.

Morales-Gálvez, C., Arrimadas Gómez, I., Ramirez Nueda, E., López Gayarre, A. and Ocana Villuendas, L. (2000) *La Enseñanza de Lenguas Extranjeras en España*, Madrid: Ministerio de Educación y Deporte, CIDE.

Morris, S. (2007) 'Mapping the journal publishing landscape: how much do we know?', *Learned Publishing*, 20(4): 299–309.

Myers, G. (1990) *Writing Biology: texts in the social construction of scientific knowledge*, Madison: University of Wisconsin Press.

National Science Foundation, Division of Science Resource Statistics (2007a) *Asia's Rising Science and Technology Strength: comparative indicators for Asia, the European Union, and the United States*. NSF 07-319, Arlington, VA: Author.

—— (2007b) *NSF InfoBrief: Brazil, China, India, Russia and Taiwan lead S&E article output of non-OECD countries*. NSF 07-328, Arlington, VA.

Naysmith, J. and Palma, A. (1997) 'Learning and teaching English in the Portuguese primary school', *Language Learning Journal*, 15: 44–46.

Nederhof, A. J. and van Wijk, E. (1997) 'Mapping the social and behavioural sciences worldwide: use of maps in portfolio analysis of national research efforts', *Scientometrics*, 40(2): 237–276.

Newell, G. (1984) 'Learning from writing in the content areas: a case study/protocol analysis', *Research in the Teaching of English*, 18: 205–287.

New London Group (1996) 'A pedagogy of multiliteracies: designing social futures', *Harvard Educational Review*, 66(1): 60–92.

Newman, M. (2001) 'The structure of scientific collaboration networks', *Proceedings of the National Academy of Sciences*, 98(2): 404–409.

Nisbet, J. (2005) 'What is educational research? Changing perspectives through the 20th century', *Research Papers in Education*, 20(1): 25–44.

Nomdo, G. (2006) 'Identity, power and discourse: the socio-political self-representations of successful "black" students', in L. Thesen and E. Van Pletzen (eds), *Academic Literacy and the Languages of Change*, London: Continuum (180–206).

Norton, B. (2000) *Identity and Language Learning: gender, ethnicity and educational change*, London: Longman.

Norton, B. and Starfield, S. (1997) 'Covert language assessment in academic writing', *Language Testing*, 4(3): 278–294.

OECD (Organization for Economic Cooperation and Development) (2007) *Science, Technology and Industry Scoreboard*, available at www.lysander.sourcoeecd.org, accessed 15 June 2009.

—— (2008) *Science, Technology and Industry Outlook 2008 Highlights*, available at www.oecd.org, accessed 20 July 2009.

—— (2009a) *Factbook*, available at www.oecd.org, accessed 20 July 2009.

—— (2009b) *Science, Technology and Industry Scoreboard*, available at www.oecd.org, accessed 14 December 2009.

Olson, K. (2002) 'Content for conversation partners', *ESL Magazine*, 5(1): 22–24.

Open Society Institute (2002) *Budapest Open Access Initiative*, available at www.soros.org/openaccess/read/shtml, accessed 11 October 2009.

Over, A., Maiworm, F. and Schelewsky, A. (2005) *Publishing Strategies in Transformation? Results of a study on publishing habits and information acquisition with regard to open access*, Deutsche Forschungsgemeinschaft Information Management (IM) Bonn, available at www.dfg.de/en/dfg_profile/facts_and_figures, accessed 17 July 2009.

Paulston, C. B. (1992) *Linguistic and Communicative Competence: topics in ESL*, Clevedon, UK: Multilingual Matters.

Pennycook, A. (1998) *English and the Discourses of Colonialism*, London: Routledge.

—— (2007) *Global Englishes and Transcultural Flows*, London: Routledge.

Peritz, B. C. (1983) 'Are methodological papers more cited than theoretical or empirical ones? The case of sociology', *Scientometrics*, 5(4): 211–218.

Peters, D. P. and Ceci, S. J. (1982) 'Peer-review practices of psychological journals: the fate of published articles, submitted again', *The Behavioural and Brain Sciences*, 5: 187–255.

Petzold, R. and Berns, M. (2000) 'Catching up with Europe: speakers and functions of English in Hungary', *World Englishes*, 19(1): 113–124.

Phillipson, R. (1992) *Linguistic Imperialism*, Oxford: Oxford University Press.

—— (2003) *English-Only Europe? Challenging language policy*, London: Routledge.

Portes, A. (1998) 'Social capital: its orgins and applications in modern sociology', *Annual Review of Sociology*, 24: 1–24.

—— (2000) 'The two meanings of social capital', *Sociological Forum*, 15(1): 1–12.

Pringle, J. (2004, November) 'Thomson Scientific finds new opportunities in Open Access', *KnowledgeLink* newsletter, available at http://science.thomsonreuters.com/m/pdfs/klnl/2004-11/open-access, accessed 1 March 2010.

Prior, P. (1998) *Writing/Disciplinarity: a sociohistoric account of literate activity in the academy*, Mahwah, NJ: Lawrence Erlbaum.

—— (2003) 'Are communities of practice really an alternative to discourse communities?', Paper presented at the meeting of the American Association of Applied Linguistics, Arlington, VA.

Räisanen, C. and Fortanet-Gomez, I. (2008) 'The state of ESP teaching and learning in Western European higher education after Bologna', in C. Räisanen and I. Fortanet-Gomez (eds), *ESP in European Higher Education: integrating language and content*, Amsterdam: John Benjamins (11–54).

Rajagopalan, K. (2009) '"World English" and the Latin analogy: where we get it wrong', *English Today*, 25(2): 49–54.

Ramanathan, V. (1999) 'English is here to stay: a critical look at institutional and educational practices in India', *TESOL Quarterly*, 33(2): 211–233.

Rampton, B. (1997) 'A sociolinguistic perspective on L2 communication strategies', in G. Kasper and E. Kellerman (eds), *Communication Strategies: Psycholinguistic and sociolinguistic perspectives*, London: Longman (279–303).

Reddy, M. J. (1979) 'The conduit metaphor – a case of conflict in our language about language', in A. Ortony (ed.), *Metaphor and Thought*, Cambridge: Cambridge University Press (284–324).

Ren, S. and Rousseau, R. (2004) 'The role of China's English-language scientific journals in scientific communication', *Learned Publishing*, 17(2): 99–104.

Roberts, C. (1997) 'Transcribing talk: issues of representation', *TESOL Quarterly*, 31(1): 167–172.

Robertson, R. (1995) 'Glocalization: time–space and heterogeneity–homogeneity', in M. Featherstone, S. Lash and R. Robertson (eds), *Global Maternities*, London: Sage (25–44).

Rose, M. (1989) *Lives on the Boundary*, New York: Penguin.

Rousseau, R. (2002) 'Journal evaluation: technical and practical issues', *Library Trends*, 50(3): 418–439.

Russell, D., Lea, M., Parker, J., Street, B. and Donahue, T. (2009) 'Exploring notions of genre in "academic literacies" and "writing across the curriculum": approaches across countries and contexts', in C. Bazerman, A. Bonini and Débora Figueiredo (eds), *Genre in a Changing World*, WAC Clearinghouse: Parlor Press. Available online at http:// wac.colostate.edu/books/genre/, accessed 9 September 2009.

Said, E. (1993) *Culture and Imperialism*, New York: Alfred A.Knopf.

Salager-Meyer, F. (1997) 'Scientific multilingualism and the "lesser" languages', *Interciencia*, 22(4): 197–201.

—— (2008) 'Scientific publishing in developing countries: challenges for the future', *Journal of English for Academic Purposes*, 7:121–132.

Sano, H. (2002) 'The world's lingua franca of science,' *English Today*, 8: 45–49.

Sarangi, S. (2006) 'The conditions and consequences of professional discourse studies', in R. Kiely, P. Rea-Dickins, H. Woodfield and G. Clibbon (eds), *Language, Culture and Identity in Applied Linguistics*, London: Equinox (199–220).

—— (2007) 'The anatomy of interpretation: coming to terms with the analyst's paradox in professional discourse studies [Editorial]', *Text*, 27(5): 567–584.

Sassen, S. (2009) 'Digging in the shadows', in J. Kenway and J. Fahey (eds), *Globalizing the Research Imagination*, London: Routledge (115–134).

Scollon, R. and Scollon, S. B. K. (1981) *Narrative, Literacy and Face in Interethnic Communication*, Norwood, NJ: Ablex.

Sebastián, J. and Muñoz, E. (eds) (2006) *Radiografía de la investigación publica en España*, Madrid: Biblioteca Nueva.

Seglen, P. (1997) 'Why the impact factor of journals should not be used for evaluating research', *British Medical Journal*, 314: 498–502.

Sehlaoui, A. (2001) 'Developing cross-cultural communicative competence in pre-service ESL/EFL teachers: a critical perspective', *Language, Culture and Curriculum*, 14(1): 42–57.

Seidlhofer, B. (2001) 'Closing a conceptual gap: the case for a description of English as a lingua franca', *International Journal of Applied Linguistics*, 11(2): 133–158.

Shashok, K. (1992) 'Educating international authors', *European Science Editing: Bulletin of the European Association of Science Editors*, 45:5–7.

—— (2001) 'Author's editors – facilitators of science information transfer', *Learned Publishing*, 14(2): 113–121.

—— (2008) 'Content and communication: how can peer review provide helpful feedback about the writing?', *BMC Medical Research Methodology*, 8: 3.

—— (2009) 'Editing around the World. AuthorAID in the Eastern Mediterranean: a communication bridge between mainstream and emerging research communities', *European Science Editing*, 106(35): 4.

Shashok, K. and Kerans, M. (2000) 'Translating the unedited science manuscript: who fixes what shortcomings?', in *I Congrés Internacional de Traducción Especialitzada: Actes*, Barcelona: Universitat Pompeu Fabra (101–104).

Shelton, R. and Holdridge, g. (2004) 'The US-EU race for leadership of science and technology: qualitative and quantitative indicators', Scientometrics, 60(3): 353–363.

Silverstein, M. and Urban, G. (1996) 'The natural history of discourses', in M. Silverstein and G. Urban (eds), *Natural Histories of Discourse*, Chicago: University of Chicago Press (1–17).

Sousa Santos, B. (1994) *Pela mão de Alice: o social eo político na pós-modernidade*, Porto: Edicões Afrontamento.

Spack, R. (1988/1998) 'Initiating ESL students into the academic discourse community: how far should we go?', *TESOL Quarterly*, 22: 29–51; reprinted in V. Zamel and R. Spack (eds), *Negotiating Academic Literacies: teaching and learning across languages and cultures*, Mahwah, NJ: Lawrence Erlbaum (85–104).

Stainton-Rogers, W. (2004) *Social Psychology: experimental and critical approaches*, Maidenhead, UK: Open University Press.

Street, B. (1984) *Literacy in Theory and Practice*, Cambridge: Cambridge University Press.

—— (2003) 'What's new in New Literacy Studies?' *Current Issues in Comparative Education*, 5(2): 1–14.

—— (2004) 'Academic literacies and the new orders: implications for research and practice in student writing in higher education', *Learning and Teaching in the Social Sciences*, 11: 9–20.

—— (2005) *Literacies across Educational Contexts: mediating learning and teaching*, Philadelphia, PA: Caslon.

Swales, J. (1985) 'English language papers and authors' first language: preliminary explorations', *Scientometrics*, 8: 91–101.

—— (1987) 'Utilizing the literature in teaching the research paper', *TESOL Quarterly*, 21: 41–68.

—— (1988) 'Language and scientific communication: the case of the reprint request', *Scientometrics*, 13: 93–101.

—— (1990) *Genre Analysis: English in Academic and Research Settings*, Cambridge: Cambridge University Press.

—— (1996) 'Occluded genres in the academy: the case of the submission letter', in E. Ventola and A. Mauranen (eds), *Academic Writing: intercultural and textual issues*, Amsterdam: John Benjamins (45–58).

—— (1997) 'English as Tyrannosaurus Rex', *World Englishes*, 16(3): 373–382.

—— (1998) *Other Floors, Other Voices: a textography of a small university building*, Mahwah, NJ: Lawrence Erlbaum.

—— (2004) *Research Genres*, Oxford: Oxford University Press.

Tardy, C. (2004) 'The role of English in scientific communication: lingua franca or Tyrannosaurus Rex?', *Journal of English for Academic Purposes*, 3(3): 247–269.

Tardy, C. and Matsuda, P. (2009) 'The construction of author voice by editorial board members', *Written Communication*, 26(1): 32–52.

Teichler, U. and Gaǧci, Y. (2009) 'Changing challenges of academic work: concepts and observations', in V. L. Meek, U. Teichler and M. L. Kearney (eds), *Higher Education, Research and Innovation: changing dynamics*, Report on the UNESCO Forum on Higher Education, Research and Knowledge, 2001–2009 (83–147).

TESOL Quarterly Mentoring Program (2009) Available at www.tesol.org/s_tesol/seccss.asp? CID=632&DID=2461, accessed 1 September 2009.

Testa, J. (2003) 'The Thomson ISI journal selection process', *Serials Review*, 29(3): 210–212.

Thesen, L. and Van Pletzen, E. (eds) (2006) *Academic Literacy and the Languages of Change*, London: Continuum.

Thomson Reuters (2008a) 'Thomson Reuters journal selection process', available at http://scientific.thomson.com/free/essays/selectionofmaterial/journalselection/date, accessed 8 February 2008.

—— (2008b) *Journal Citation Reports*, available at www.ThomsonReuters.com, accessed 15 September 2009.

—— (2009) 'Current contents', available at www.ThomsonReuters.com, accessed 22 June 2009.

Tomlinson, J. (1999) *Globalization and Culture*, Chicago, IL: University of Chicago Press.

Truchot, C. (1994) 'The spread of English in Europe', *Journal of European Studies*, 25: 141–151.

Turner, J. (1999) 'Problematising the language problem', in H. Bool and P. Luford (eds), *Academic Standards and Expectations: the role of EAP*, Nottingham: Nottingham University Press (59–66).

—— (2003) 'Academic literacy in post-colonial times: hegemonic norms and transcultural possibilities', *Language and Intercultural Communication*, (3): 187–197.

—— (2008) 'Proofreading: a case of protecting pristine prose?' Paper given in a symposium entitled: *What is 'proofreading' in academic text production?* Writing Development in Higher Education Conference, University of Strathclyde, Glasgow, UK.

—— (2009) 'The contested spaces of proofreading', Paper presented at the Canadian Association for the Study of Discourse and Writing, Carleton University, Ottawa.

—— (forthcoming a) 'Supporting academic literacy: issues of proofreading and language proficiency', in George Blue (ed.), *Developing Academic Literacy*, Bern: Peter Lang.

—— (forthcoming b) *Language and Intercultural Communication in Higher Education*, Clevedon, UK: Multilingual Matters.

Turner, J. and Scott, M. (2007) 'English as a lingua franca and the rise of proofreading in the academy', Paper presented at the BALEAP conference, University of Durham, UK.

—— (2008) Paper given in panel entitled: 'Get the English corrected': an investigation of the relationships, meanings, and practices behind 'proof-reading' in four European universities. Writing Research Across Borders conference, University of California, Santa Barbara.

Uitermark, J. (2002) 'Re-scaling, "scale fragmentation" and the regulation of antagonistic relationships', *Progress in Human Geography*, 26(6): 743–765.

Ulrich's Periodicals Directory (2009a) Available at www.Ulrichsweb.com, accessed 24 June 2009.

—— (2009b) 'New in 2006: more than 14,700 individual serials added to the Ulrich's knowledgebase', available at www.ulrichsweb.com/ulrichsweb/news.asp, accessed 10 October 2009.

UNESCO DARE Database, available at http://databases.unesco.org, accessed 22 July 2009.

UNESCO Forum on Higher Education, Research and Knowledge (2001–2009), available at www.unesco.org, accessed 29 July 2009.

UNESCO Institute for Statistics, *Bulletin on Science and Technology Statistics (2005)*, available at www.unesco.org, accessed 29 May 2009.

UNESCO Statistical Yearbook 2008, available at www.unesco.org, accessed 22 July 2009.

Uzuner, S. (2008) 'Multilingual scholars' participation in core/global academic communities: a literature review', *Journal of English for Academic Purposes*, 7: 250–263.

Van Dijk, T. A. (1997) 'Editorial: the imperialism of English', *Discourse and Society*, 8: 291–292.

Van Leeuwen, T., Moed, H., Tijssen, R., Visser, M. and van Raan, A. (2001) 'Language biases in the coverage of the Science Citation Index and its consequences for international comparisons of national research performance', *Scientometrics*, 51(1): 335–346.

Ventola, E. and Mauranen, A. (1991) 'Non-native writing and native revising of scientific articles', in E. Ventola (ed.), *Functional and Systemic Linguistics: approaches and uses*, Berlin: Mouton de Gruyter (457–492).

Waddell, H. (1932/2000) *The Wandering Scholars of the Middle Ages*, New York: Dover.

Wallerstein, I. (1991) *Geopolitics and Geoculture*, Cambridge: Cambridge University Press.

Ware, M. (2006) *Scientific Publishing in Transition: an overview of current developments*, Bristol: Mark Ware Consulting.

Weedon, C. (1997, 2nd edn) *Feminist Practice and Poststructuralist Theory*, Malden, MA: Blackwell.

Wellman, B. and Berkowitz, S. D. (1988) 'Introduction', in B. Wellman and S. D. Berkowitz (eds), *Social Structures: a network approach*, Cambridge: Cambridge University Press (1–13).

Wellman, B., Koku, E. and Hunsinger, J. (2006) 'Networked scholarship', in J. Weiss, J. Nolan, J. Hunsinger and P. Trifonas (eds), *The International Handbook of Virtual Learning Environments*, The Netherlands: Springer (1429–1447).

Wen, Q. and Gao, Y. (2007) 'Dual publication and academic inequality', *International Journal of Applied Linguistics*, 17(2): 221–225.

Wenger, E. (1998) *Communities of Practice: learning, meaning, and identity*, Cambridge: Cambridge University Press.

Widdowson, H. (1983) *Learning Purpose and Language Use*, Oxford: Oxford University Press.

Wilson, A. (2000) 'There's no escape from Third-space Theory', in D. Barton, M. Hamillon and R. Ivanič (eds) *Situated Literacies*, London: Routledge.

Wilson, L. (1942/1995) *The Academic Man: a study in the sociology of a profession*, New Brunswick, NJ: Transaction Publishers; originally published by Oxford University Press.

World Bank (2008) *World Development Indicators*, Washington, DC: World Bank Development Data Group.

Wormell, I. (1998) 'Informetric analysis of the international impact of scientific journals: how "international" are the international journals?', *Journal of Documentation*, 54(5): 584–605.

Young, S. S. C. (2003) 'Integrating ICT into second language education in a vocational high school', *Journal of Computer Assisted Learning*, 19(4): 447–461.

Zhou, P. and Leydesdorff, L. (2006) 'The emergence of China as a leading nation in science', *Research Policy*, 35: 83–104.

Index

Related titles from Routledge

Applied Linguistics in Action
A Reader
Edited by Guy Cook and Sarah North

'This is an expertly put together collection of articles that represent some of the most important and exciting work in applied linguistics. It offers the reader a comprehensive and up-to-date survey of the key areas of the field today. It is an excellent resource for students and instructors alike.'

Li Wei, *University of London, Birkbeck College, UK*

Applied Linguistics in Action: A Reader presents students with an applied linguistics framework for the analysis of real-world problems in which language is a central issue. The Reader allows students to develop both the theoretical and empirical skills crucial to an understanding of language teaching and other language-related professional practices.

Part One brings together seven key discussions of the nature and direction of contemporary applied linguistics, relating theory and description of language in use to educational and other professional contexts. Issues include the politics of applied linguistics, its responses to globalisation, and its relation to social theory.

While the discussions in Part One are largely theoretical, Part Two, through abridged versions of thirteen case studies, demonstrates at a much more practical level how general principles formulated in Part One can be applied to a range of specific real-world problems. While the majority of studies are from educational settings, the breadth of current applied linguistic enquiry is illustrated by others relating to legal forensics, literary analysis, translation, language therapy, lexicography, and workplace communication.

The editors' introductions, both to the volume as a whole and to each individual part, guide the student through the difficult transition from general discussion to specific application, highlighting the most significant issues, and helping the student to see the relevance of both general theory and specific applications to the needs of their own studies, and their professional practice beyond.

Applied Linguistics in Action: A Reader is essential reading for advanced level undergraduates and postgraduates on applied linguistics, English language, and TESOL/TEFL courses.

ISBN13: 978-0-415-54546-4 (hbk)
ISBN13: 978-0-415-54547-1 (pbk)

Available at all good bookshops
For further information on our English Language and Linguistics series, please visit
http://www.routledgelinguistics.com/
For ordering and further information please visit:
www.routledge.com

Related titles from Routledge

Applied Linguistics Methods
A Reader
Edited by Caroline Coffin, Theresa Lillis and Kieran O'Halloran

'This book distils into a single volume the rich traditions of systemic functional linguistics, critical discourse analysis and ethnography to show how language analysis can be applied to a wide range of real-world issues. It offers graduate students and researchers a useful guide to help them navigate and appreciate the diverse, ever expanding and exciting landscape of applied linguistics.'

Peter Teo, *National Institute of Education, Singapore*

Applied Linguistics Methods: A Reader presents the student with three contemporary approaches for investigating text, practices and contexts in which language-related problems are implicated. Divided into three parts, the reader focuses in turn on the different approaches, showing how each is relevant to addressing real-world problems, including those relating to contemporary educational practices.

Part One introduces the reader to systemic functional linguistics (SFL) as an approach particularly well suited to the description of language and language-related problems in social contexts.

Part Two examines critical discourse analysis (CDA) as a means of uncovering the relationships between language use, power and ideology.

Part Three presents ethnography (and linguistic ethnography) as a methodology for observing the use and significance of language in real-life events as they unfold.

The book begins by introducing the student to the tools of SFL, CDA and ethnography and explains how aspects of the three approaches can work in complementary ways. Each part is made up of theoretical readings reflecting the key epistemological and methodological issues of the specific approach, along with readings which centre on a specific language problem. Introductions to each part provide synopses of the individual chapters, making the Reader highly usable on courses.

Applied Linguistics Methods: A Reader is key reading for advanced level undergraduates and postgraduates on applied linguistics, English language, and TESOL/TEFL courses.

ISBN13: 978-0-415-54544-0 (hbk)
ISBN13: 978-0-415-54545-7 (pbk)

Available at all good bookshops
For further information on our English Language and Linguistics series, please visit
http://www.routledgelinguistics.com/
For ordering and further information please visit:
www.routledge.com

Related titles from Routledge

Intercultural Communication
2nd edition

An advanced resource book for students

Adrian Holliday, John Kullman and Martin Hyde

Part of the Routledge Applied Linguistics series, edited by Ronald Carter, University of
Nottingham, UK and Christopher N. Candlin, Macquarie University, Australia.

**'This book helps the reader to gain a greater understanding of intercultural
communication, of their own culture and of themselves. It does so by
presenting engaging case studies of problematic intercultural "events", by
providing enlightening explanations and by inviting the reader to connect
these cases to their own thinking and their lives.'**

Brian Tomlinson, *Leeds Metropolitan University, UK*

The 2nd edition of *Intercultural Communication*:

- Updates key theories of intercultural communication.

- Explores the ways in which people communicate within and across social groups
  around three themes. These include identity, Othering, and representation – which are
  developed through the book's three sections.

- Contains new examples from business, healthcare, law and education.

- Presents an updated and expanded set of influential readings including James Paul Gee,
  James Lantolf, Les Back, Richard Dyer, Jacques Derrida and B. Kumaravadivelu, with
  new critical perspectives from outside Europe and North America.

Written by experienced teachers and researchers in the field, *Intercultural Communication*
is an essential resource for students and researchers of English language and applied
linguistics.

ISBN13: 978-0-415-48941-6 (hbk)
ISBN13: 978-0-415-48942-3 (pbk)
ISBN13: 978-0-203-09158-6 (ebk)

Available at all good bookshops
For further information on our English Language and Linguistics series, please visit
http://www.routledgelinguistics.com/
For ordering and further information please visit:
www.routledge.com

Related titles from Routledge

Introducing Applied Linguistics
Concepts and Skills
Susan Hunston and David Oakey

'For those of us involved in teaching postgraduate students where resources are limited, this is an ideal book to have at hand. The topics are varied and presented in such a way as to stimulate discussion in a very thought-provoking way. I teach postgraduate courses in Thailand, Vietnam and China and this book will be "a must" on my reading list.'

Professor Joseph Foley, *Assumption University, Thailand*

Introducing Applied Linguistics provides in-depth coverage of key areas in the subject, as well as introducing the essential study skills needed for academic success in the field.
Introducing Applied Linguistics:

- is organised into two sections: the first introducing key concepts in applied linguistics; and the second devoted to the study skills students need to succeed.
- features specially commissioned chapters from key authorities who address core areas of applied linguistics, including both traditional and more cutting edge topics, such as: grammar, vocabulary, language in the media, forensic linguistics, and much more.
- contains a study skills section offering guidance on a range of skills, such as: how to structure and organise an essay, the conventions of referencing, how to design research projects, plus many more.
- is supported by a lively companion website, which includes interactive exercises, information about the contributors and why they've written the book, and annotated weblinks to help facilitate further independent learning.

Ideal for advanced undergraduate and postgraduate students of applied linguistics and TEFL/TESOL, *Introducing Applied Linguistics* not only presents selected key concepts in depth, but also initiates the student into the discourse of applied linguistics.

ISBN13: 978-0-415-44768-3 (hbk)
ISBN13: 978-0-415-44767-6 (pbk)
ISBN13: 978-0-203-87572-8 (ebk)

Available at all good bookshops
For further information on our English Language and Linguistics series, please visit
http://www.routledgelinguistics.com/
For ordering and further information please visit:
www.routledge.com

Language as a Local Practice
Alastair Pennycook

'*Language as a Local Practice* is one of the most refreshing linguistics books to appear in a decade. Weaving together different strands of current research, Alastair Pennycook provides new framings and directions for the study of language.'

David Barton, *University of Lancaster, UK*

Language as a Local Practice addresses the questions of language, locality and practice as a way of moving forward in our understanding of how language operates as an integrated social and spatial activity.

By taking each of these three elements – language, locality and practice – and exploring how they relate to each other, *Language as a Local Practice* opens up new ways of thinking about language. It questions assumptions about languages as systems or as countable entities, and suggests instead that language emerges from the activities it performs. To look at language as a practice is to view language as an activity rather than a structure, as something we do rather than a system we draw on, as a material part of social and cultural life rather than an abstract entity.

Language as a Local Practice draws on a variety of contexts of language use, from bank machines to postcards, Indian newspaper articles to fish-naming in the Philippines, urban graffiti to mission statements, suggesting that rather than thinking in terms of language use in context, we need to consider how language, space and place are related, how language creates the contexts where it is used, how languages are the products of socially located activities and how they are part of the action.

Language as a Local Practice will be of interest to students on advanced undergraduate and post graduate courses in applied linguistics, language education, TESOL, literacy and cultural studies.

ISBN13: 978-0-415-54750-5 (hbk)
ISBN13: 978-0-415-54751-2 (pbk)
ISBN13: 978-0-203-84622-3 (ebk)